THE BOOK OF DRAWINGS+SKETCHES ARCHITECTURE

THE BOOK OF DRAWINGS+SKETCHES ARCHITECTURE

CHRIS VAN UFFELEN

BRAUN

Contents

The Story of Hand Drawings

by Chris van Uffelen

Scriptorium Reichenau (?)
Plan of St. Gall (Library of St.
Gall, Codex Ms 1092)
Red ink on parchment
112 x 77.5 cm
ca. 819–826
Stiftsbibliothek, St. Gall

Architectural drawings are one of the most direct forms of expression available to architects. With just a few strokes of the brush or pencil, the famous first sketch on a paper napkin can capture the initial composition, where the volume is presented or the spatial concept is roughly outlined. More comprehensive drawings with light and shading, color and texture portray the spatial effect and suggest appearance and haptic. This form of expression is much more sensual than a computer graphic and a lot less technical than a plan. The choice of medium – felt-tip pen or watercolors, Indian ink or even oil paints – expresses emotion.

Despite this, it appears that there is some anxiety and an unwillingness to publish project sketches and drawings. During the research phase, several architects stated that these were not intended for publication, were not stored, or even that they had been systematically destroyed. Some even avoided hand drawings altogether for architectural theory reasons. Because of this, this volume limits itself to architects who understand and support the use of sketches and the importance of this technique in the design process.

Drafts and work copies were already found in ancient civilizations and the occidental antiquity era. They were used to determine the three-dimensional shape of the building to be constructed as specifically as possible via schematic two-dimensional presentations. They can be found on Mesopotamian clay tablets as well as on ancient Egyptian papyrus. Engraved drawings have been preserved from the Greek and Roman antiquity, along with decorative architectural drawings on Pompeian murals. In addition to drawings, models were also used for visualization. These include both original-sized details as well as entire buildings on a proportionately smaller scale.

Medieval Architectural Drawings

The oldest medieval plan drawing is that of the monastery of St. Gall, which was created between the years 819 and 826 at the Abbey of Reichenau. Measuring 112 x 77.5 cm, it consists of five sewn-together parchments. However, the red

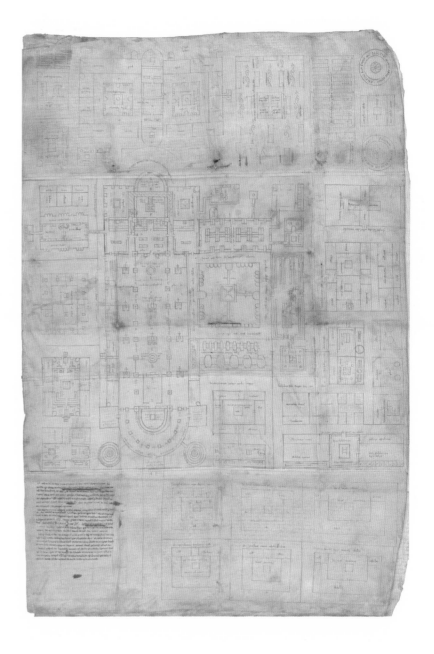

Villard de Honnecourt
From the Sketchbook
Re-drawing by Jules Quicherat: Notice sur l'Album
de Villard de Honnecourt architecte du XIIIe siècle
1230

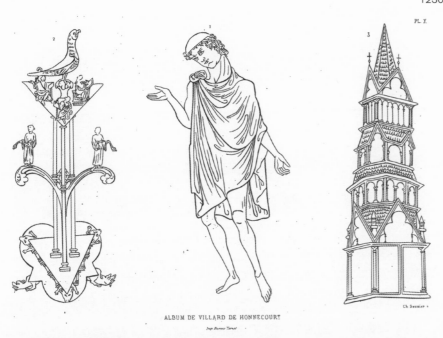

PL. X.

ALBUM DE VILLARD DE HONNECOURT
Imp. Becquet Paris

Ch. Saunier .

ink drawing probably only represents an ideal plan for a monastery with which Abbott Gozbert was to "practice his innovative skills", according to the inscription. The subsequent new construction of the St. Gall monastery had little in common with the details of the drawing. Thus the first post-medieval architectural drawing is an architectural theory depiction of which few records were found later. Rather, medieval architectural drawings mainly consisted of blue prints in remote sections of the constructed buildings, drafts for the precise implementation of entire building sections (Strasbourg cathedral; Ulrich von Ensingen's draft of the tower for the cathedral of Ulm) on the one hand, and by model books on the other. The drafts were so precise that they could be used for the completion of abandoned buildings, such as the cathedral of Cologne in the 19th century. Measuring more than four meters in height, the draft of the cathedral façade, dating to the late 13th century, was found in two parts – in 1814 the draft for the northern tower was found in the attic of the inn 'Zur Traube' in Darmstadt, and in 1816 the draft for the middle section and southern tower was found at an antique dealer in Paris. This indicates that the drawings were possibly already

used in the Middle Ages for architectural purposes. A function, however, that was mainly fulfilled by model books. The oldest architectural model book, actually a sketch book, is the so-called "lodge-book" portfolio of Villard de Honnecourt, which dates back to around 1240. On 33 pages it contains drawings and sketches of buildings, figures, building tools and techniques. It is not known whether it was used as an instruction book or a private record or if it can be considered as a lodge book. It were such drawings, however, that conveyed architectural styles across large distances independent of their place of origin, and which led to the emergence of the international Late Gothic style a century and a half later.

Architectural Drawings in the Modern Era

With the advent of the modern era, architectural hand drawings assumed all functions they have today. They maintained the purpose of conveying architectural information, extensively utilizing their illustrative role for architectural theories in treatises, they are used to gain insights in architectural surveys, and as an aid for the generation of ideas as sketches and for decision making as presentation drawings. Architectural drawings as guidelines for buildings to be implemented later, but also as vedutas and architectural fantasies, emerged as an independent genre. Compilations of engravings, such as Fischer von Erlach's "Plan of Civil and Historical Architecture," Piranesi's frequently stage-like visionary images of ancient buildings and own creations, as well as paintings and cityscapes such as those of the Canalettos (Giovanni Antonio Canal in Venice and England, Bernardo Bellotto in Warsaw and Dresden), showcase a wide range of presentation options for architecture in the modern era. From strict, objectified architectural portraits, wide-angle "recorded" limited spaces, up to atmospheric landscapes, all PC rendering methods known from other sectors are also applicable to architectural illustration. Ever since Giotto, even devotional and historical subjects could include architecture, as prior to that they merely contained schematic building structures. Following Giotto's lead, in the Renaissance era, the rediscovered perspective with its mathematical principles became the basic of the "realistic" spatial effect of image spaces. For example, the secular and sacral scenes of Piero della Francesca were structured by buildings. Sometimes it even seems as though the architecture is more important than the actual topic of the painting – such as Raphael's "Wedding of the Virgin" in which the polygonal temple dominates half the painting. Architectural pictures were used to introduce real-life space to the image space, which in the Baroque era led to the illusionary breaking open of the mirrored vaults through apotheoses and views of a Christian Olympus. However, in a more limited sense, pure architectural images were created in the Netherlands as a succession of sacral interiors (Jan van Eyck) and within the context of genre paintings, still lifes and landscapes. Church interiors (Hendrik Cornelisz van Vliet) and secular exteriors (Hans Vredeman de Vries) were discovered as models for paintings, while after 1600 the fantastical elements were eliminated in favor of great realism (Pieter Jansz Saenredam). The portrayed buildings were not necessarily only well-known grand buildings, but also included unremarkable buildings. A well-known example is Jan Vermeer's "Street in Delft," a so-called urban interior, a small section of a cityscape as opposed to his "View of Delft." The Dutch dominated the architectural painting genre during the 17th century, though the Italians took over once more in the 18th century.

Repercussion on Architecture

As soon as painters discovered the use of perspective to depict architecture, the architects also began to use this optical illusion in their buildings. While the backdrop of Palladio's Teatro Olimpico in Vicenza still rather ineptly presented room depth, Giovanni Lorenzo Bernini was able to dramatically extend the Scala Regia at the Vatican by means of perspective. Michelangelo's floor plan sketches for the Milanese Capella Sforza already deliberately added dynamics to the room by means of perspective. The illusionary spatial room depiction of architectural ideas revolutionized the presentation of architectural concepts. Now, architects were able to present illusionary depictions of their designs, add assisting figures to them, dramatize them through lighting and shadow effects, and also utilize all other architectural tricks to make their buildings appear more vivid and beautiful, larger or better than those of others. Even the effects of new buildings

Jacob Isaaksz. Ruisdael
Inside View of the Oude Kerk Amsterdam
Graphite and Indian ink on paper
Bibliothèque de l'École des Beaux-Arts, Paris

Matthäus Merian the Elder
Lübeck
Etching from the book: Topographia Saxoniae Inferioris, Frankfurt/Main
1653

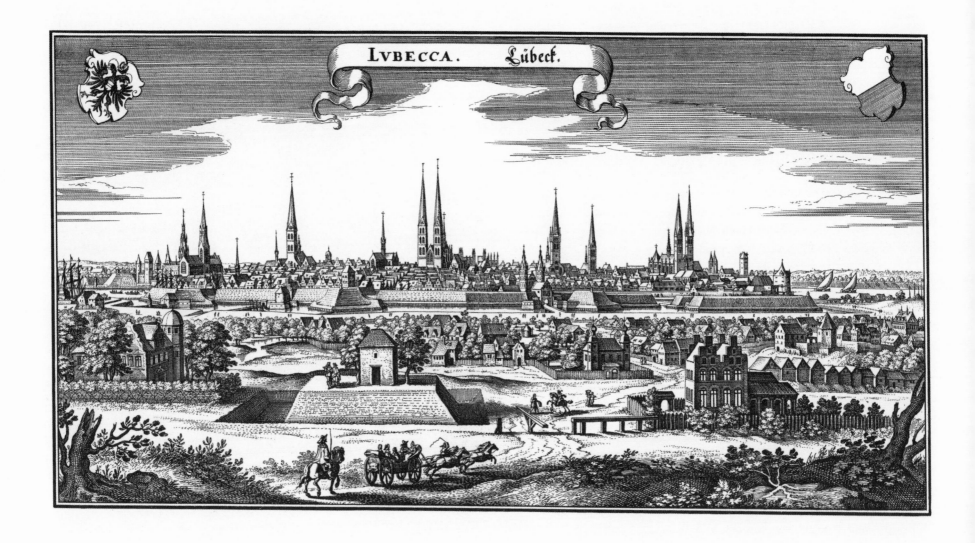

as future ruins in a new Arcadia could already be shown (Hubert Robert: Grande Galerie in the Louvre, 1796). Painter architects designed entire settings of potential or utopian buildings (Karl Friedrich Schinkel: Gothic cathedral by the water, 1813), which also allowed non-professionals to be creative like architects. In line with the development of painting styles, architectural surveys were perfected in a more or less ornamented manner by various architects, especially based on antique buildings in Rome, and implemented in drawings and paintings. Yet not only through these, but primarily through manuals and compilations of engravings, repertoire of building designs quickly spread across the entire occident – as the revolution of letterpress printing and graphic prints allowed the production of large circulations of illustrated works. The cityscapes of Merian became widely known along with theoretical essays by Vitruv and treatises by Leon Battista Albert or Vincenzo Scamozzi. The compilations of engravings by Ledoux and Boullée were more influential than the few buildings they constructed, and there was a general tendency of architectural reception to shift away from the actual buildings to their reproduction. Despite all study trips and Rome Prizes, this did not change until the widespread use of photography, even though only affecting the means of indirect reception. In the era of photography the image conveyed by the media dominated the view of the original. However, a new era also began for structural engineering drawings after the year 1800, as the "unique copy" along with individual drawings was lost in favor of a more "rational" presentation through lithographic reproduction. During the last third of the century, diazo copying further increased this trend. The academies additionally contributed to establishing a canon of "correct" construction drawings. Finally, with the end of Classicism (Friedrich David Gilly), and Romanticism (Caspar David Friedrich), architectural illustration directly related to construction was largely disengaged from the general style development of the fine arts. Realism was widely used as a form of presentation but reduced to an objective presentation of the visible. Even though buildings were still portrayed in subsequent art styles – cityscapes were the most important subject of all in Impressionism – the artistic depiction of architecture no longer influenced construction, while current artistic trends were no longer relevant to architects in their drawings. They either created "objective" technical drawings or, in the artistic depiction of buildings, with their high correspondence to reality, continued to adhere to the "realistic" style of the 18th and early 19th century. Despite H. P. Berlage's passion for impressionist architecture, the requirements of architectural drawings are not conducive to buildings dissolving in the shimmering light of a sweltering day or emerging as hidden silhouettes against back lighting. It was not until the Art Nouveau era that an independent style emerged for architecture as exemplified by Hector Guimard, Charles Rennie Mackintosh and Joseph Maria Olbrich. It is a strongly linear style with clear and simple contours and surface decoration, which also distinguishes the prints of the era and which later reemerged in classic Modernism.

Rationality, Decoration and Propaganda

Mackintosh's architectural works are among the first to be primarily recognized by drawings. However, around the late 19th century, another development affected visualization, which, combined with the Art Nouveau movement, brought about a major change in architecture. The increased use of rational technical drawings, horizontal and upright projections with clear lines and their advantages for printed reproduction were incorporated into presentation drawings. The three-volume publication "The English House" by Hermann Muthesius (1904) and the two-volume portfolio with around 100 lithographs by Frank Lloyd Wright (Ernst Wasmuth, 1910) are two of the key publications on the way to objectification of architectural drawings. The development of architectural style no longer relied on realized buildings as a requirement for a positive critical reception. This reduced style with precise sharp lines shaped the decade of Reform Classicism that was based on logic, intellect and artisanship, such as the work of Tony Garnier or Heinrich Tessenow. However, during the following Expressionism era, innovative projects were rarely implemented and opposed this sober style with a picturesque spirit – as exemplified by the amorphous watercolor architectural fantasies of Hermann Finsterlin and colorful city crests of Bruno Taut. At the same time, the first Bauhaus manifesto by Walter Gropius featuring the image of a crystal cathedral (by Lyonel Feininger) and the thick lines of Erich Mendelsohn demonstrates the expressive freedom of drawings, albeit in pure black and white. In both types of work the external contour dominates the nearly or entirely non-existent internal drawing.

The line loses its anonymity and no longer exists as a line among a group of lines that constitute the image, but becomes a means of expression. This emancipation of the line, the soberness of Reform Classicism and the sprawling ornamentation of the Art Nouveau style shaped architectural drawings of the classical Modern era. Contours and laterally applied local colors without gradations distinguish De Stijl, Russian Avantgarde and Bauhaus. What's more, these styles focused on axonometry, and in particular isometry, as an unusual – and for amateurs often incomprehensible – view at the center of many presentations. These depictions have a high decorative value, as they reduce the reproduction of construction to a quickly constructible set of lines and areas within a coordinate system with three axes and combine the horizontal and upright projections in an easily perceptible uniform 1:1:1 axial measure. The perspective illusion of depth is forsaken in favor

of technical measurable values. These linear visualizations, implemented with compass and straightedge, have few details, do not include settings or persons and bear witness to the "machine esthetics," which remained heroic, expressionist and individualistic among the futurists, but was now evolving into a focus on rationality and serial production – Le Corbusier's "Après le cubism" manifesto was published in 1918, the same year in which the (still expressionist) Bauhaus was established. In 1923 the first axonometry was published by De Stijl, eight years after Kasimir Malewitsch introduced it to art. Subsequently, when the conflict between romantic, conservative and expressionist architects on the one hand, and Neues Bauen (New Building) on the other was becoming more heated, especially in Germany, not only did the proposed and implemented buildings become more radical, but their geometrical drawings became increasingly linear. Similar to the often polemic choice of words, the buildings served to theoretically cement the views of their creators as well as establish their own historical derivation from the pre-rational tendencies in Art Nouveau and Reform Classicism. The pure white walls of the International Style served the self-fulfillment of the much older architectural draw-

Giovanni Antonio Canal
Campo San Giovanni e Paolo in Venice
18th century

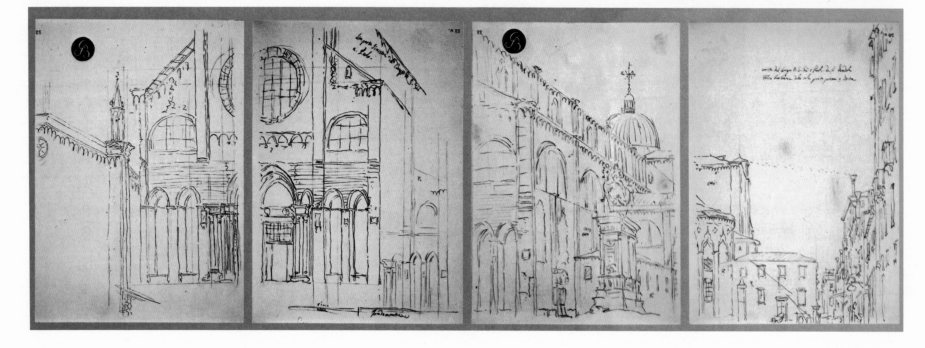

12

Construction and Imagination

The monumental style of the 1930s/1940s – in both totalitarian and democratic nations – derived from Classicism on the one hand and the reduction of rational tendencies on the other. Yet in contrast to Reform Classicism at the beginning of the century, it did not combine the two into constructions based on intellect and logic, but rather into a megalomaniac style aimed at heroics and monumentality. However, columns and pillars freed of bases and capitals (mostly cylinders) as well as geometrical constructions also applied the principles of Neues Bauen, especially if they involved whitewashed buildings. Nevertheless, apart from the Washington monument tradition, rustic or smooth hewn cyclopean masonry resembling machine production was more common. The stylistic variation of drawings from this era are as varied as its architectural elements – heroic, expressive sketches, presentation drawings with functional lines (without image contents) as well as impersonal technical drafts, which had previously only been present in Neues Bauen. In the technical drawing area, such as the semi-industrialized construction of temporary buildings, the visualization and application of Neues Bauen survived even in totalitarian states such as Germany, which refused the expression of International Style and New Rationalism. Modern architects such as Egon Eiermann could survive in the niches of industrial architecture, while their drawing style survived as technical drawings.

After 1945, Neues Bauen made a powerful comeback and largely replaced the previous corrupt conservative architecture. In the United States, the subjective artistic expression of architectural drawings also survived into the post-WWII era (William Lescaze, Richard Neutra, Rudolf Schindler). Eventually, expressive illustration (Böhm family) as well as building styles (Le Corbusier's church in Ronchamp) returned to Europe. It is remarkable that particularly the engineering architects of the era (Konrad Wachsman) were looking for a powerful means of expression. The architectural utopists of the 1960s/1970s introduced new ways of presentation to architectural drawings, adopted the schematic drawings and diagrams of Neues Bauen, however, transforming the graphic elements into decorative ones (Haus-Rucker-Co), or creating collages in emulation of Dada (Coop Himmelb(l)au). The fact that the pointed pen drawings of high-tech architecture resemble those of the early postmodern era of all styles (but with far

ing style with sharp contours without interior drawings described above. While this type of drawing became even more mathematical at this time, it still can be said that the drawing style of the first two decades of the 20th century led to the International Style of the 1920s/1930s.

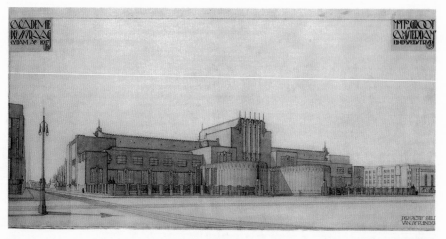

Michel de Klerk
Competition Design for an Academy of Fine Arts, Amsterdam
Pencil and ink on paper
45 x 86 cm
1918
Netherlands Architecture Institute, Rotterdam

Hector Guimard
Perspective View of a Villa
Graphite, pen and brown and black ink on tracing paper
1900–1905
Smithsonian Cooper-Hewitt, National Design Museum

more complex rooms) is among the most unusual aspects of the history of visualization. However, they soon introduced figures and colors, albeit in a very two-
dimensional and decorative form. A third option located between the technically
impeccable perspectives and isometrics of Neues Bauen and the experimental
illustration of the utopists, were classic linear perspectives (Rob Krier) with one
to three vanishing points as well as horizontal and upright projection (multiview
orthographic projection) that now experienced a revival: the latter were either
linked decoratively next to each other like a cut-out sheet (Giorgio Grassi) or in
a complicated avant-garde style within each other (Stanley Tigerman). As seen
in the work of Aldo Rossi, they are autonomous works of art within the context
of construction.

Rendering as a Challenge

Autonomous architectural illustrations survived to the postmodern era, whether
in the context of architectural theory, planned construction, or as an independent practice of visualization or potential building concepts. Since the 1990s and
Frank O. Gehry's first work processes from CAD to CAM, freehand sketches are
also in imminent danger of being entirely replaced by three-dimensional computer aided design models. However, the introduction of computers as drawing and
presentation tools in the late 20th century challenged their preeminence in the
area of two-dimensional visualization. Plans, linear perspective views and axono-
metric projections are now simply "released" from the computer. PC renderings
with the claim of being photographic realistic presentations dominate competition presentations and animations allow three-dimensional experiences in the
world of virtual data. A completely new form of visualization is emerging here,

which will be made even more impressive through special three-dimensional glasses in the future. The difference this makes to the entire construction sector was first visible at the Mercedes-Benz Museum, which was created by UNStudio 2006 in Stuttgart. Not the plan, but the dynamic data model from which new and altered plans could be generated were now considered binding for all participants. This goes far beyond Gehry's sketch-CAD-CAM process, as every craftsperson had to adjust to a spontaneously alterable concept. The design was only completed at the turnkey stage. Prior to this, the data model remained as alterable as a clay sculpture prior to firing – it could be stretched and twisted and all parts of the virtual building adjusted accordingly. This combines the spontaneity of a hand drawing with the perfection of technical rendering while forfeiting (personal) abstraction.

Hand drawings have qualities that even the most perfect rendering can't reproduce. Above all, these can be seen in the deliberate imperfections and abstractions. An abstract computer rendering is always a perspective view of a volume model. An abstract drawing or sketch gives the imagination and freedom to develop. A wireframe model might have no complete walls, but a pencil drawing allows the viewer to complete these themselves, albeit in their imagination. While a number of lines can capture an almost ideal image, a rendering has to choose just one angle. The remarkable power inherit in this means of architectural presentation becomes visible in the paintings of Zaha Hadid. She considered the possibilities of horizontal and upright projection, perspective and isometrics to be insufficient for portraying the expression of her experimental spatial constructions, and therefore used paintings to create abstract compositions, which, when objectively seen, partially create architectural space, but do not reflect a clear and discernable architectural reality in the eye of the beholder. The architectural image is detached from the physical structure, does not feature the (potentially) built reality, but portrays the effect of the space. Not only the construction details are abstracted, but also the concept of being able to grasp a construction with all its aspects. Computer renderings cannot show the true future, they just pretend that they can. Maybe it is because these appear so near to reality that they often lead to disappointment in the end.

This volume is a collection of very different artistic drawings, paintings and sketches, executed with different techniques. Everything has its place, from preliminary sketches to comprehensive drawings, from small realizations to huge utopias. Within the pages of this book are numerous sketches of various sizes from all corners of the international architectural scene, as well as from freelance architectural sketchers and a few less well-known architects who nevertheless show an original approach to architectural drawings. These show a range of different styles, not only in terms of buildings, but also in terms of artistic style. The role the drawing process played in the development of the project is also often visible: sometimes functioning as a note about the basic idea, and sometimes as a meditative expression of the entire design. Dramatic perspectives alternate with harmonic views, or illustrations with a drawn manifesto. Often these drawings are accompanied by photographs of the realized buildings, allowing a direct comparison between the design process presented in the drawing and the final building. This volume shows the never ending possibilities that hand drawn illustrations open up for the building process, the wealth of forms and ideas that hide behind the empty canvas, and how a non rendered surface introduces huge diversity to the development of the final building.

Frank Lloyd Wright
Concrete House
Published in Ladies' Home Journal, 1907

Collection of Architectural Visions

ARTHUR W. ANDERSSON

Arthur W. Andersson (born in Gillette, WY, USA, 1957) has practiced architecture throughout the United States for more than three decades. He was educated at the University of Kansas and the University of London (United Kingdom), and has taught design at Tulane University, The University of Texas at Austin, and the University of Houston. Through his Austin-based practice, Andersson has successfully expanded the impressive tradition established by his mentor, the late Charles W. Moore. The collaborative of Andersson-Wise Architects has grown into an energetic young firm of twelve designers and architects with a commitment to producing consistently significant work by reinforcing the physical and historical connections that give specificity to a place.

Cabin on Flathead Lake
Polson, MT, USA
Pencil
12 x 9 cm
Sketch: 2008
Building: 2009
Arthur W. Andersson/Andersson-Wise Architects

Cabin on Flathead Lake
Polson, MT, USA
Watercolor
30 x 28 cm
Sketch: 2008
Building: 2009
Arthur W. Andersson/Andersson-Wise Architects

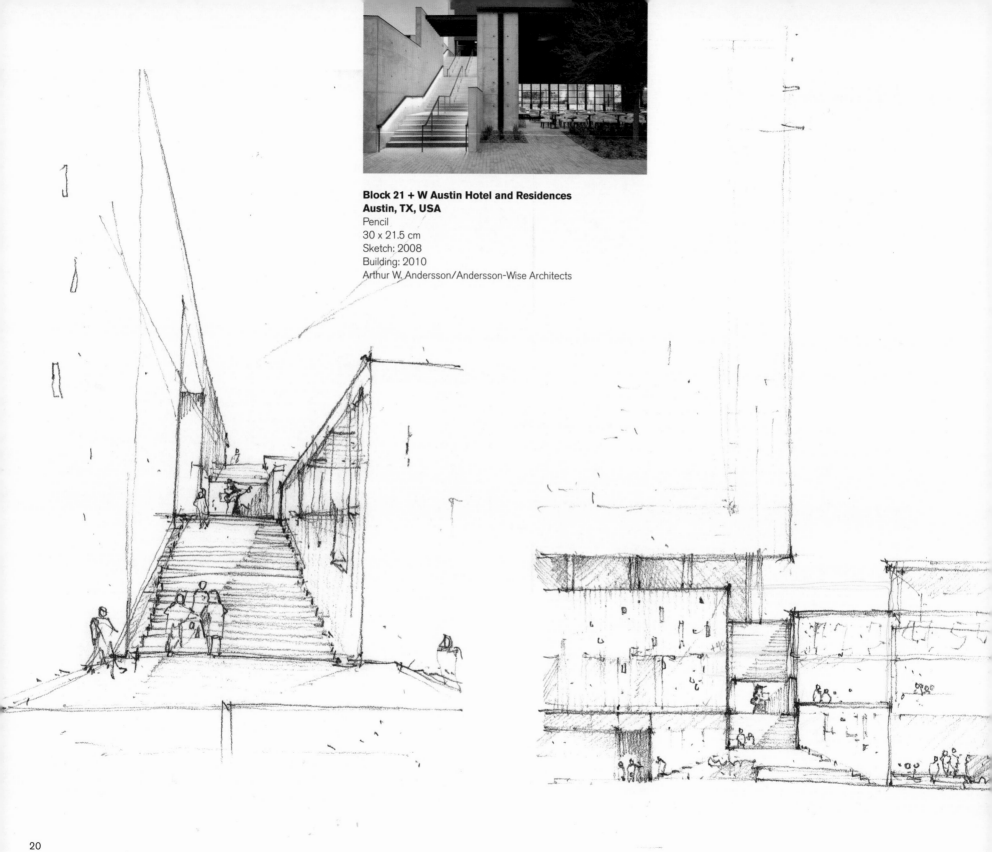

Block 21 + W Austin Hotel and Residences
Austin, TX, USA
Pencil
30 x 21.5 cm
Sketch: 2008
Building: 2010
Arthur W. Andersson/Andersson-Wise Architects

VIEW FROM PLAZA LOOKING EAST
ANDERSSON·WISE ARCHITECTS 2009

Topfer Theatre at ZACH
Austin, TX, USA
Watercolor
43 x 30 cm
Sketch: 2008
Building: 2012
Arthur W. Andersson/Andersson-Wise Architects

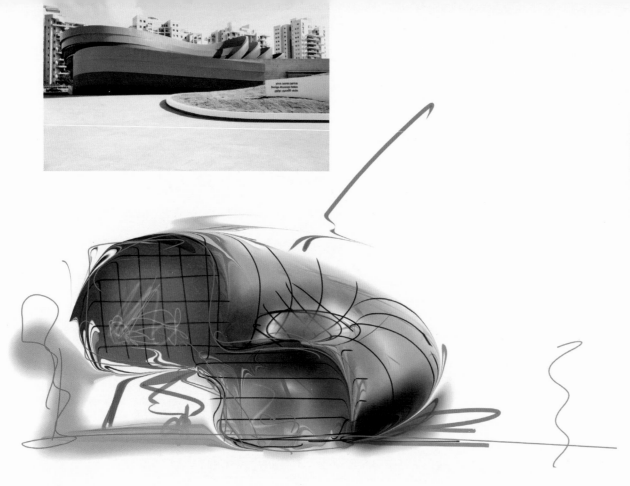

RON ARAD

Ron Arad (born in Tel Aviv, Israel, 1951) was educated at Bezalel Academy of Art and Design, Jerusalem, and the Architectural Association, London. He co-founded the One Off Studio with Caroline Thorman in 1981, Ron Arad Associates in 1989 and Ron Arad Architects in 2008. Arad held various influential academic roles around Europe, and until 2009, acted as professor and head of the design products department at the Royal College of Art in London. His experimentation with the use and potential of material and form, and the radical questioning of the limits of structure, discipline and convention in the making of studio pieces, art and architecture, has placed him at the forefront of contemporary creative culture.

Design Museum Holon
Holon, Israel
Digital sketch on pen tablet
Sketch: 2004
Building: 2010
Ron Arad/Ron Arad Architects

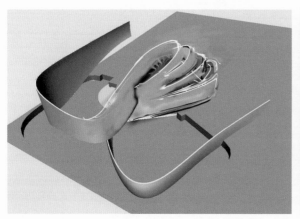

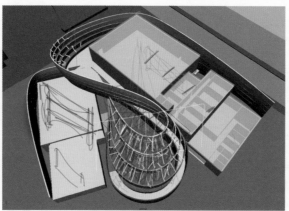

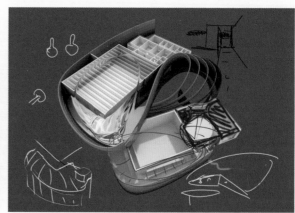

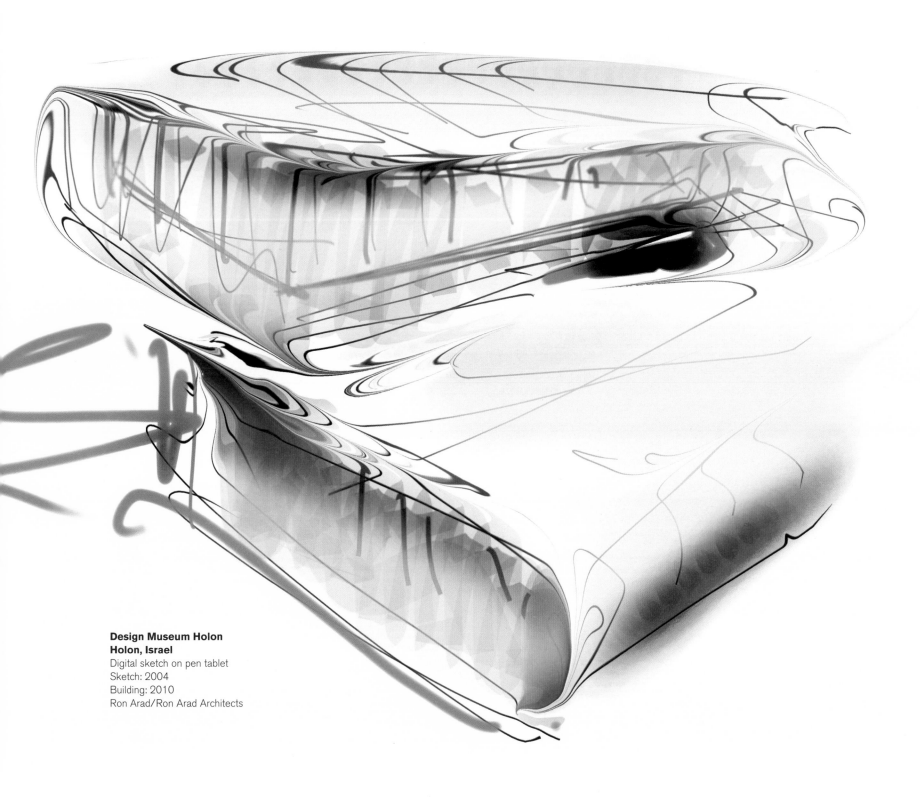

Design Museum Holon
Holon, Israel
Digital sketch on pen tablet
Sketch: 2004
Building: 2010
Ron Arad/Ron Arad Architects

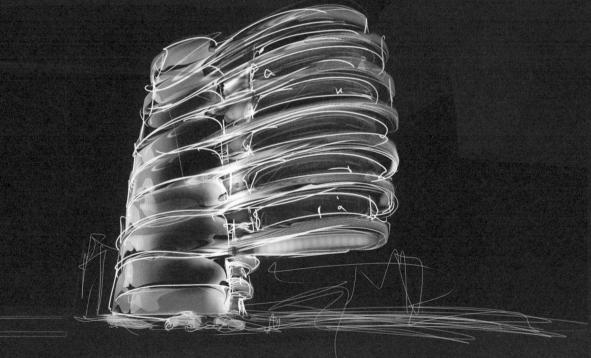

154 Ha Yarkon Street
Tel Aviv, Israel
Digital sketch on pen tablet
Sketch: 2006
Building: ongoing
Ron Arad/Ron Arad Architects

Willow Street Hotel
London, United Kingdom
Digital sketch on pen tablet
2011
Ron Arad/Ron Arad Architects

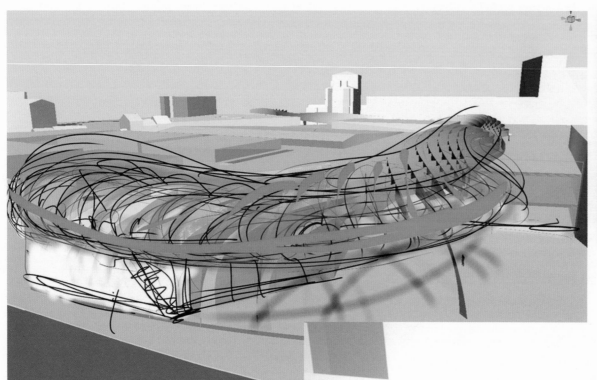

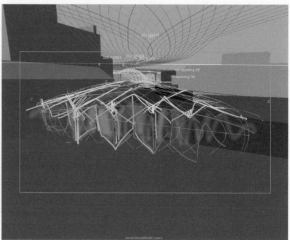

Médiacité
Liège, Belgium
Digital sketch on pen tablet
Sketch: 2007
Building: 2009
Ron Arad/Ron Arad Architects

Médiacité
Liège, Belgium
Digital sketch on pen tablet
Sketch: 2007
Building: 2009
Ron Arad/Ron Arad Architects

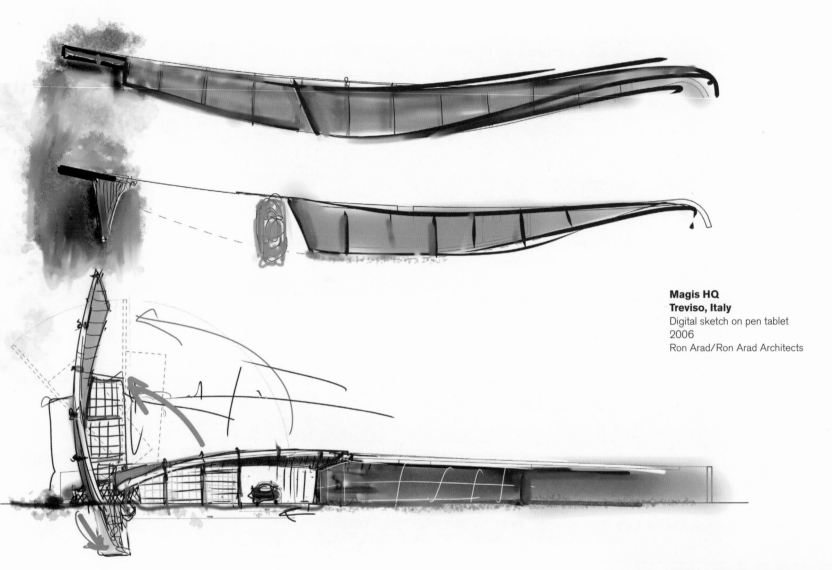

Magis HQ
Treviso, Italy
Digital sketch on pen tablet
2006
Ron Arad/Ron Arad Architects

Crystal Side
Mountain Side
Sky
not alpine?

Hotel Wattens
Innsbruck, Austria
Digital sketch on pen tablet
2004
Ron Arad/Ron Arad Architects

ARCHITECTURE PARADIGM

Architecture Paradigm was established in the year 1996 by Manoj Ladhad, Sandeep J and Vimal Jain. Sandeep J (born in Bangalore, India, 1973) completed his Bachelor of Architecture at BMS College of Engineering, Bangalore in 1995 and also attended Glenn Murcutt Master Class 2012 in Australia. As one of the founders of Architecture Paradigm, he has been involved in a wide range of projects, ranging from small residential dwellings to large-scale housing projects, as well as commercial establishments and hospitality projects. Sandeep J firmly believes that architecture is about people and sensitivity to the idea of place. He uses sketching and drawing as a means of developing a connection with place, helping in anticipating the quality of space, tactility and experience.

Brigade Millenium Club
Colored pencil and felt-tip pen
21 x 29.7 cm
2006
Sandeep J/Architecture Paradigm

Brigade Millenium Club
Colored pencil and felt-tip pen
21 x 29.7 cm
2006
Sandeep J/Architecture Paradigm

MLR Convention Center
Pencil and colored pencil
21 x 29.7 cm
Sketch: 2003
Building: 2005
Sandeep J/Architecture Paradigm

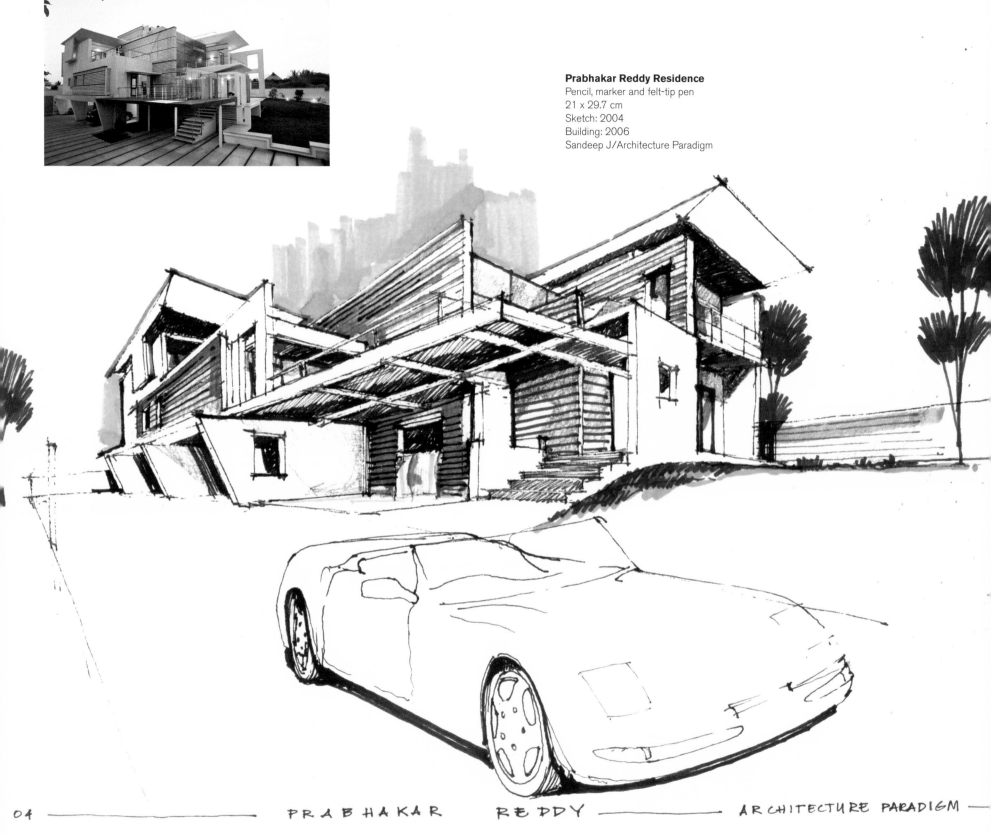

Prabhakar Reddy Residence
Pencil, marker and felt-tip pen
21 x 29.7 cm
Sketch: 2004
Building: 2006
Sandeep J/Architecture Paradigm

04 ———————— P R A B H A K A R   R E D D Y ———— ARCHITECTURE PARADIGM

Manoj Jain Residence
Pencil, marker and felt-tip pen
21 x 29.7 cm
Sketch: 2005
Building: 2007
Sandeep J/Architecture Paradigm

FEB 2005   MANOJ JAIN   ARCHITECTURE PARADIGM

Anil Kush Residence
Pencil, marker and felt-tip pen
21 x 29.7 cm
Sketch: 2006
Building: 2008
Sandeep J/Architecture Paradigm

FEB 2006 — RESIDENCE FOR MR KUSH - 2 — ARCHITECTURE PARADIGM

MAIN OPERATION ROOM

JEREMY HUGH ASTON

Jeremy Hugh Aston (born in Doncaster, South Yorkshire, United Kingdom) graduated from Northumbria University with a bachelors degree in 1994, before completing his Masters in 1996 at the Royal College of Art, London. Aston is a partner and creative director of Simpli Design, a Portuguese based Design Consultancy, and also works as a lecturer at ESAD, ESEIG and IPCA, all in the north of Portugal.

RECEPTION AREA

PRODUCT WALL

WAITING SEATING

Clínica Veterinária Santa Luzia (CVSL)
Guimarães, Portugal
Pencil and Photoshop coloring
18 x 25 cm
Sketches: 2006
Building: 2007
Jeremy Hugh Aston/Simpli Design

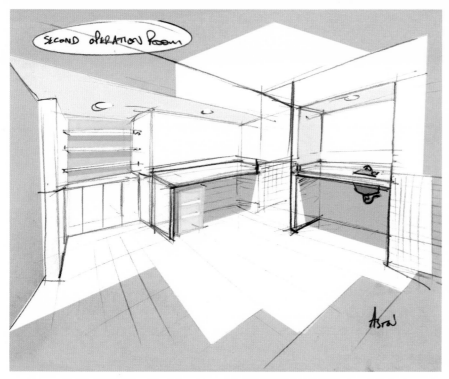

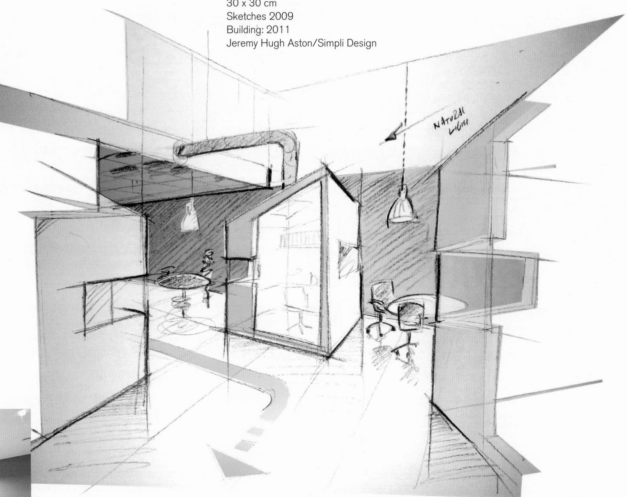

Factory Business Center
Braga, Portugal
Permanent marker and black pencil
30 x 30 cm
Sketches 2009
Building: 2011
Jeremy Hugh Aston/Simpli Design

Factory Business Center
Braga, Portugal
Markers and colored pencils with
Photoshop coloring
10 x 25 cm
Sketches: 2009
Building: 2011
Jeremy Hugh Aston/Simpli Design

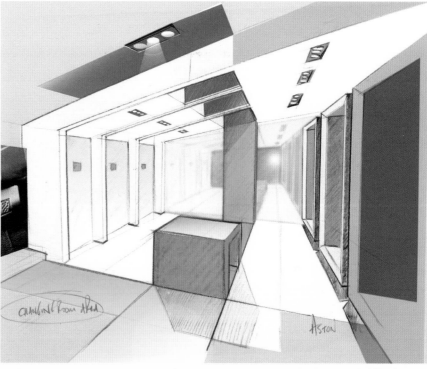

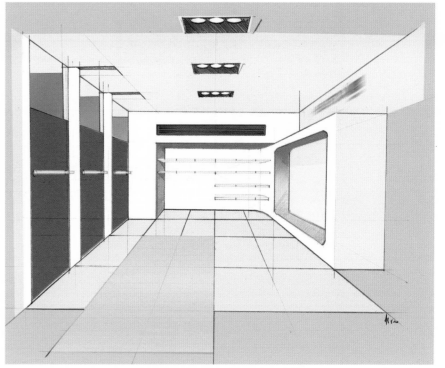

Various Store Interiors
Lisbon, Portugal
Colored pencils with Photoshop coloring
18 x 25 cm
Sketches: 2003/2005
Buildings: 2005/2007
Jeremy Hugh Aston/Simpli Design

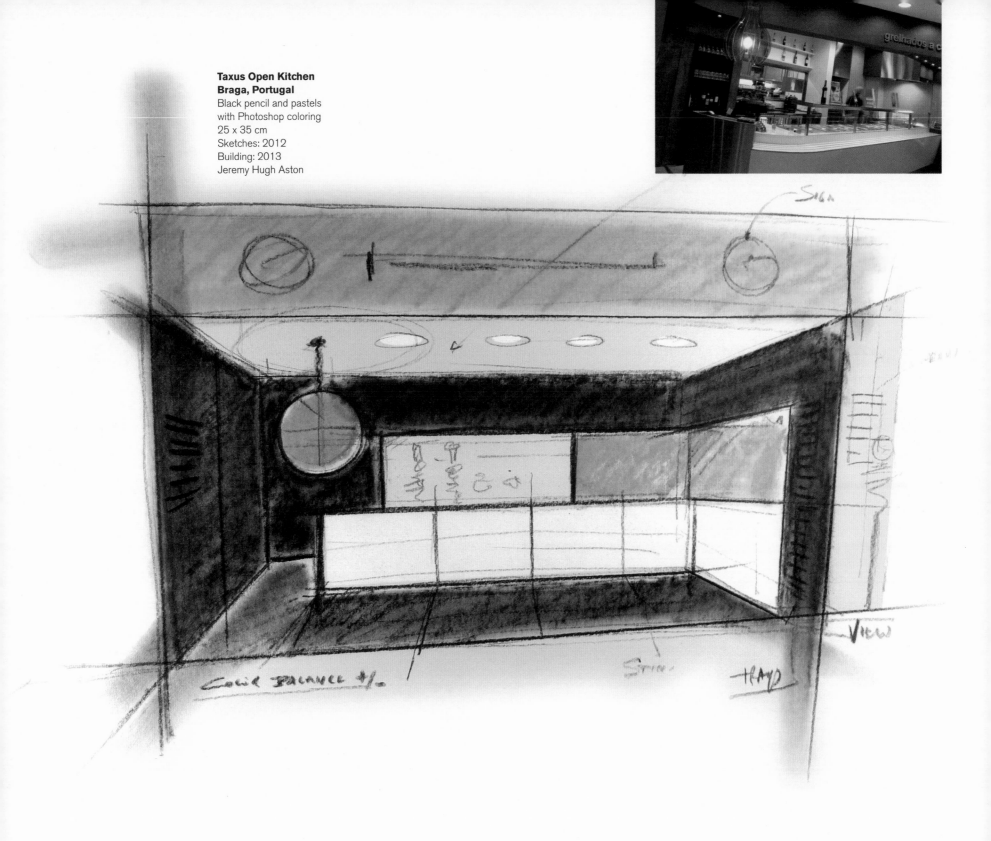

Taxus Open Kitchen
Braga, Portugal
Black pencil and pastels
with Photoshop coloring
25 x 35 cm
Sketches: 2012
Building: 2013
Jeremy Hugh Aston

40

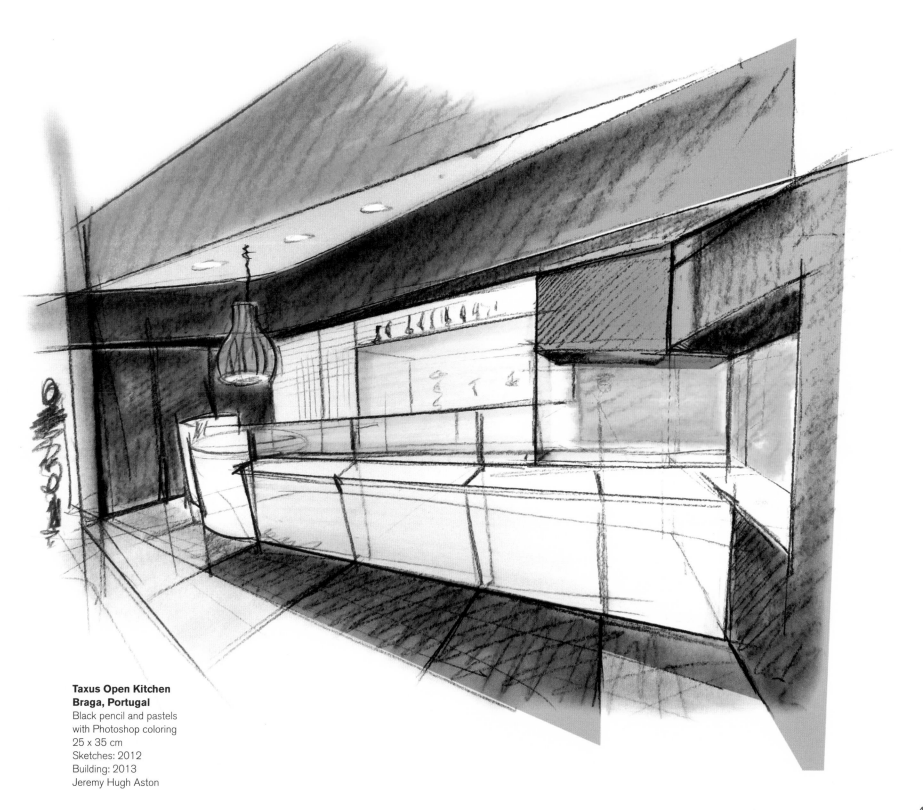

Taxus Open Kitchen
Braga, Portugal
Black pencil and pastels
with Photoshop coloring
25 x 35 cm
Sketches: 2012
Building: 2013
Jeremy Hugh Aston

ATELIER BOW-WOW

Atelier Bow-Wow is a Tokyo-based firm founded by Yoshiharu Tsukamoto (born in Kanagawa Prefecture, Japan, 1965) and Momoyo Kaijima (born in Tokyo, Japan, 1969) in 1992. Their interest lies in diverse fields ranging from architectural design to urban research and the creation of public artworks, which are produced based on the theory called behaviorology. The practice has designed and built houses, public and commercial buildings mainly in Tokyo, as well as Europe and the USA.

Miyashita Park
Tokyo, Japan
Pencil
1,188 x 2,523 cm
2012
Atelier Bow-Wow + Tokyo Institute of
Technology Tsukamoto Lab

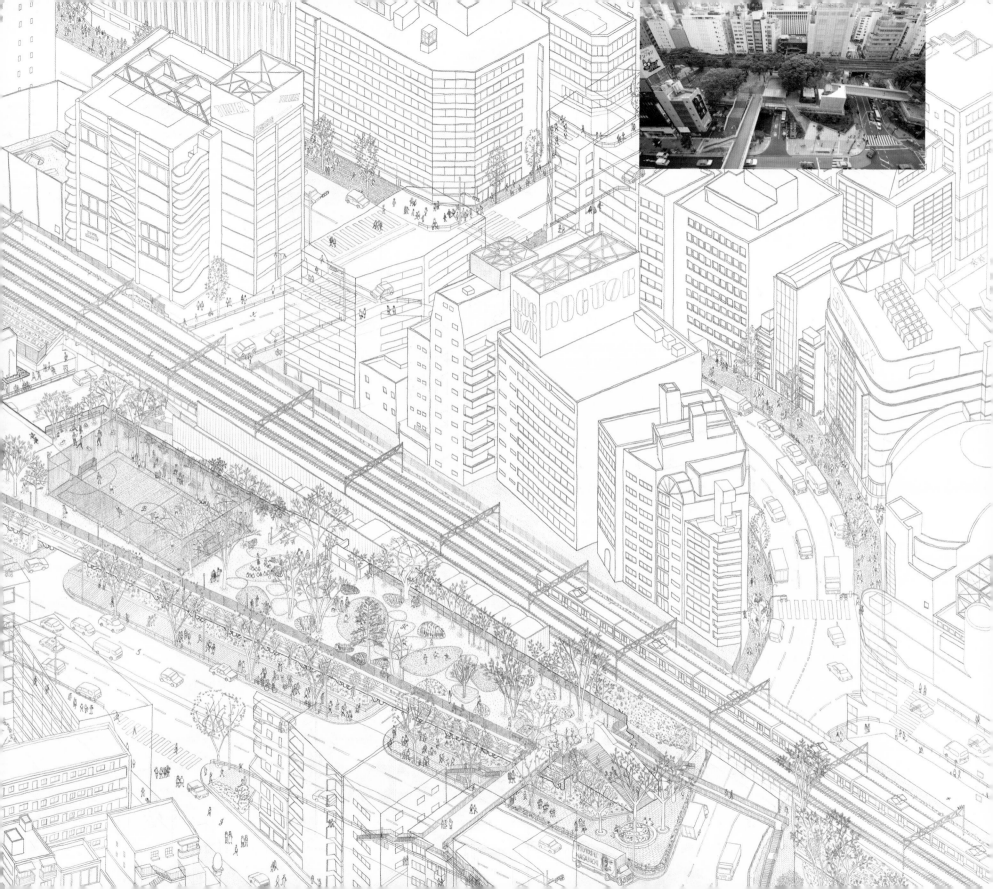

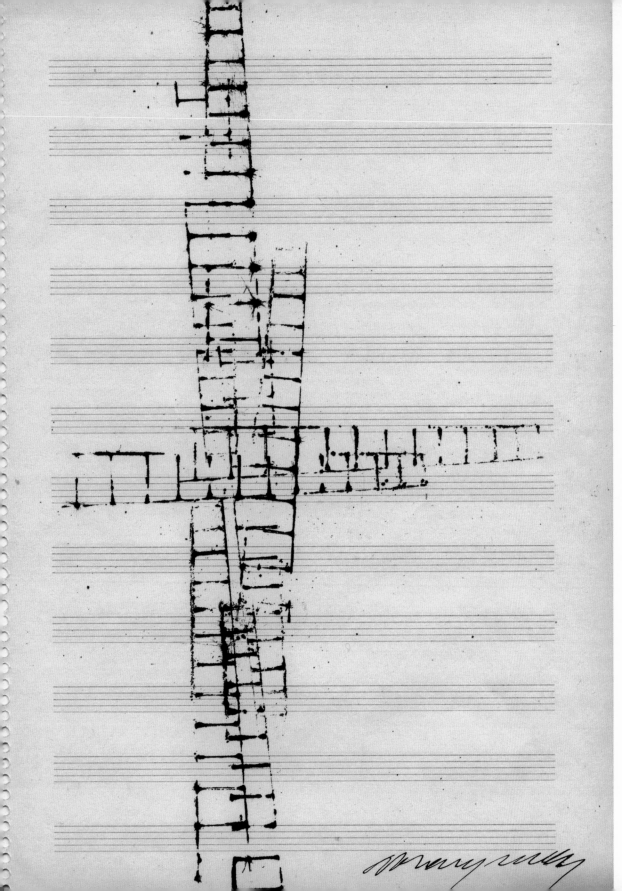

YURI AVVAKUMOV

Yuri Avvakumov (born in Tiraspol, Moldova, 1957) graduated from the Moscow Architectural Institute in 1981. He set up his own studio, Agitarch, in 1988 and established the Utopia Foundation in 1993. He has curated and participated in various international exhibitions and also took part in the Venice Biennale in 1996, 2003, and 2008. Public collections of his work are on display in various locations, including the State Russian Museum, Deutsches Architekturmuseum, Victoria & Albert Museum and the ZKM Museum of New Art, Karlsruhe.

La Scala
Monotype prints
on music paper
29 x 20 cm
1989–2005
Yuri Avvakumov

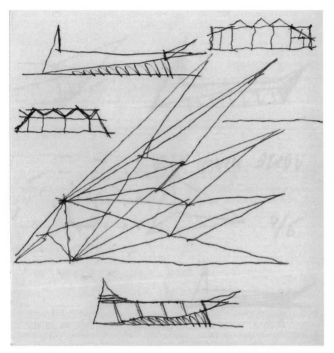

Park Pavilion
Abu Dhabi Guggenheim Biennale
Abu Dhabi, United Arab Emirates
Concept design
6 x 6 cm
2007
Yuri Avvakumov (with Andrei Savin)

Aerobridge
Solovki island, Russia
Ink on tracing paper
21 x 30 cm
2001
Yuri Avvakumov

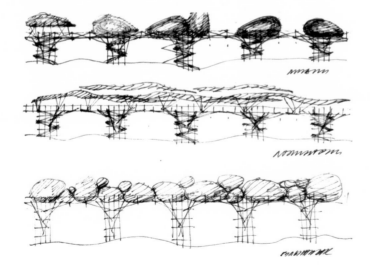

Krasnaya Gorka Bridge
Krasnaya Gorka, Russia
Concept design
3.2 x 21 cm
1997
Yuri Avvakumov

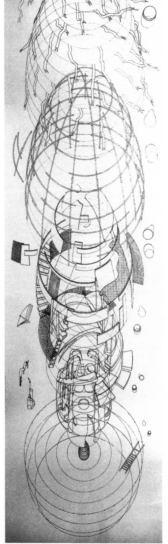

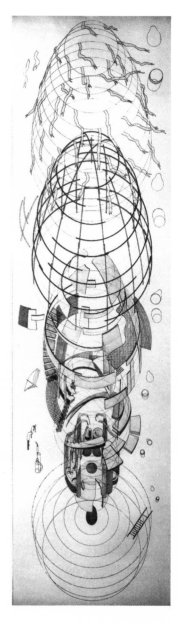

Matrioshka House
Concept design
120 x 32 cm
1984
Yuri Avvakumov (with I. Pischukevich)

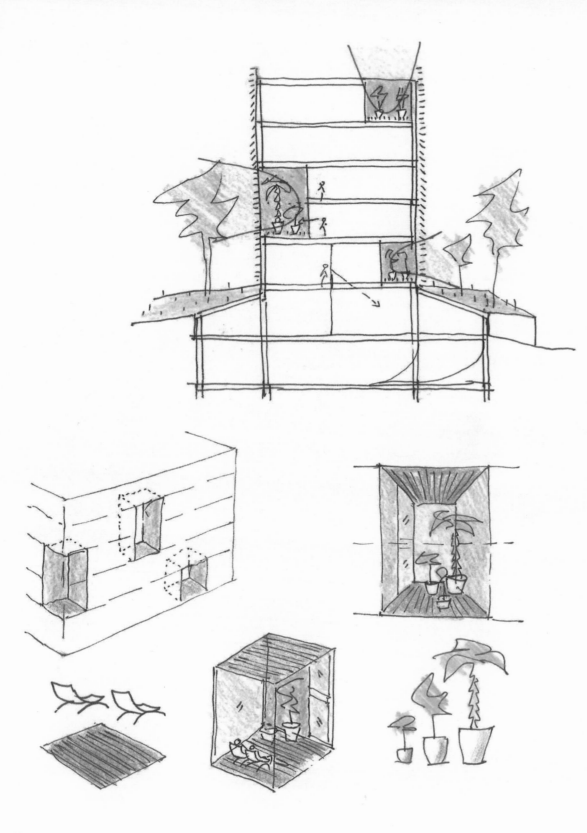

3LHD

Saša Begović (born in Bjelovar, Croatia, 1967) completed his studies at the Architectural Technical High School in Zagreb in 1986. He later graduated from the Faculty of Architecture, University of Zagreb. In 1994 he founded architectural studio 3LHD with partners Marko Dabrovi , Tanja Grozdani and Silvije Novak. He currently works as a guest lecturer and critic of architecture faculties in Europe and Croatia and periodically writes for architectural and art journals. He is also a member of CAA's Court of Honor, the commission for sports buildings and landscape of the Croatian Olympic committee.

Polyclinic St
Split, Croatia
Felt-tip pen, crayon, colored pencil
28.8 x 20.49 cm
2009
Saša Begović/3LHD

atrium / logia

Polyclinic St
Split, Croatia
Felt-tip pen, crayon and colored pencil
29.65 x 20.97 cm
2009
Saša Begović/3LHD

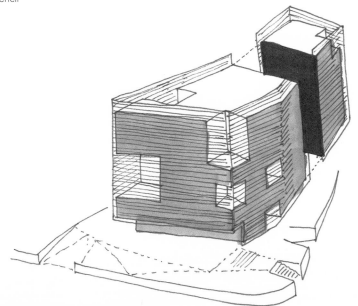

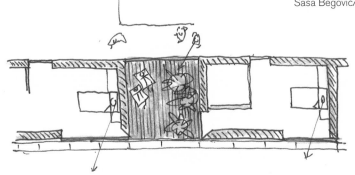

Polyclinic St
Split, Croatia
Felt-tip pen
14.12 x 15.62 cm
2009
Saša Begović/3LHD

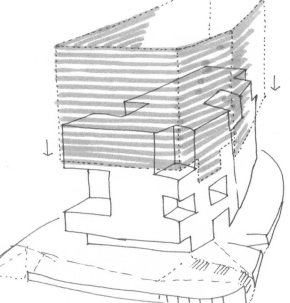

Polyclinic St
Split, Croatia
Felt-tip pen, crayon and colored pencil
14.43 x 18.72 cm
2009
Saša Begović/3LHD

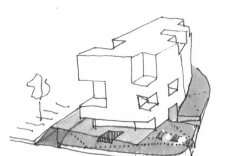

Polyclinic St
Split, Croatia
Felt-tip pen, crayon and colored pencil
8.06 x 11.32cm
2009
Saša Begović/3LHD

Park Muzil
Pula, Croatia
Felt-tip pen
10.22 x 27.08 cm
2011
Bence Pasztor/3LHD

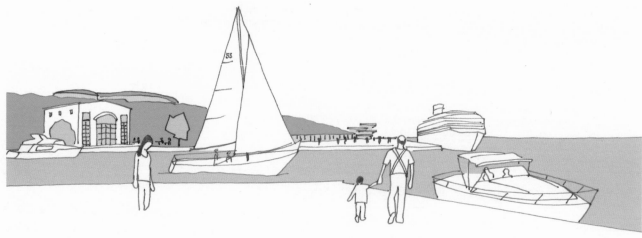

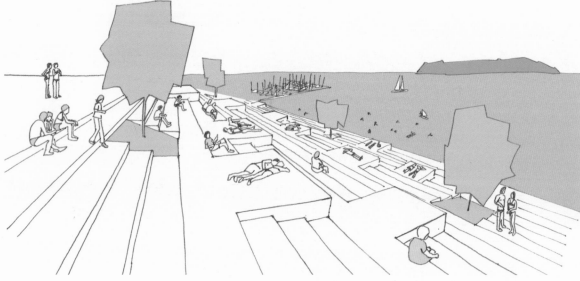

Park Muzil, Pula
Pula, Croatia
Felt-tip pen
15.47 x 27.89 cm
2011
Bence Pasztor/3LHD

Park Muzil
Pula, Croatia
Felt-tip pen
10.88 x 28.97 cm
2011
Bence Pasztor/3LHD

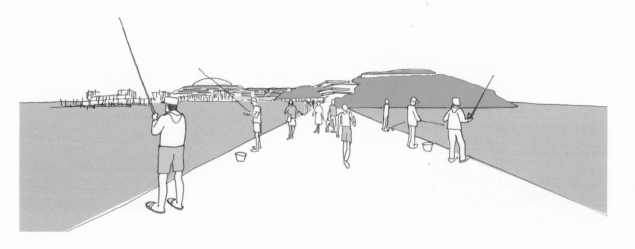

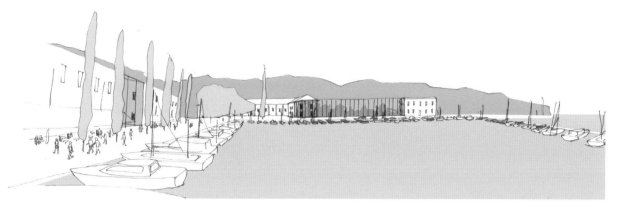

Park Muzil
Pula, Croatia
Felt-tip pen
14.49 x 30.06 cm
2011
Bence Pasztor/3LHD

Park Muzil
Pula, Croatia
Felt-tip pen
13.5 x 41.95 cm
2011
Bence Pasztor/3LHD

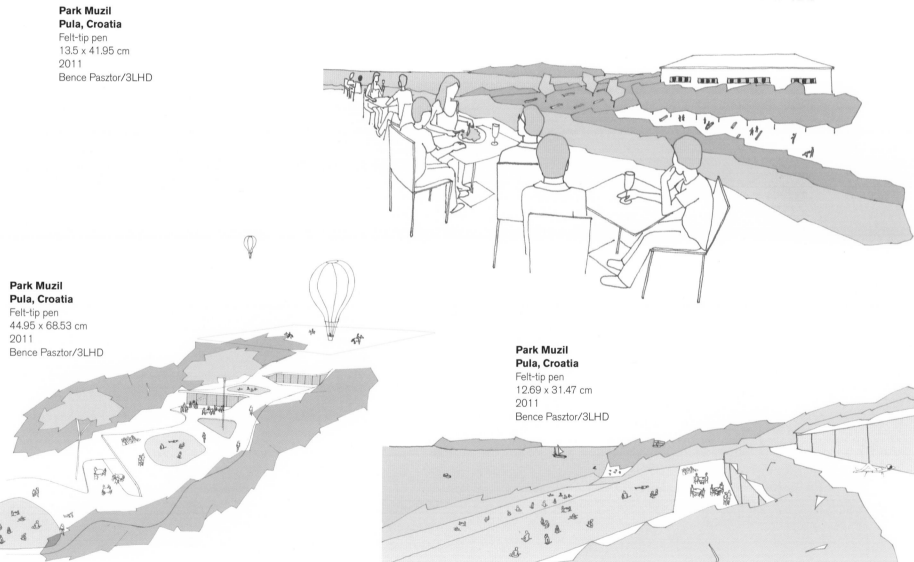

Park Muzil
Pula, Croatia
Felt-tip pen
44.95 x 68.53 cm
2011
Bence Pasztor/3LHD

Park Muzil
Pula, Croatia
Felt-tip pen
12.69 x 31.47 cm
2011
Bence Pasztor/3LHD

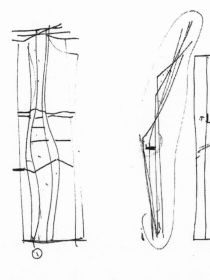

Five Franklin Place
New York City, NY, USA
Felt-tip pen on paper
42 x 29.7 cm
2007
Ben van Berkel

BEN VAN BERKEL

Ben van Berkel (born in Utrecht, the Netherlands, 1957) is the Co-Founder and Principal Architect of UNStudio in Amsterdam and Shanghai. He studied architecture at the Rietveld Academy in Amsterdam and at the Architectural Association in London, receiving the AA Diploma with Honours in 1987. UNStudio is a network of specialists in architecture, urban development and infrastructure. Current projects include restructuring the station area of Arnhem, the Raffles City mixed-use development in Hangzhou and a dance theater for St. Petersburg. Currently he is Professor of Conceptual Design at the Staedelschule in Frankfurt/Main and was recently awarded the Kenzo Tange Visiting Professor's Chair at Harvard University GSD.

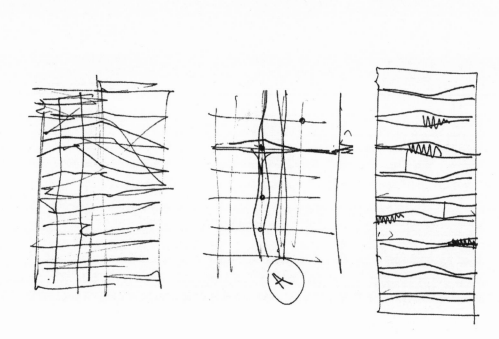

The Scotts Tower
Singapore
Felt-tip pen on paper
42 x 29.7 cm
2010
Ben van Berkel

pattern

pattern

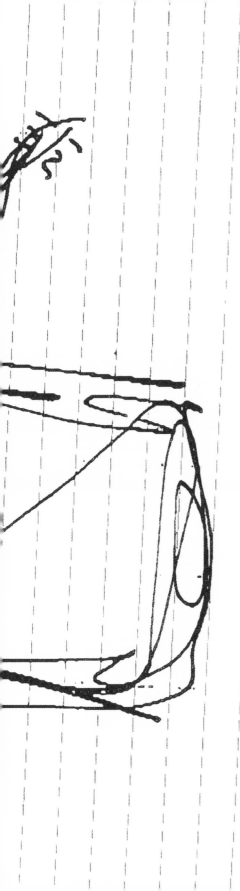

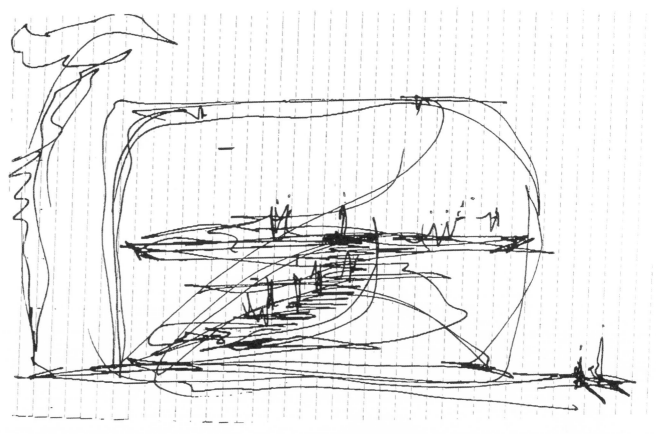

Music Theatre
Graz, Austria
Felt-tip pen on notepaper
Sketch: approx. 2005
Building: 2008
Ben van Berkel

Music Theatre
Graz, Austria
Felt-tip pen on notepaper
Sketch: approx. 2005
Building: 2008
Ben van Berkel

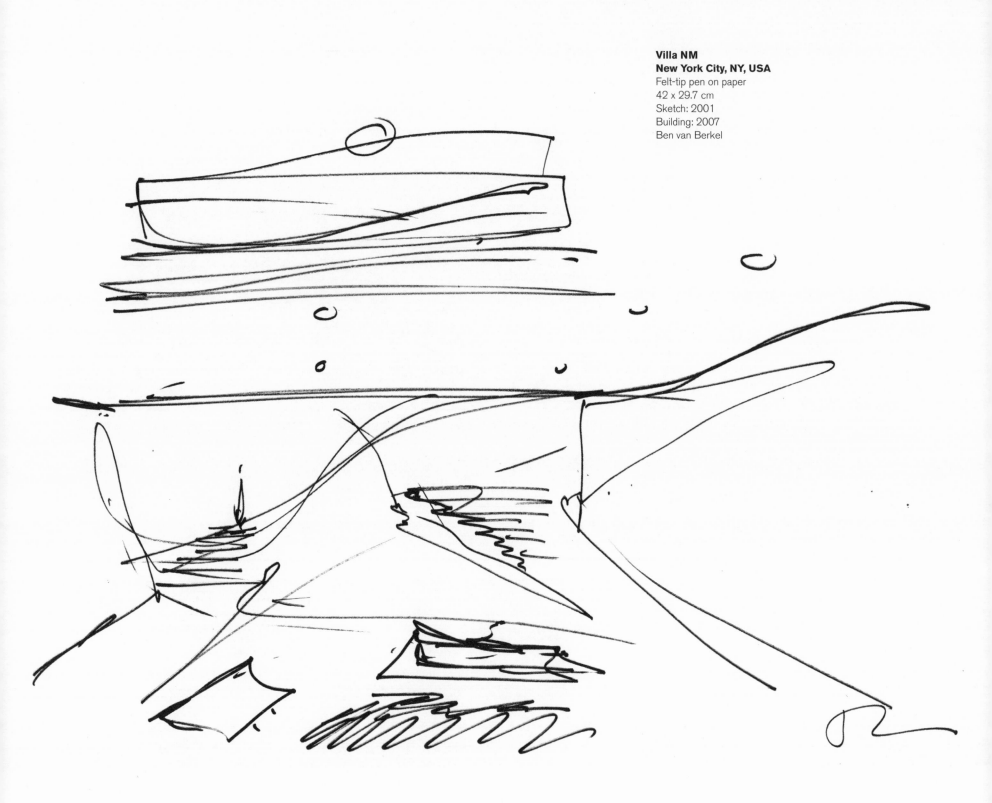

Villa NM
New York City, NY, USA
Felt-tip pen on paper
42 x 29.7 cm
Sketch: 2001
Building: 2007
Ben van Berkel

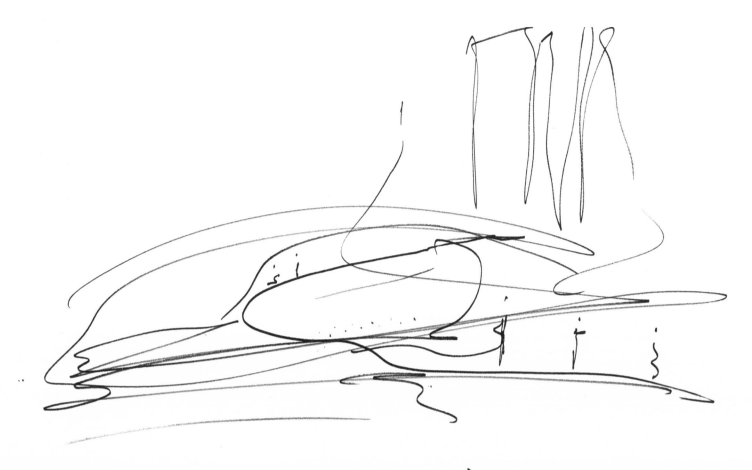

Villa NM
New York City, NY, USA
Felt-tip pen on paper
42 x 29.7 cm
Sketch: 2001
Building: 2007
Ben van Berkel

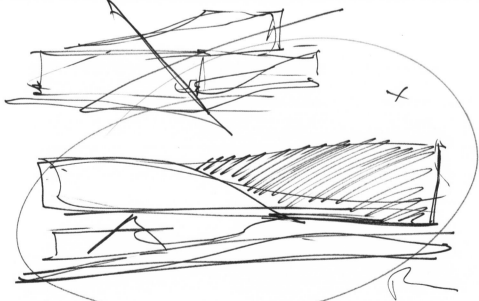

Villa NM
New York City, NY, USA
Felt-tip on paper
42 x 29.7 cm
Sketch: 2001
Building: 2007
Ben van Berkel

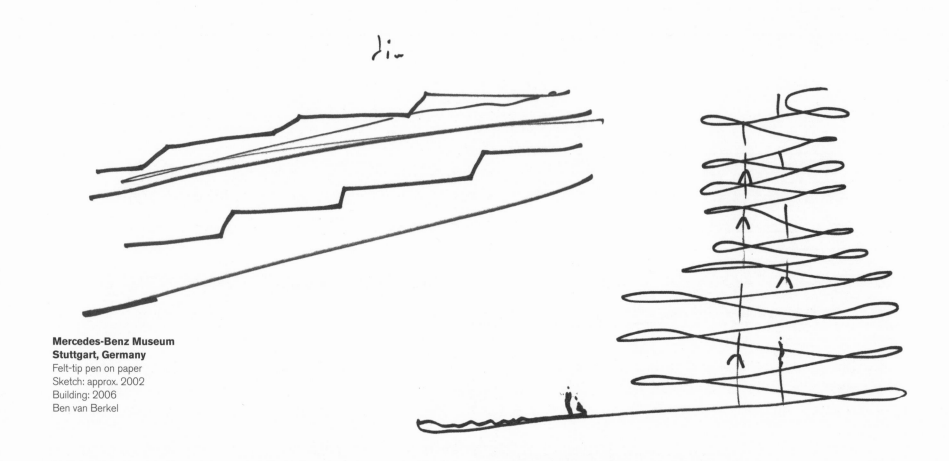

**Mercedes-Benz Museum
Stuttgart, Germany**
Felt-tip pen on paper
Sketch: approx. 2002
Building: 2006
Ben van Berkel

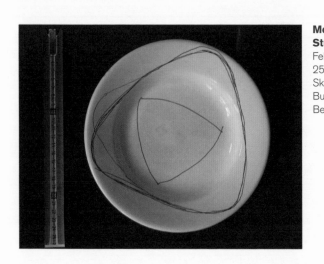

**Mercedes-Benz Museum
Stuttgart, Germany**
Felt-tip pen on ceramic bowl
25 x 25 cm
Sketch: approx. 2002
Building: 2006
Ben van Berkel

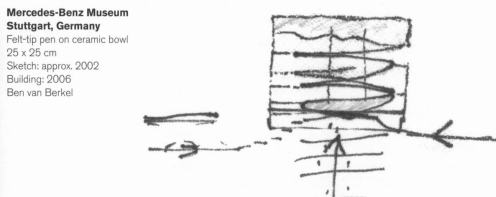

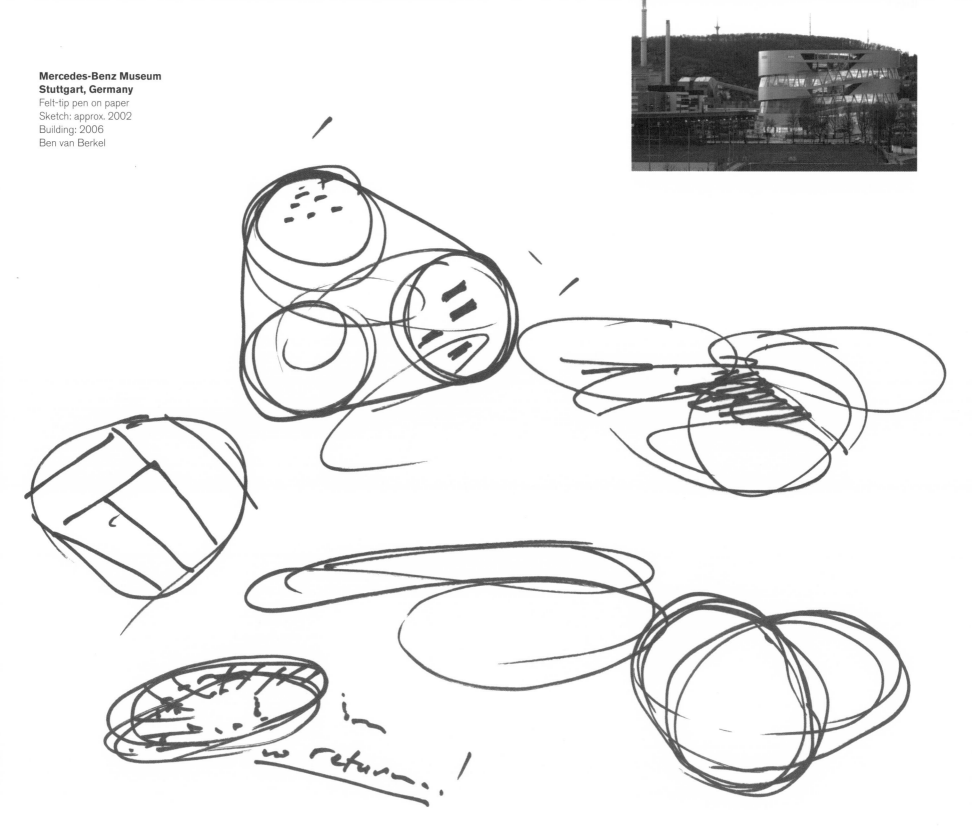

Mercedes-Benz Museum
Stuttgart, Germany
Felt-tip pen on paper
Sketch: approx. 2002
Building: 2006
Ben van Berkel

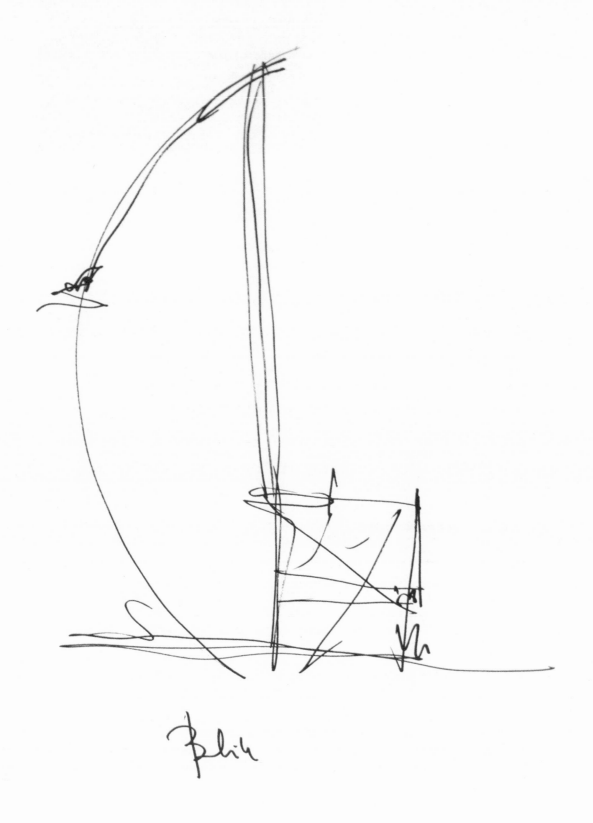

RICARDO BOFILL

Ricardo Bofill (born in Barcelona, Spain, 1939) is a Catalan architect. He studied in Switzerland at the School of Architecture in Geneva. In 1963 he gathered together a multidisciplinary group of people, from a range of different fields, including architects, engineers, planners, sociologists, writers, moviemakers, and philosophers; this group formed the basis for what would later become Taller de Arquitectura. Bofill's early work focused on the characteristic craft elements of traditional Catalan architecture, whereas his later work dealt with urban planning problems. In 1971 he formed a team in Paris, and from 1979 on, the activities of Bofill's Taller de Arquitectura took place mainly in France. In 2000 Bofill regrouped his activity in Spain. Bofill's many international projects validate his capacity to design in harmony with different local cultures as the result of combining know-how and global experience.

W Barcelona
Barcelona, Spain
Felt-tip pen on transparent paper
59.4 x 84.1 cm
Sketch: 2007
Building: 2010
Ricardo Bofill/Taller de Arquitectura

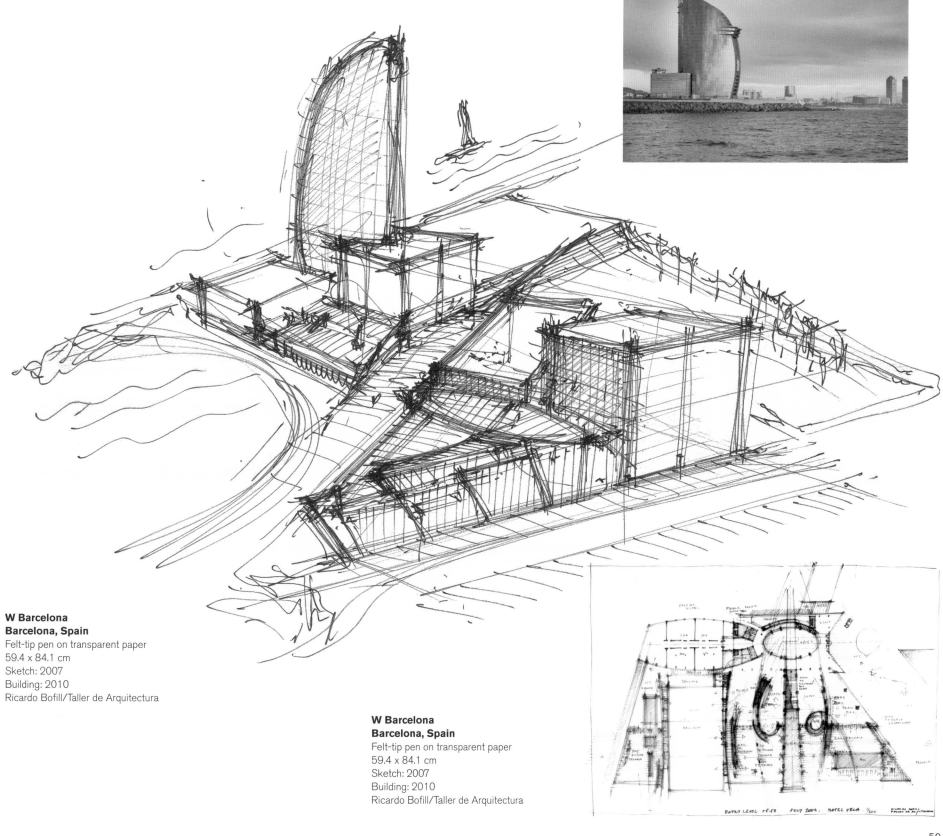

W Barcelona
Barcelona, Spain
Felt-tip pen on transparent paper
59.4 x 84.1 cm
Sketch: 2007
Building: 2010
Ricardo Bofill/Taller de Arquitectura

W Barcelona
Barcelona, Spain
Felt-tip pen on transparent paper
59.4 x 84.1 cm
Sketch: 2007
Building: 2010
Ricardo Bofill/Taller de Arquitectura

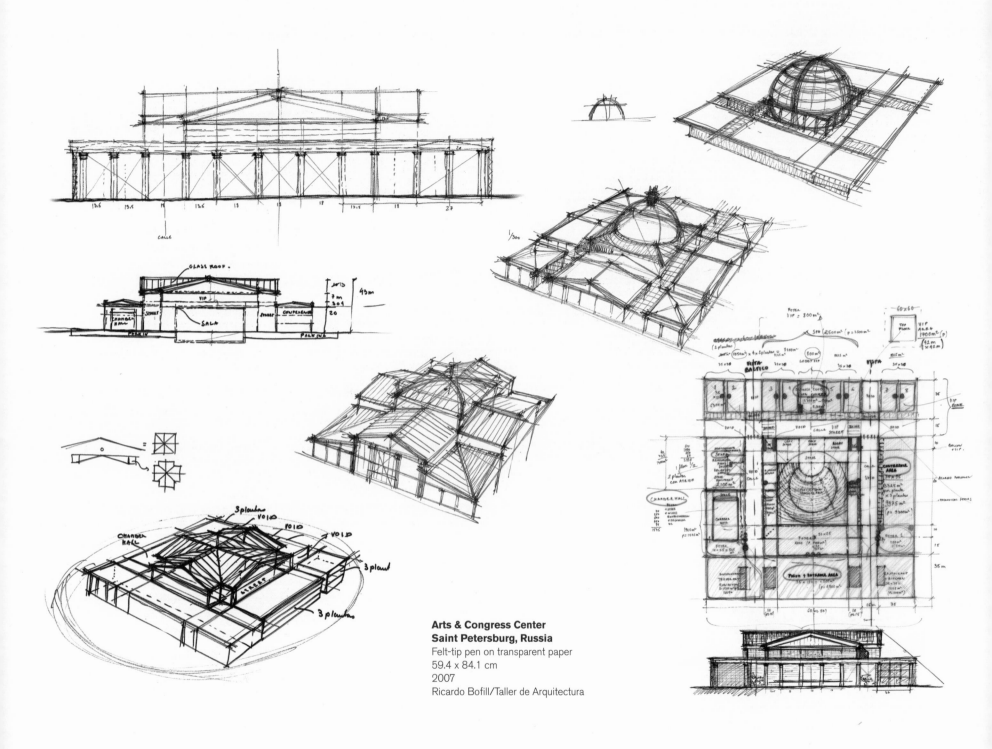

**Arts & Congress Center
Saint Petersburg, Russia**
Felt-tip pen on transparent paper
59.4 x 84.1 cm
2007
Ricardo Bofill/Taller de Arquitectura

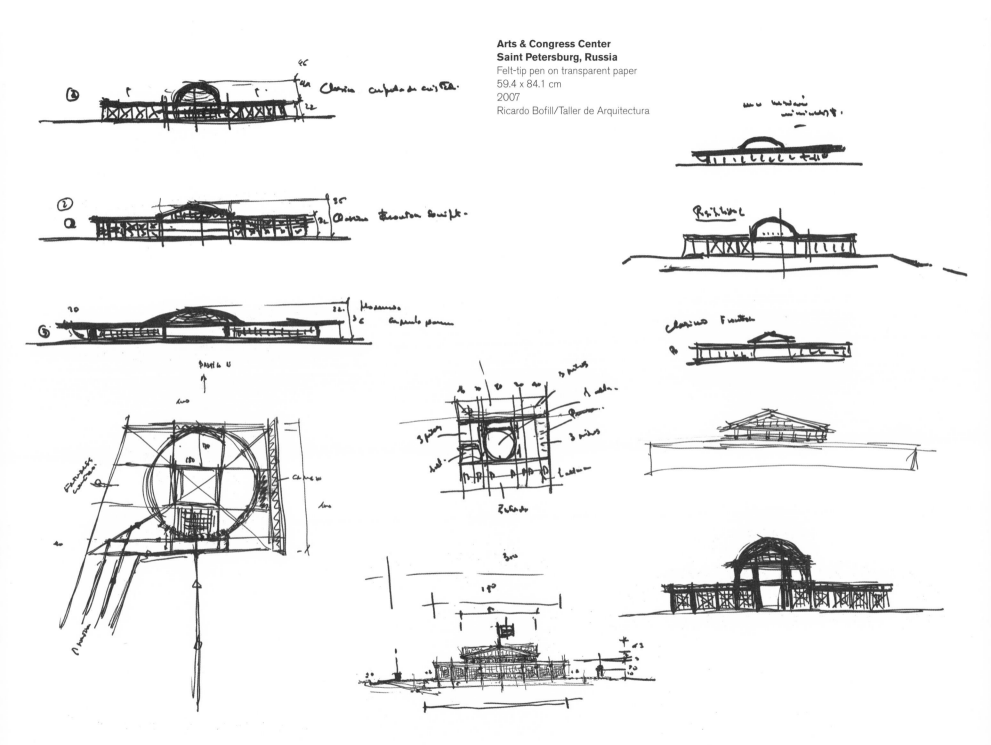

Arts & Congress Center
Saint Petersburg, Russia
Felt-tip pen on transparent paper
59.4 x 84.1 cm
2007
Ricardo Bofill/Taller de Arquitectura

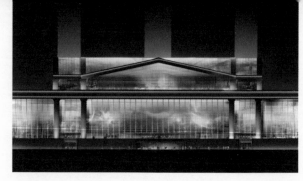

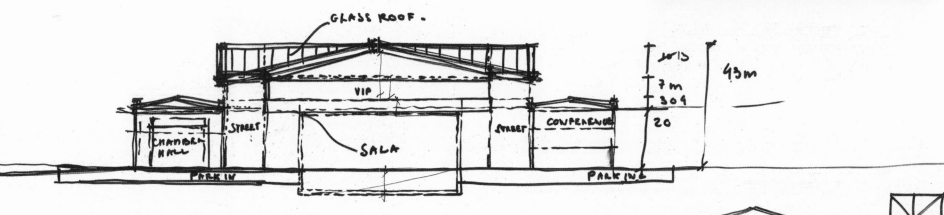

GLASS ROOF.

VIP

STREET   SALA   STREET   CONFERENCE

CHAMBER
HALL

PARKIN   PARKING

10'3
7 m
30 q
20

43 m

Arts & Congress Center
Saint Petersburg, Russia
Felt-tip pen on transparent paper
59.4 x 84.1 cm
2007
Ricardo Bofill/Taller de Arquitectura

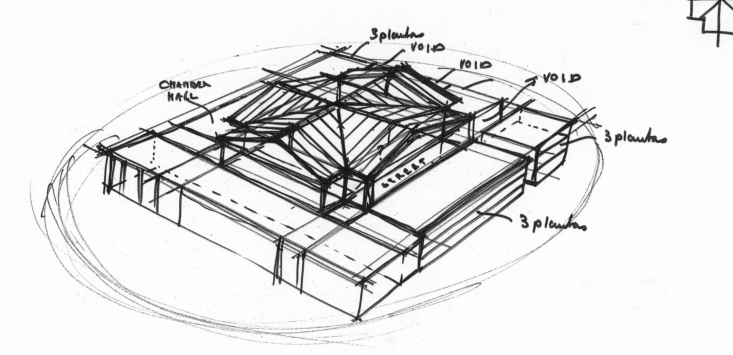

3 plantas   VOID

VOID

VOID

CHAMBER
HALL

3 plantas

STREET

3 plantas

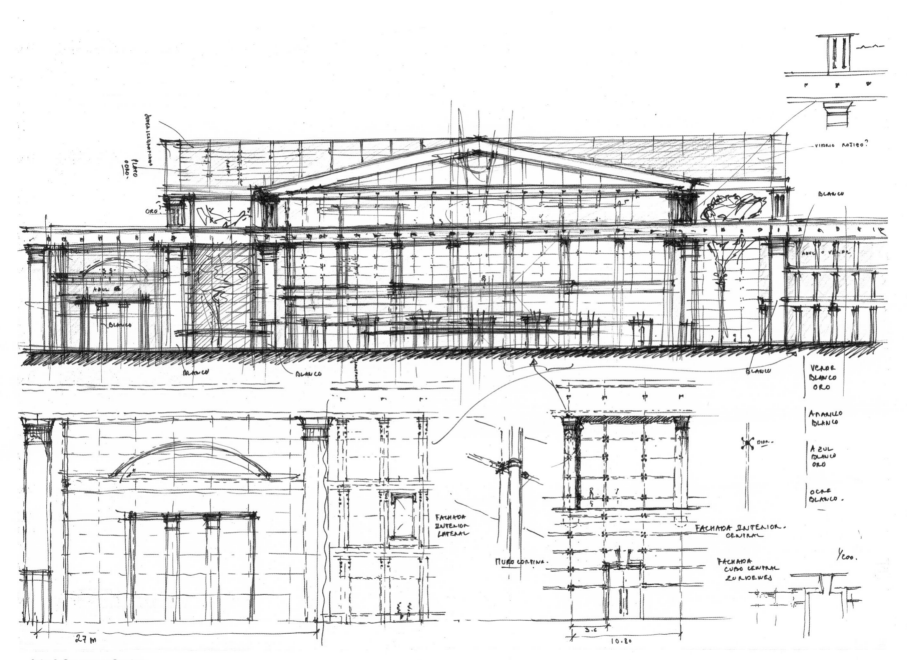

Arts & Congress Center
Saint Petersburg, Russia
Felt-tip pen on transparent paper
59.4 x 84.1 cm
2007
Ricardo Bofill/Taller de Arquitectura

Karlin Hall
Prague, Czech Republic
Felt-tip pen and red pencil
on transparent paper
59.4 x 84.1 cm
2011–2012
Ricardo Bofill/Taller de Arquitectura

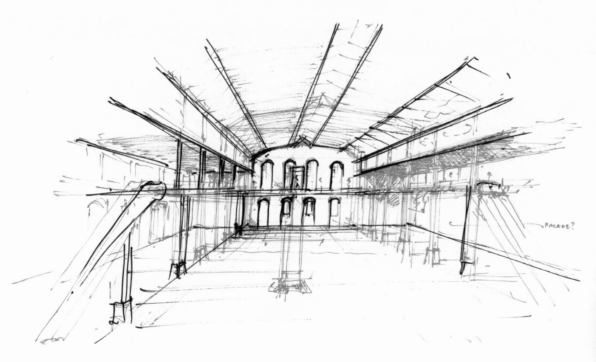

Karlin Hall
Prague, Czech Republic
Felt-tip pen and red pencil
on transparent paper
59.4 x 84.1 cm
2011–2012
Ricardo Bofill/Taller de Arquitectura

Karlin Hall
Prague, Czech Republic

Felt-tip pen and red pencil
on transparent paper
59.4 x 84.1 cm
2011–2012
Ricardo Bofill/Taller de Arquitectura

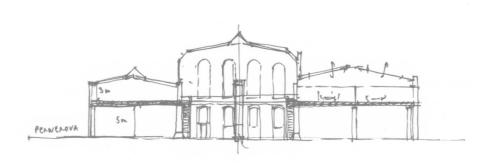

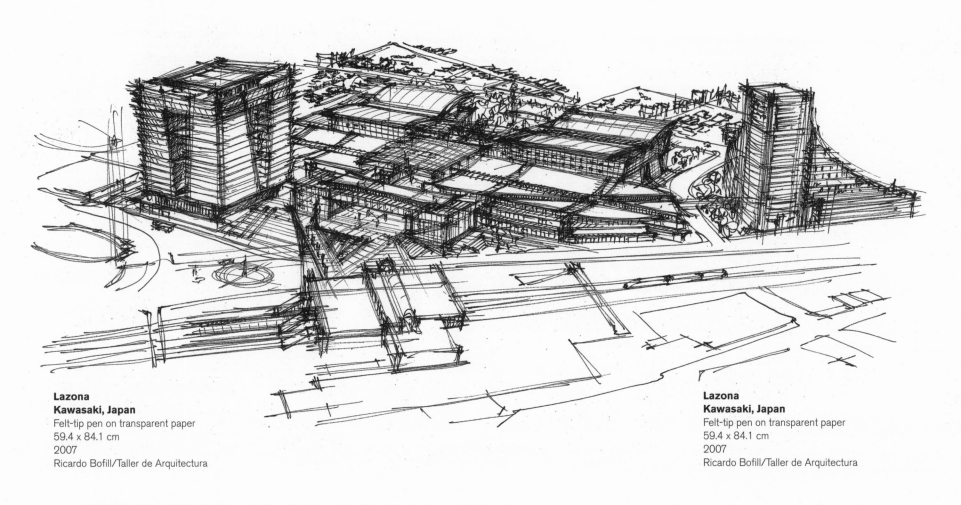

Lazona
Kawasaki, Japan
Felt-tip pen on transparent paper
59.4 x 84.1 cm
2007
Ricardo Bofill/Taller de Arquitectura

Lazona
Kawasaki, Japan
Felt-tip pen on transparent paper
59.4 x 84.1 cm
2007
Ricardo Bofill/Taller de Arquitectura

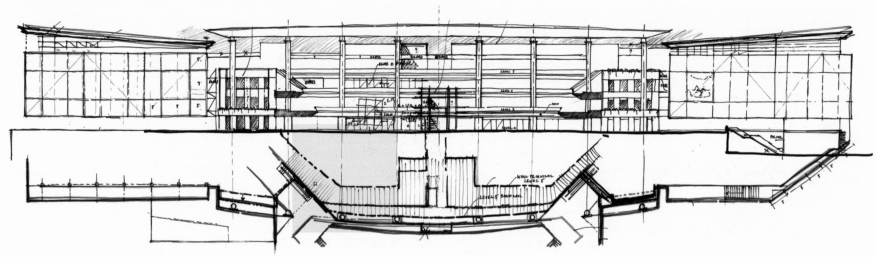

Lazona
Kawasaki, Japan
Felt-tip pen on transparent paper
59.4 x 84.1 cm
2007
Ricardo Bofill/Taller de Arquitectura

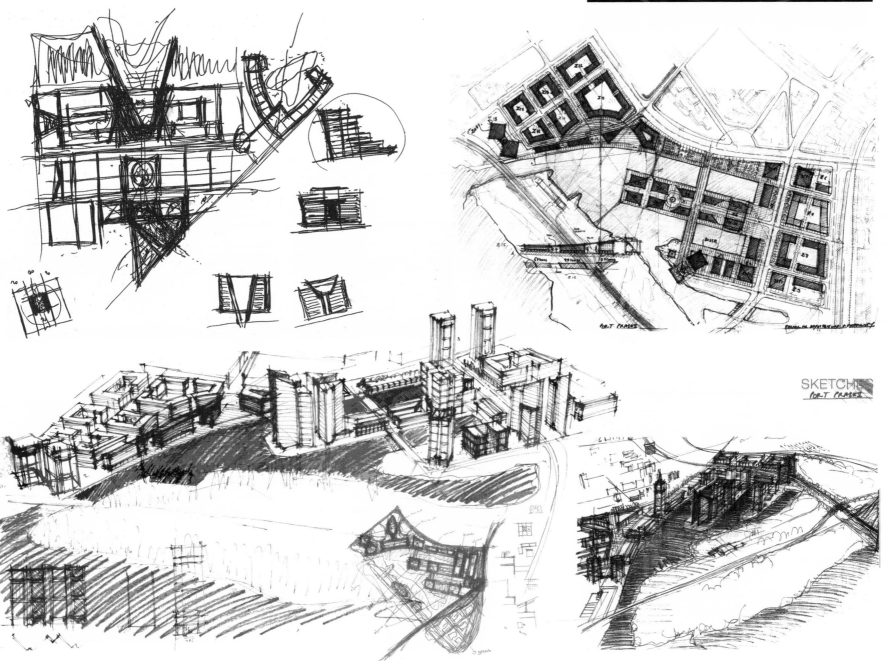

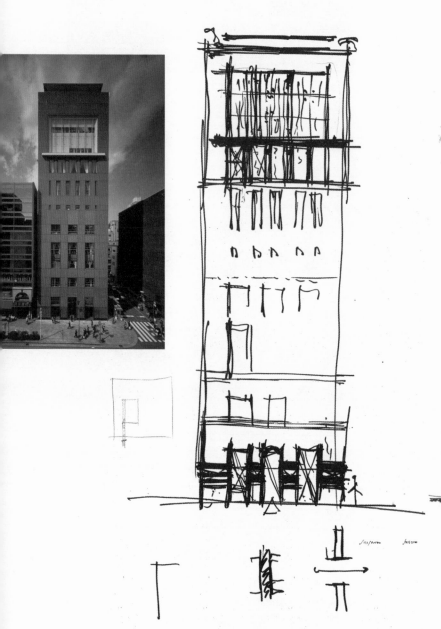

**Tokyo Ginza Shiseido Building
Tokyo, Japan**
Felt-tip pen and red pencil
on transparent paper
59.4 x 84.1 cm
1999
Ricardo Bofill/Taller de Arquitectura

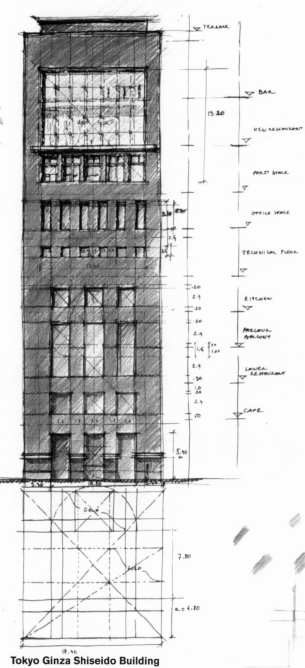

**Tokyo Ginza Shiseido Building
Tokyo, Japan**
Felt-tip pen and red pencil
on transparent paper
59.4 x 84.1 cm
1999
Ricardo Bofill/Taller de Arquitectura

Tokyo Ginza Shiseido Building
Tokyo, Japan
Felt-tip pen and red pencil
on transparent paper
59.4 x 84.1 cm
1999
Ricardo Bofill/Taller de Arquitectura

SECTION & ELEVATIONS- SHISEIDO - MG PROJECT - RICARDO BOFILL TALLER DE ARQUITECTURA - MARCH 1997

Antigone Quarter
Montpellier, France
Felt-tip pen on transparent paper
59.4 x 84.1 cm
1978–1980
Ricardo Bofill/Taller de Arquitectura

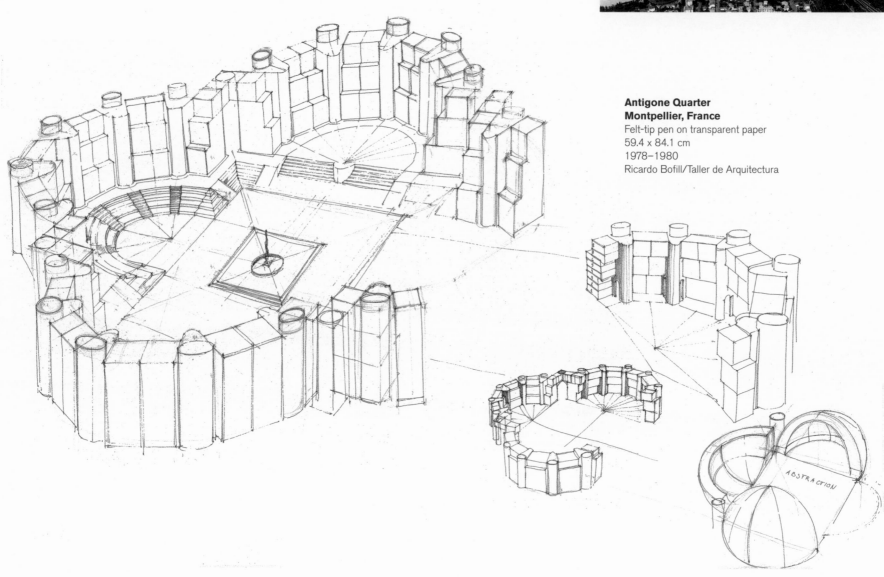

ABSTRACTION

**Antigone Quarter
Montpellier, France**
Indian ink on transparent paper
59.4 x 84.1 cm
1978–1980
Ricardo Bofill/Taller de Arquitectura

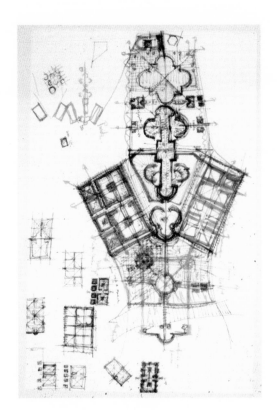

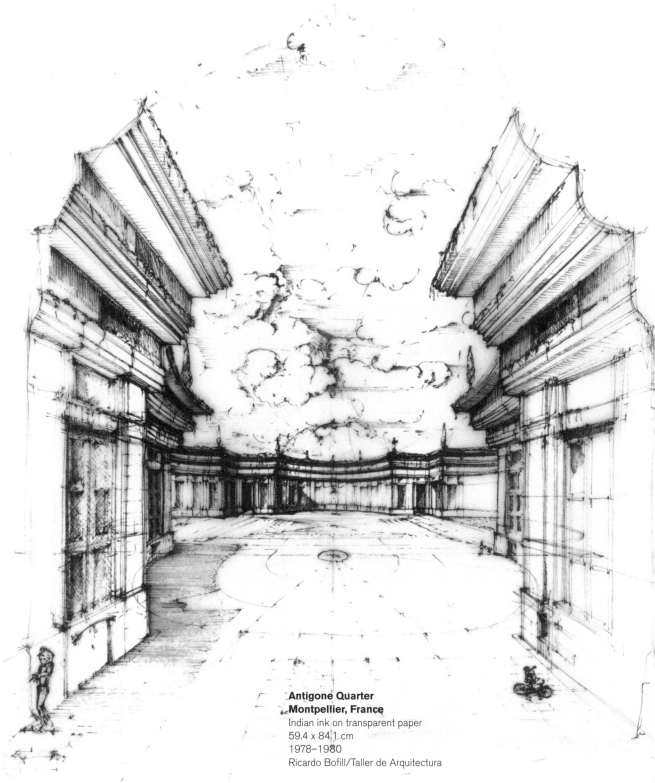

**Antigone Quarter
Montpellier, France**
Indian ink on transparent paper
59.4 x 84.1 cm
1978–1980
Ricardo Bofill/Taller de Arquitectura

DAVID BÜLOW-JACOBSEN

David Bülow-Jacobsen (born in Copenhagen, Denmark, 1973) graduated from the Royal Academy of Fine Arts, School of Architecture, Copenhagen in 2002. He was a partner of Witraz architects + landscape, before founding primus architects in 2008 with architect and trained carpenter Per Appel. The company's office philosophy is based on the combination of studio work and construction. This approach to architecture allows a hands on presence throughout all project phases. Bülow-Jacobsen's intention is to create a laboratory for the tailor-made solution. Knowledge and understanding of materials is an integrated part of the design process, which presents the opportunity to explore new spatial organization and materials. The understanding of the aesthetical and physical importance of light is at the core of each design.

Plan/Section/Elevation Studies
Community Center
Copenhagen, Denmark
Ink on paper
13 x 18 cm
2013
David Bülow-Jacobsen

Spatial Jam Session
Community Center
Copenhagen, Denmark
Ink on paper
13 x 18 cm
2013
David Bülow-Jacobsen

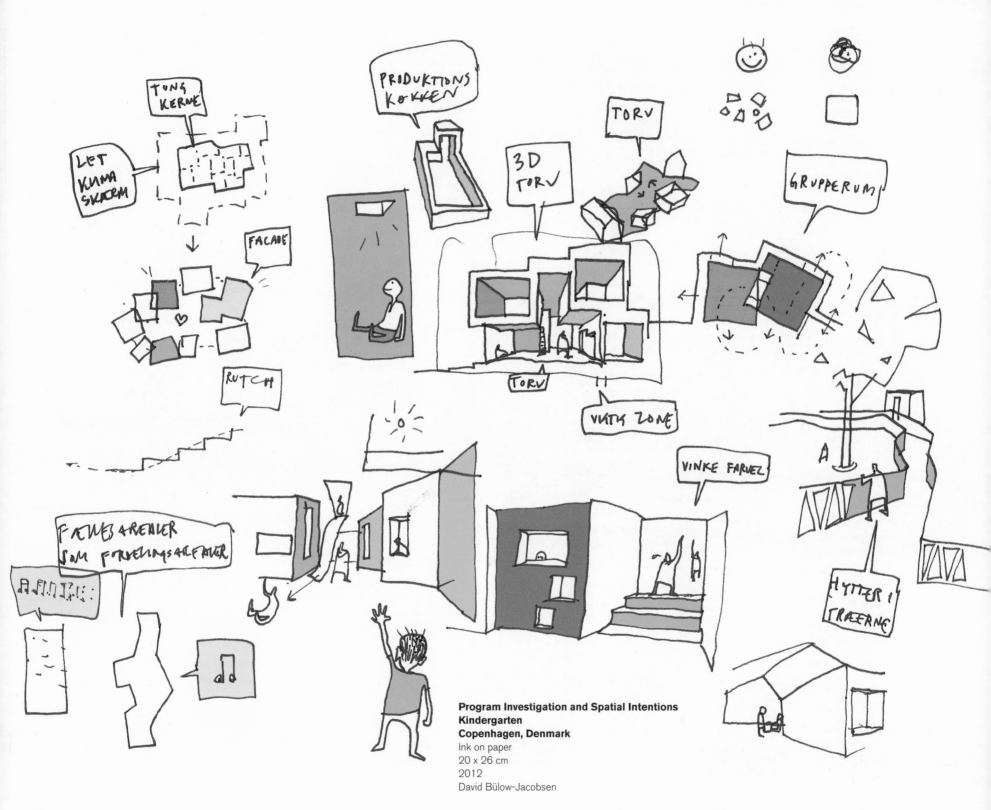

Program Investigation and Spatial Intentions
Kindergarten
Copenhagen, Denmark
Ink on paper
20 x 26 cm
2012
David Bülow-Jacobsen

Social Events in Architecture
Kindergarten
Copenhagen, Denmark
Ink on paper
Each 12 x 12 cm
2012
David Bülow-Jacobsen

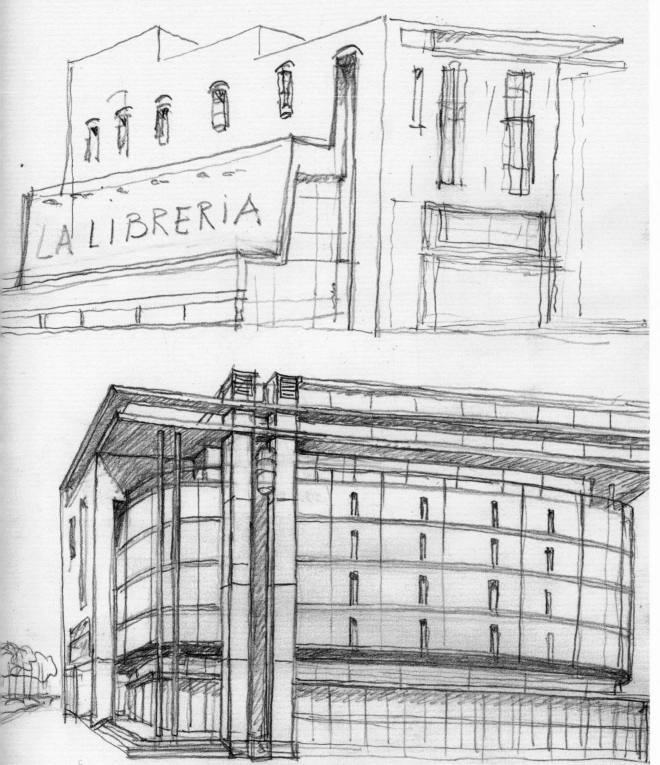

Tessin Aidon Maastricht
19 Sept 2002

JO COENEN

Jo Coenen (born in Heerlen, the Netherlands, 1949) stud-ied architecture at the Technical University in Eindhoven, where he graduated in 1975. Between 1977 and 1987 he studied with Luigi Snozzi in Locarno, Switzerland, and with James Stirling in Düsseldorf. In 1979 he worked with Aldo van Eyck and Theo Bosch in Amsterdam and that same year set up his own office in Eindhoven, which he moved to Maastricht in 1990. In 1999 he set up a second office in Berlin, followed by two more offices in Luxembourg and Amsterdam and in 2007 his latest studio in Milan. The office has gained an international reputation, thanks to a number of projects that earned a lot of press cover-age, such as the Public Library in Amsterdam, the Dutch Architecture Institute, and the Vesteda Tower in Eindhoven. Jo Coenen's architecture and architectonic-urban designs do not only fit well into their environment, they are also embedded in them – they absorb, reinforce and reflect the characteristics of the surroundings.

Library Amsterdam (OBA)
Amsterdam, The Netherlands
Pencil on sketch paper
21 x 14.8 cm
2002
Jo Coenen/Jo Coenen Architects &
Urbanists

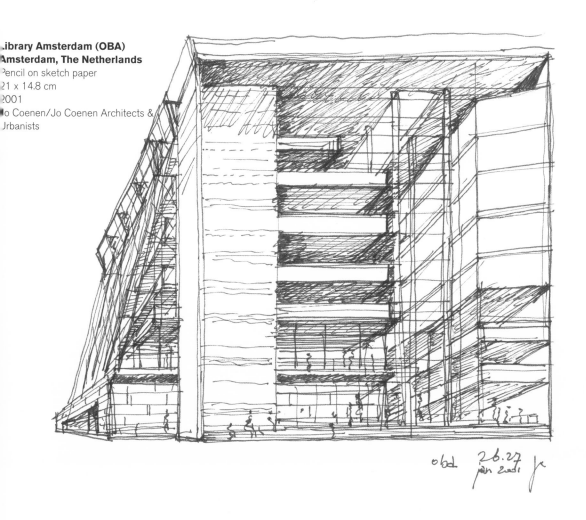

Library Amsterdam (OBA)
Amsterdam, The Netherlands
Pencil on sketch paper
21 x 14.8 cm
2001
Jo Coenen/Jo Coenen Architects &
Urbanists

Library Amsterdam (OBA)
Amsterdam, The Netherlands
Pencil on sketch paper
21 x 14.8 cm
2001
Jo Coenen/Jo Coenen Architects &
Urbanists

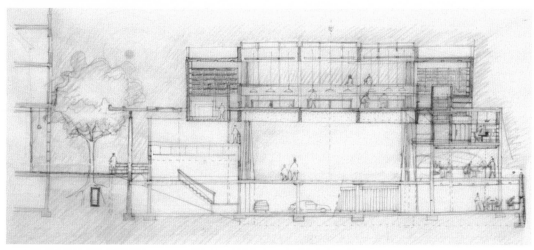

Library Amsterdam (OBA)
Amsterdam, The Netherlands
Pencil on sketch paper
29.7 x 21 cm
2003
Jo Coenen/Jo Coenen Architects &
Urbanists

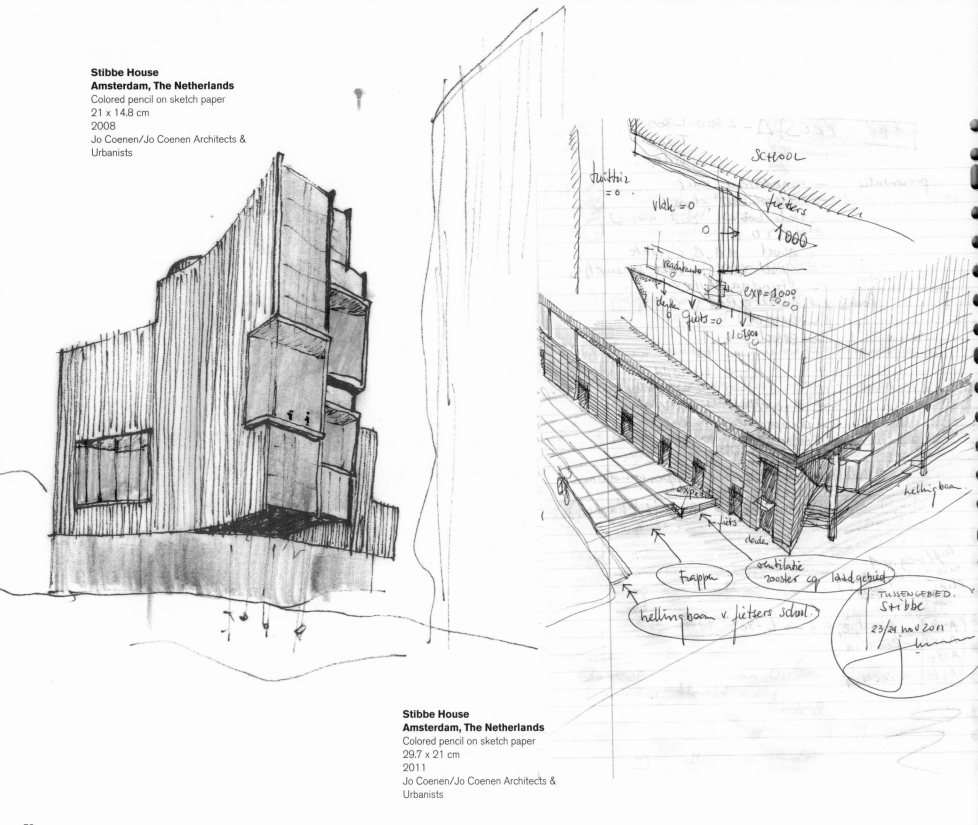

Stibbe House
Amsterdam, The Netherlands
Colored pencil on sketch paper
21 x 14.8 cm
2008
Jo Coenen/Jo Coenen Architects &
Urbanists

Stibbe House
Amsterdam, The Netherlands
Colored pencil on sketch paper
29.7 x 21 cm
2011
Jo Coenen/Jo Coenen Architects &
Urbanists

78

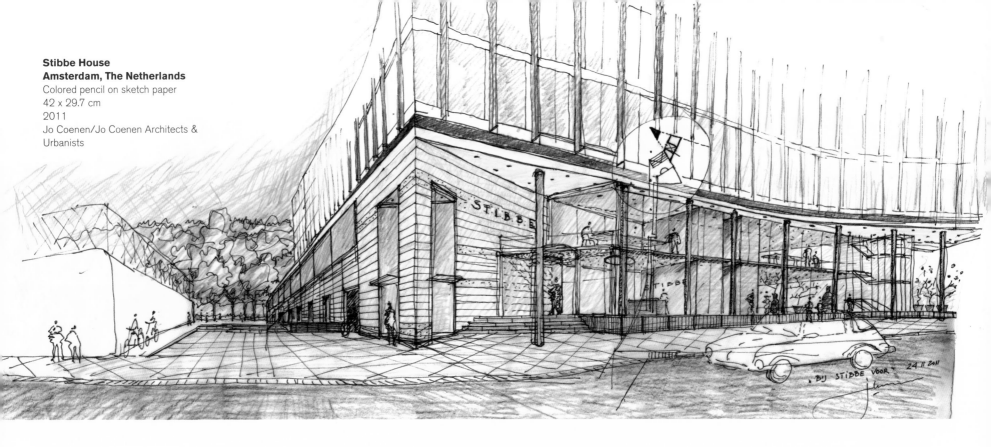

Stibbe House
Amsterdam, The Netherlands
Colored pencil on sketch paper
42 x 29.7 cm
2011
Jo Coenen/Jo Coenen Architects &
Urbanists

Stibbe House
Amsterdam, The Netherlands
Colored pencil on sketch paper
29.7 x 21 cm
2011
Jo Coenen/Jo Coenen Architects &
Urbanists

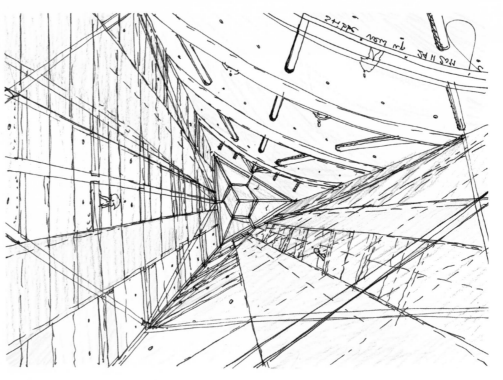

Hong Kong Design Institute
Hong Kong, China
Felt-tip pen
35 x 9 cm
Sketch: 2010
Building: 2011
Thomas Coldefy/CAAU

THOMAS COLDEFY

Thomas Coldefy (born in Paris, France, 1978) was appointed as principal of CAAU in 2011. In 2006 he won the international architectural design competition for the Hong Kong Design Institute. In 2010 Thomas was awarded the Europe 40 Under 40 prize by the European Center for Architecture, Art Design and Urban Studies. Engaged in the industry for 10 years, he has worked for several renowned architecture and urban planning firms. He graduated from the École Spéciale d'Architecture in 2002 and joined CAAU in 2006. Thomas' methodology involves experimentation with the contradictions of site and program drawing upon a deep rooted belief in green design in order to create an architecture that responds to the environment at a macro and micro scale.

Hong Kong Design Institute
Hong Kong, China
Felt-tip pen
29.72 x 21.01 cm
Sketch: 2010
Building: 2011
Jerry Geurts/CAAU

International Conference Center
Ouagadougou, Burkina Faso
Felt-tip pen
45.58 x 9.45 cm
Sketch: 2009
Building: ongoing
Thomas Coldefy/CAAU

Public Service Hall
Kobuleti, Georgia
Felt-tip pen
28.49 x 9.08 cm
2009
Thomas Coldefy/CAAU

Rue des Rogations
Hellemmes, France
Pencil
72.02 x 63.96 cm
Sketch: 2012
Building: 2012
Thomas Coldefy/CAAU

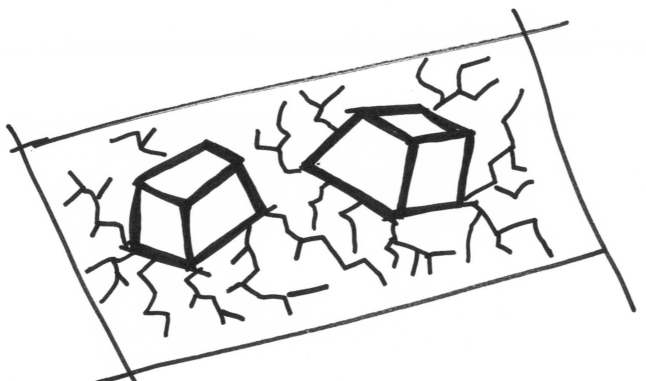

Museum of Second World War
Gdansk, Poland
Felt-tip pen
18.28 x 11.24 cm
2010
Thomas Coldefy/CAAU

Apple Fifth Avenue
New York City, NY, USA
Pencil and colored pencil
11.5 x 9 cm
2003
Peter Bohlin/Bohlin Cywinski Jackson

Apple Fifth Avenue
New York City, NY, USA
Pencil and colored pencil
9 x 9 cm
2003
Peter Bohlin/Bohlin Cywinski Jackson

BERNARD CYWINSKI, PETER BOHLIN, GREG MOTTOLA

Bohlin Cywinski Jackson, founded in 1965, is an architecture practice with offices in Wilkes-Barre, Pittsburgh, Philadelphia, Seattle, and San Francisco. The firm is recognized for elegant and humane design, ranging in scale and circumstance from major academic, civic, cultural, and corporate buildings to private homes both large and small. Its architecture responds to the subtleties of place, both manmade and natural; to the varied natures of people; to the character of institutions; and to the rich possibilities of material and means of construction. Bohlin Cywinski Jackson was recognized as the 1994 AIA Firm Award, and in 2010, founder Peter Bohlin was awarded the AIA Gold Medal.

Apple Fifth Avenue
New York City, NY, USA
Pencil and colored pencil
13 x 8 cm
2003
Peter Bohlin/Bohlin Cywinski Jackson

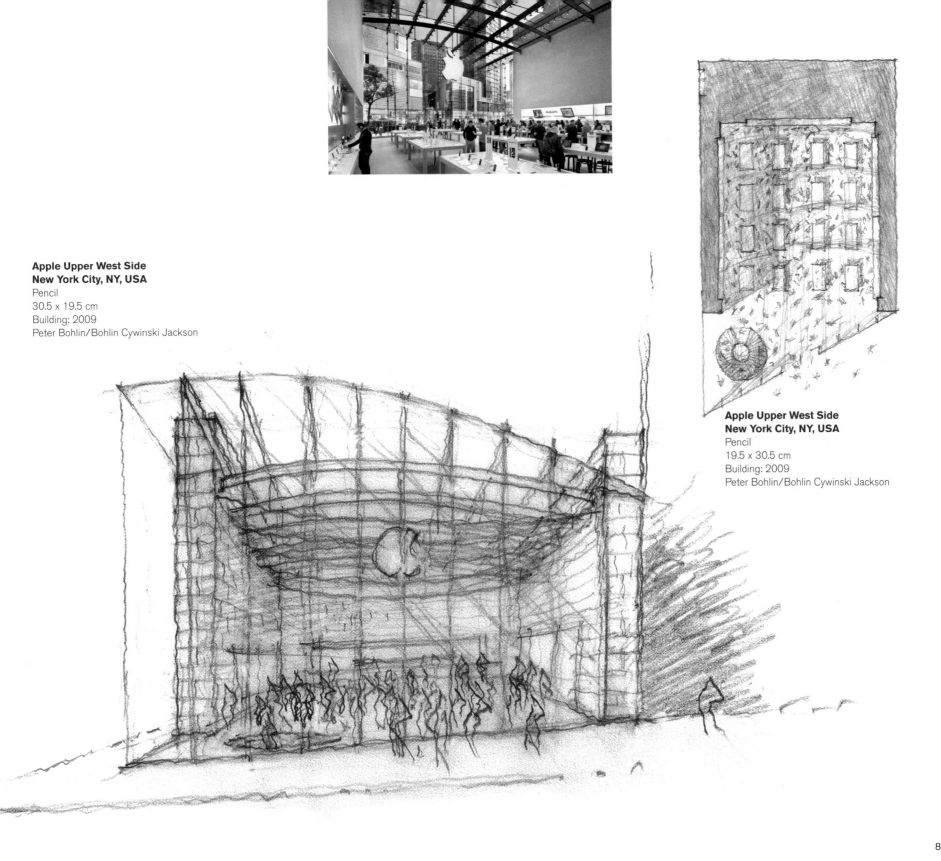

**Apple Upper West Side
New York City, NY, USA**
Pencil
30.5 x 19.5 cm
Building: 2009
Peter Bohlin/Bohlin Cywinski Jackson

**Apple Upper West Side
New York City, NY, USA**
Pencil
19.5 x 30.5 cm
Building: 2009
Peter Bohlin/Bohlin Cywinski Jackson

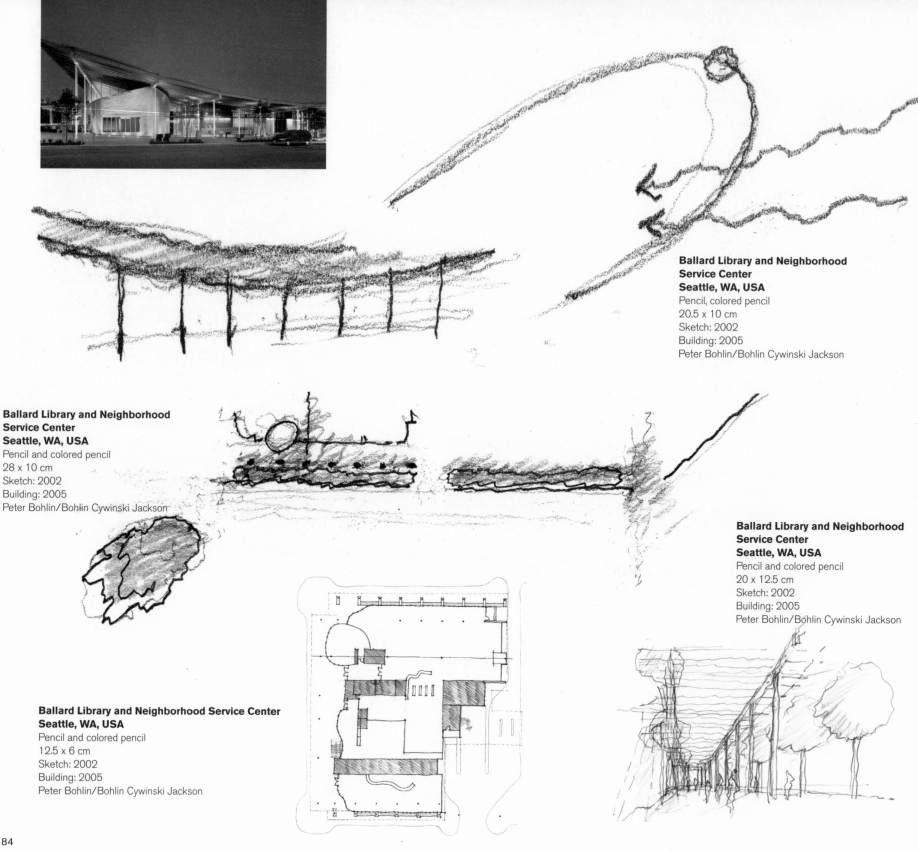

Ballard Library and Neighborhood Service Center
Seattle, WA, USA
Pencil, colored pencil
20.5 x 10 cm
Sketch: 2002
Building: 2005
Peter Bohlin/Bohlin Cywinski Jackson

Ballard Library and Neighborhood Service Center
Seattle, WA, USA
Pencil and colored pencil
28 x 10 cm
Sketch: 2002
Building: 2005
Peter Bohlin/Bohlin Cywinski Jackson

Ballard Library and Neighborhood Service Center
Seattle, WA, USA
Pencil and colored pencil
20 x 12.5 cm
Sketch: 2002
Building: 2005
Peter Bohlin/Bohlin Cywinski Jackson

Ballard Library and Neighborhood Service Center
Seattle, WA, USA
Pencil and colored pencil
12.5 x 6 cm
Sketch: 2002
Building: 2005
Peter Bohlin/Bohlin Cywinski Jackson

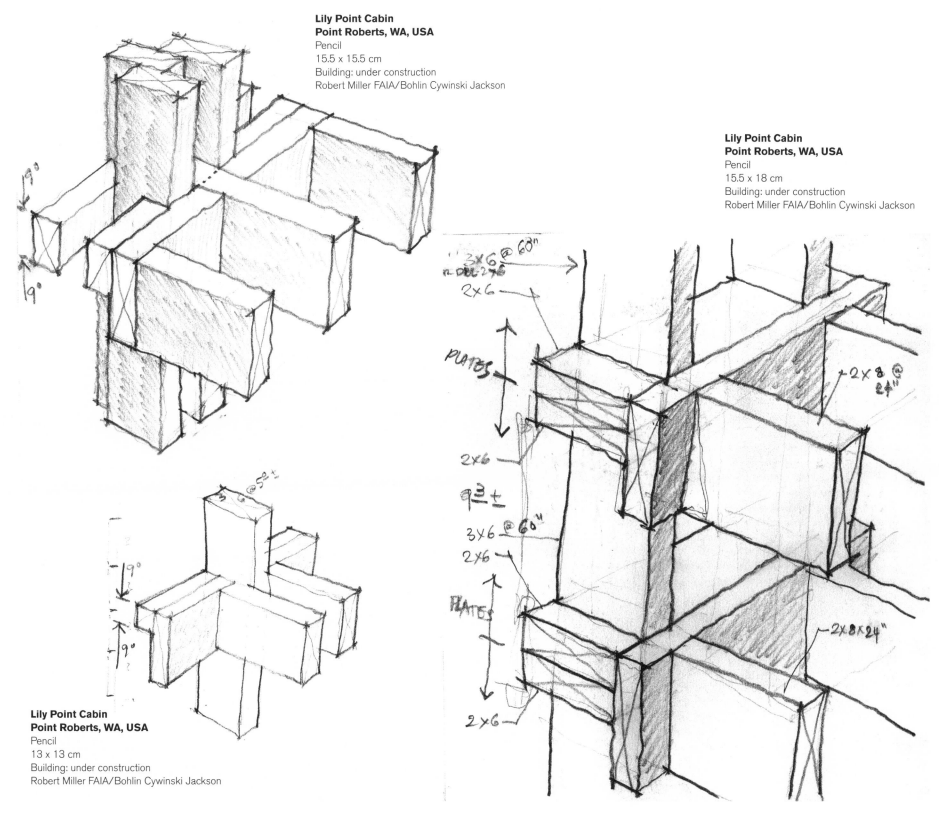

Lily Point Cabin
Point Roberts, WA, USA
Pencil
15.5 x 15.5 cm
Building: under construction
Robert Miller FAIA/Bohlin Cywinski Jackson

Lily Point Cabin
Point Roberts, WA, USA
Pencil
15.5 x 18 cm
Building: under construction
Robert Miller FAIA/Bohlin Cywinski Jackson

Lily Point Cabin
Point Roberts, WA, USA
Pencil
13 x 13 cm
Building: under construction
Robert Miller FAIA/Bohlin Cywinski Jackson

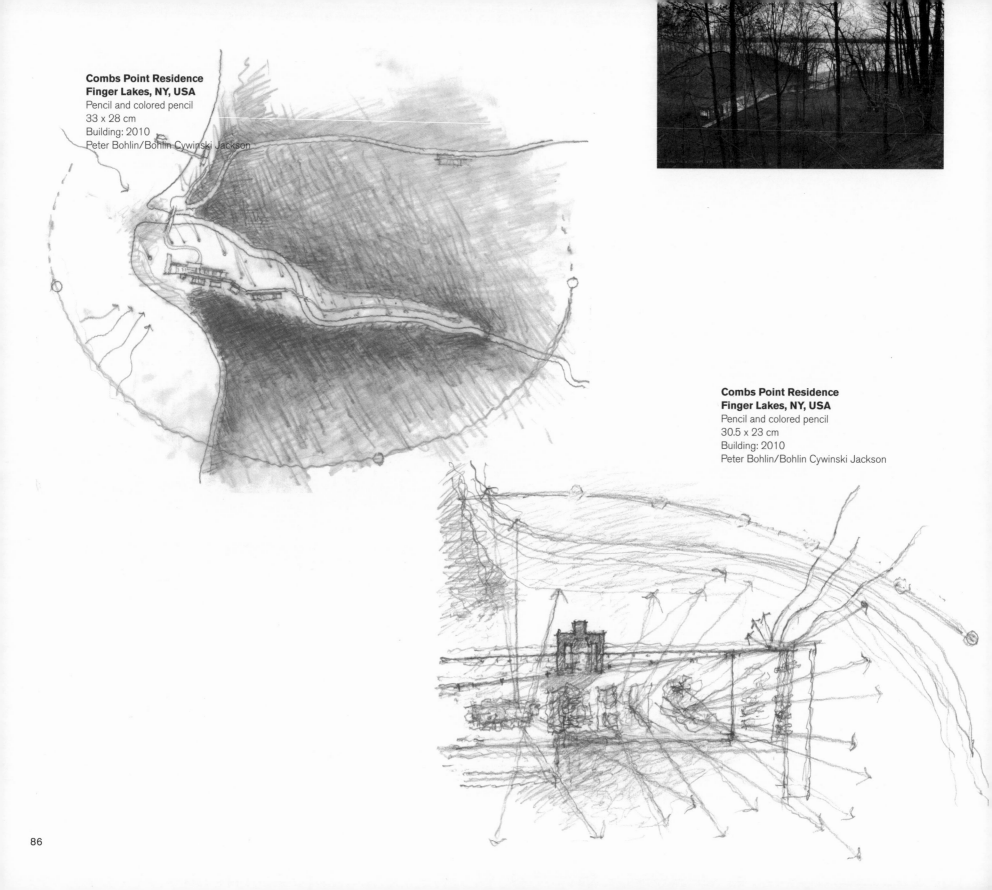

Combs Point Residence
Finger Lakes, NY, USA
Pencil and colored pencil
33 x 28 cm
Building: 2010
Peter Bohlin/Bohlin Cywinski Jackson

Combs Point Residence
Finger Lakes, NY, USA
Pencil and colored pencil
30.5 x 23 cm
Building: 2010
Peter Bohlin/Bohlin Cywinski Jackson

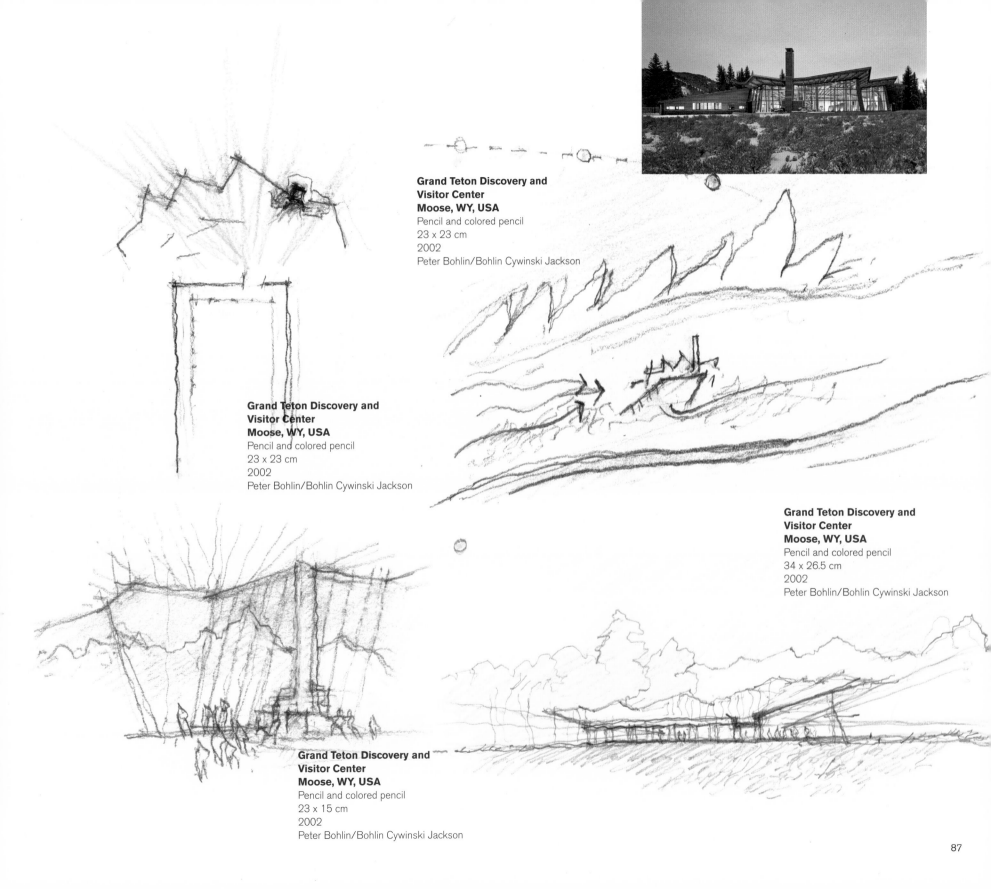

**Grand Teton Discovery and
Visitor Center
Moose, WY, USA**
Pencil and colored pencil
23 x 23 cm
2002
Peter Bohlin/Bohlin Cywinski Jackson

**Grand Teton Discovery and
Visitor Center
Moose, WY, USA**
Pencil and colored pencil
23 x 23 cm
2002
Peter Bohlin/Bohlin Cywinski Jackson

**Grand Teton Discovery and
Visitor Center
Moose, WY, USA**
Pencil and colored pencil
34 x 26.5 cm
2002
Peter Bohlin/Bohlin Cywinski Jackson

**Grand Teton Discovery and
Visitor Center
Moose, WY, USA**
Pencil and colored pencil
23 x 15 cm
2002
Peter Bohlin/Bohlin Cywinski Jackson

Creekside Residence
Woodside, CA, USA
Pencil and colored pencil
13 x 10 cm
2003
Peter Bohlin/Bohlin Cywinski Jackson

Creekside Residence
Woodside, CA, USA
Pencil and colored pencil
14 x 10 cm
2003
Peter Bohlin/Bohlin Cywinski Jackson

Creekside Residence
Woodside, CA, USA
Pencil and colored pencil
14 x 10 cm
2003
Peter Bohlin/Bohlin Cywinski Jackson

Creekside Residence
Woodside, CA, USA
Pencil and colored pencil
13 x 10 cm
2003
Peter Bohlin/Bohlin Cywinski Jackson

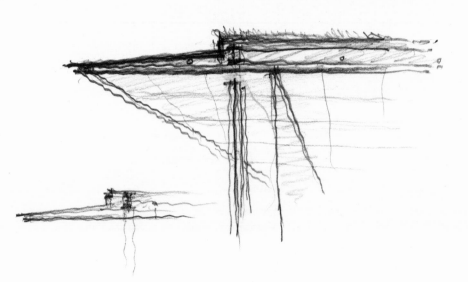

Creekside Residence
Woodside, CA, USA
Pencil and colored pencil
13 x 10 cm
2003
Peter Bohlin/Bohlin Cywinski Jackson

Creekside Residence
Woodside, CA, USA
Pencil and colored pencil
14 x 10 cm
2003
Peter Bohlin/Bohlin Cywinski Jackson

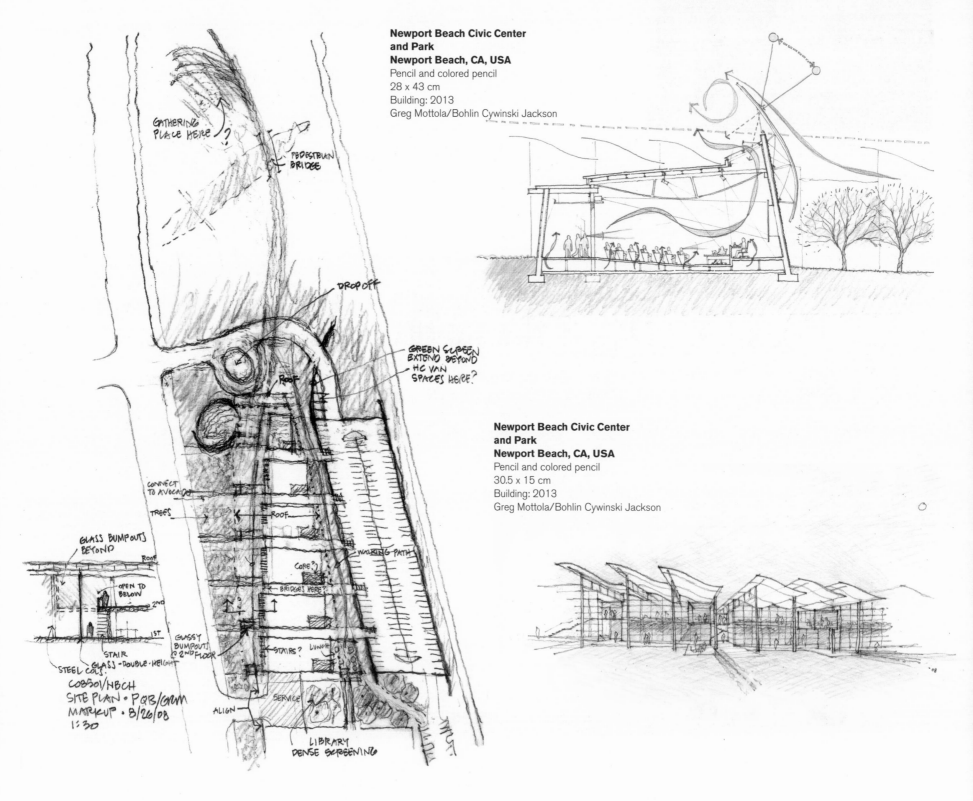

GATHERING PLACE HERE ?

PEDESTRIAN BRIDGE

DROP OFF

Roof

GREEN SCREEN EXTEND BEYOND HC VAN SPACES HERE ?

Newport Beach Civic Center and Park
Newport Beach, CA, USA
Pencil and colored pencil
28 x 43 cm
Building: 2013
Greg Mottola/Bohlin Cywinski Jackson

Newport Beach Civic Center and Park
Newport Beach, CA, USA
Pencil and colored pencil
30.5 x 15 cm
Building: 2013
Greg Mottola/Bohlin Cywinski Jackson

CONNECT TO AVOCADO

TREES

Roof

CORE ?

WALKING PATH

BRIDGES HERE ?

GLASS BUMPOUTS BEYOND

ROOF

OPEN TO BELOW

2ND

1ST

STAIR

GLASS - DOUBLE - HEIGHT

STEEL COLS.

GLASSY BUMPOUTS @ 2ND FLOOR

STAIRS ?

LUNCH ?

COBSO1/NBCH SITE PLAN • PQB/GRM MARKUP • 8/26/08 1:30

ALIGN

SERVICE

LIBRARY DENSE SCREENING

90

**Newport Beach Civic Center
and Park
Newport Beach, CA, USA**
Pencil and colored pencil
76 x 28 cm
Building: 2013
Greg Mottola/Bohlin Cywinski Jackson

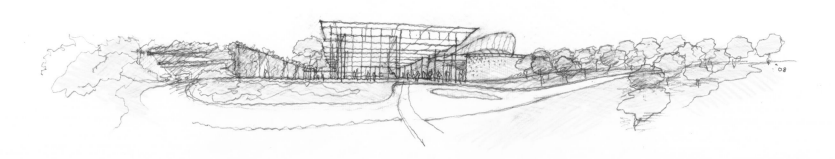

**Newport Beach Civic Center
and Park
Newport Beach, CA, USA**
Pencil and colored pencil
73.5 x 28 cm
Building: 2013
Greg Mottola/Bohlin Cywinski Jackson

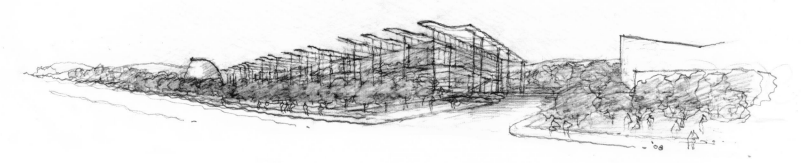

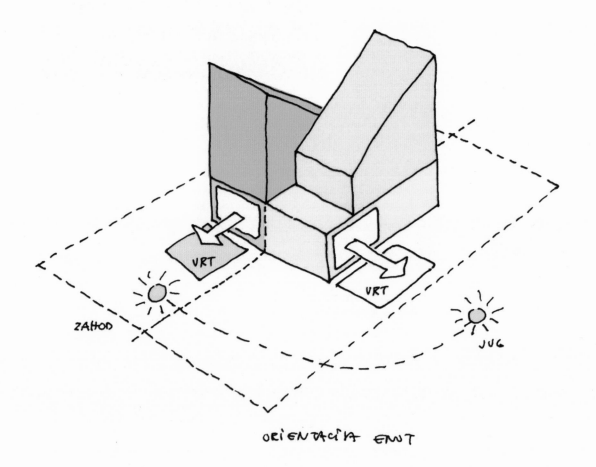

ZAHOD

VRT

VRT

JUG

ORIENTACIJA ENOT

ALJOŠA DEKLEVA

Aljoša Dekleva (born in Postojna, Slovenia, 1972) graduated from Faculty of Architecture, University of Ljubljana, Slovenia, in 1998 and later started his own architectural practice winning several competitions and realizing some distinct buildings. In 2002 he completed his master's in architecture with distinction from the Architectural Association, London. At the AA he co-founded an international architectural network RAMTV. RAMTV's master thesis on mass-customization in housing "Negotiate my Boundary!" received intense professional attention and was published as a book by first AA Publications, London and later by Birkhäuser, Basel. In 2003 he founded the architectural office dekleva gregorič arhitekti, based in Ljubljana.

Housing Razgledi Perovo
Kamnik, Slovenia
Ballpoint pen and computer graphics
14.85 x 21 cm
Sketch: 2008
Building: 2011
Aljoša Dekleva/dekleva gregorič arhitekti

PICK YOUR CHOICE!

MOVE!

TEST YOUR BATHROOM LAYOUT IN SCALE 1:1

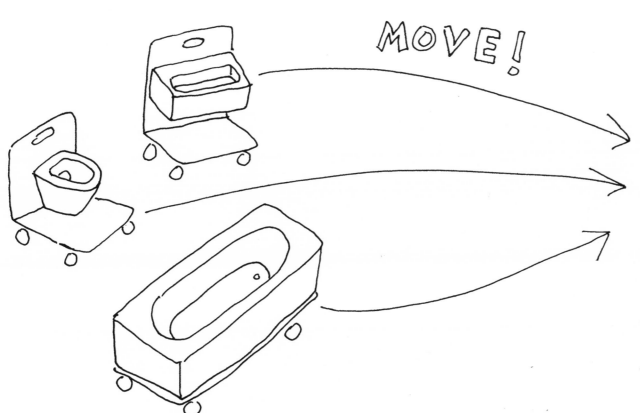

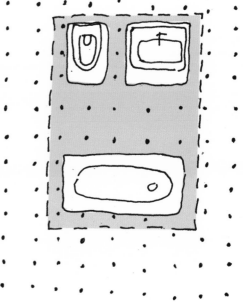

Bath Laboratory – Showroom Pertot
Trieste, Italy
Ballpoint pen and computer graphics
14.85 x 21 cm
Sketch: 2006
Building: 2007
Aljoša Dekleva/dekleva gregorič arhitekti

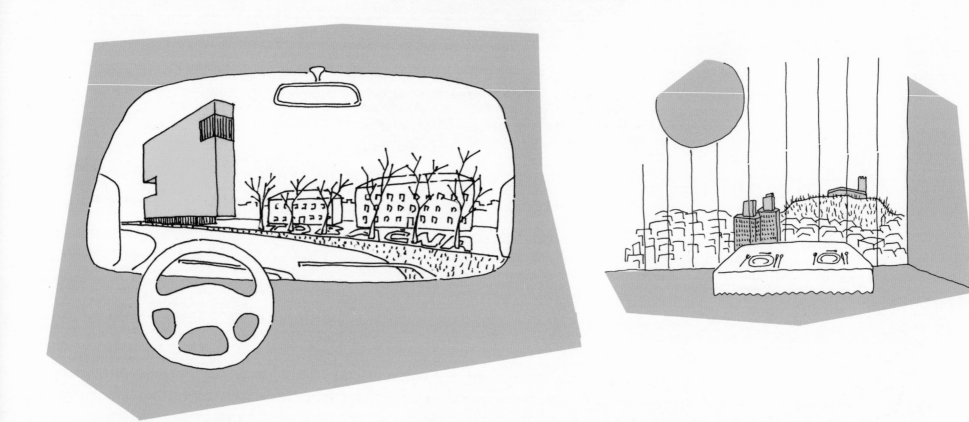

94

**Revitalizing Tobacco Factory Area
Ljubljana, Slovenia**
Ballpoint pen and computer graphics
14.85 x 21 cm
2007
Aljoša Dekleva/dekleva gregorič arhitekti

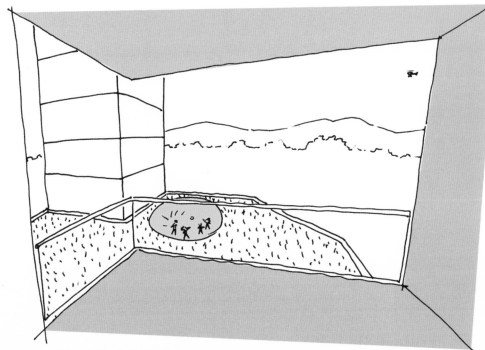

Kindergarten B
Brežice, Slovenia
Ballpoint pen and computer graphics
14.85 x 21 cm
2011
Aljoša Dekleva/dekleva gregorič arhitekti

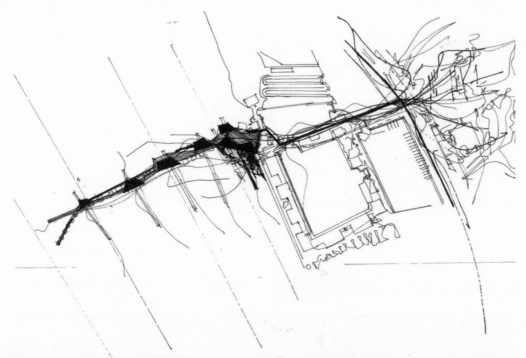

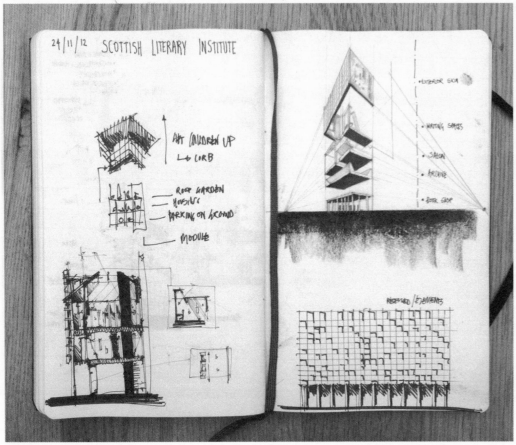

CHRIS DOVE

Chris Dove (born in Liverpool, United Kingdom, 1989), graduated with a first class honors degree in Architecture from Liverpool John Moores University in 2011. Dove is interested in design and creating on a small, humble scale and believes that good architecture must apply these principles to an urban scale. Dove and a fellow graduate won a nationwide competition and commission to design and build a large installation in central London, outside Jean Nouvel's One New Change and Saint Paul's Cathedral. He is currently undertaking post graduate studies at the Glasgow School of Art, as well as running his own design projects. He is also involved with various projects that have a deep urban historical context and connection with the city.

Gallery of Technological Artifacts
Pencil and charcoal on tracing paper
30 x 15 cm
2011
Chris Dove

Scottish Literary Institute
Sketchbook
20 x 15 cm
2013
Chris Dove

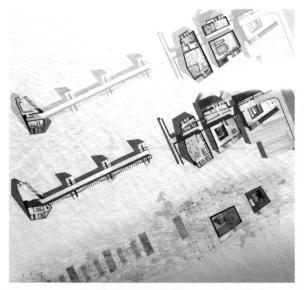

Gallery of Technological Artifacts
Pencil and charcoal on tracing paper
240 x 240 cm
2011
Chris Dove

Scottish Literary Institute
Pencil and charcoal on tracing paper
84 x 59 cm
2013
Chris Dove

Scottish Literary Institute
Pencil and charcoal on tracing paper
84 x 118 cm
2013
Chris Dove

Urban Housing
Glasgow, Scotland
Pencil on tracing paper
29 x 59 cm
2013
Chris Dove

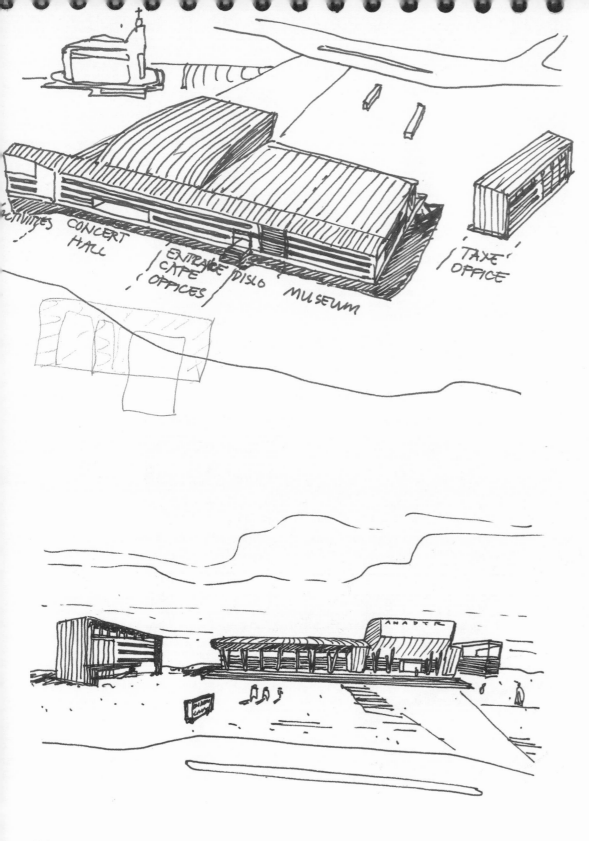

KEREM ERGINOĞLU

Kerem Erginoğlu (born in Zonguldak, Turkey, 1966) graduated from the Mimar Sinan University Faculty of Architecture in 1990. Erginoğlu conducted his postgraduate studies on 'New Building Design in Historical Textures' at Mimar Sinan University. In 1991, he went to the United States to do professional research. He founded Erginoğlu&Çalışlar Architects in 1993, together with Hasan Çalışlar.

Anadyr Cultural Center
Chukotka, Russia
Pen
16 x 22 cm
Sketch: 2001
Building: 2001
Kerem Erginoğlu/
Erginoğlu&Çalışlar Architects

**Anadyr Cultural Center,
Chukotka, Russia**
Pen
16 x 22 cm
Sketch: 2001
Building: 2001
Kerem Erginoğlu/
Erginoğlu&Çalışlar Architects

**Anadyr Cultural Center
Chukotka, Russia**
Pen
16 x 22 cm
Sketch: 2001
Building: 2001
Kerem Erginoğlu/
Erginoğlu&Çalışlar Architects

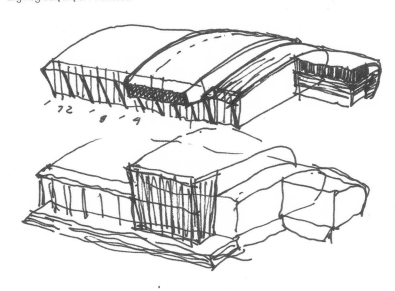

48.000.000.000.T
Sportshet Fatura berri... → 48.109.442.000 TL.+KDV

**Anadyr Cultural Center
Chukotka, Russia**
Pen
16 x 22 cm
Sketch: 2001
Building: 2001
Kerem Erginoğlu/
Erginoğlu&Çalışlar Architects

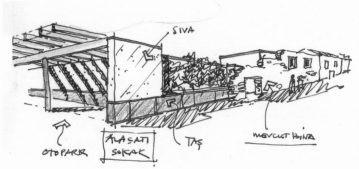

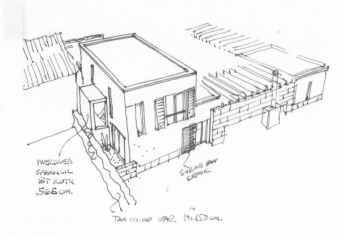

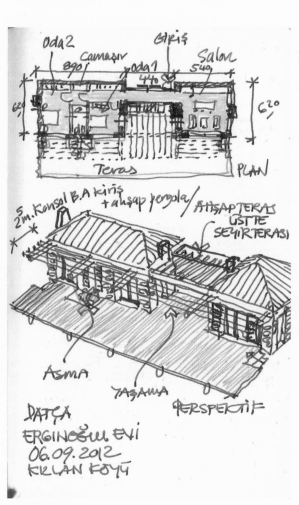

Gaziantep Shopping Center
Gaziantep, Turkey
Pen
21 x 13 cm
2014
Kerem Erginoğlu/
Erginoğlu&Çalışlar Architects

Alaçati House
Izmir, Turkey
Pen
25 x 36 cm
Kerem Erginoğlu/
Erginoğlu&Çalışlar Architects

Datça House
Datça, Turkey
Pen
21 x 13 cm
Kerem Erginoğlu/
Erginoğlu&Çalışlar Architects

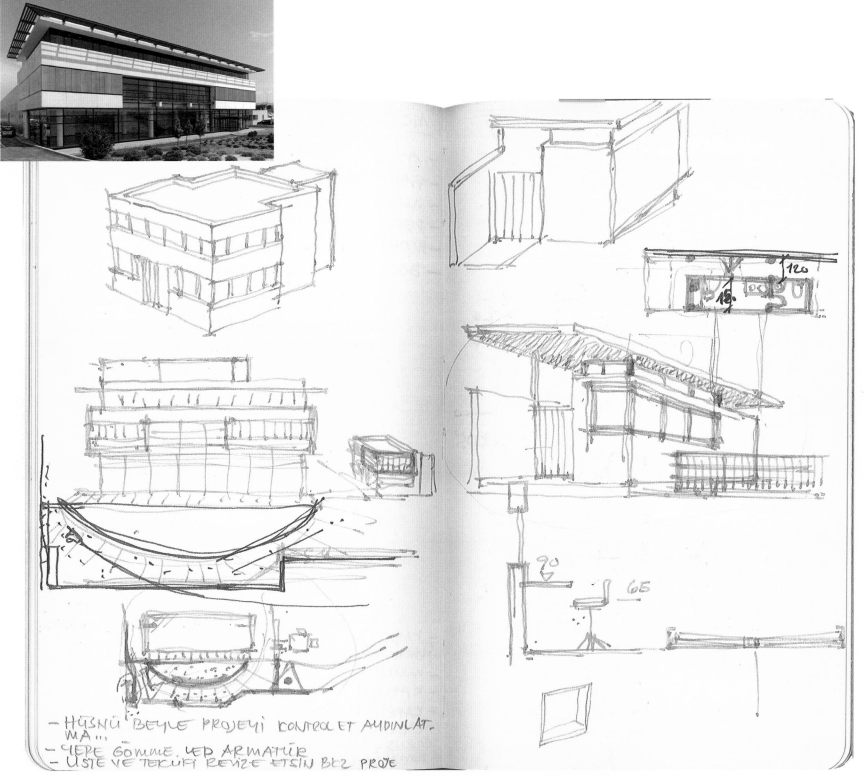

- HÜSNÜ BEYLE PROJEYİ KONTROL ET AYDINLAT.
  MA...
- ÇEPE GOMME. LED ARMATÜR
- ÜSTE VE TEKLİFİ REVİZE ETSİN BU PROJE

Suzuki Headquarters
Gebze, Turkey
Pen
26 x 20.5 cm
Kerem Erginoğlu/
Erginoğlu&Çalışlar Architects

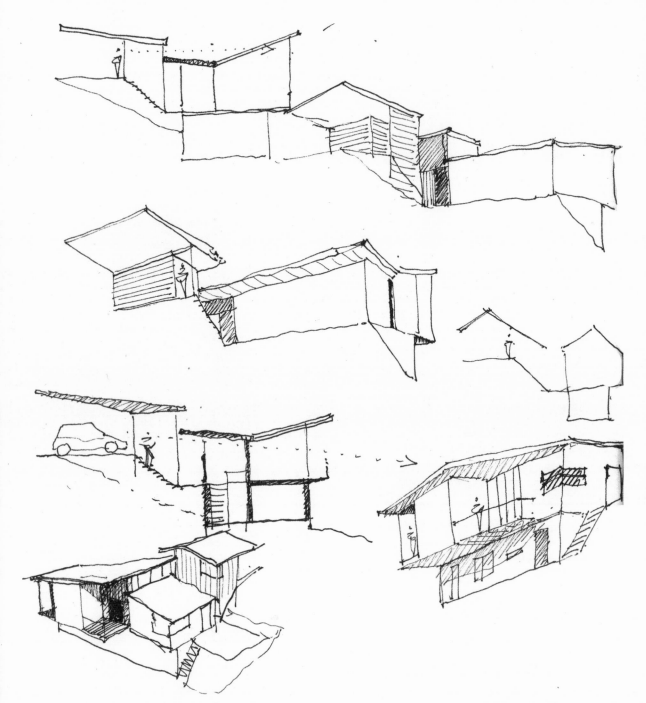

ROBERT EVANS

Robert Evans (born in Darlington, United Kingdom, 1958) founded Evans Vettori Architects with Mariangela Vettori in 1995, after gaining valuable experience working for Norman Foster and Will Alsop, as well as Studio ToniFollina in Italy. He has since built up the practice's present day reputation for high quality, sensitive, contemporary architecture, specializing in bespoke education and community projects. Evans Vettori has won many awards for education and housing projects, and Robert Evans is a strong believer in exploring design through hand-drawn sketching and modeling. He has worked as a lecturer, tutor and examiner in many schools of architecture, and currently teaches at Nottingham and Sheffield Universities. He sits on several regional design review panels and chairs the OPUN East Midlands Panel.

High Edge
Derbyshire, United Kingdom
Fiber-tip pen on paper
20 x 21 cm
Sketch: 2011
Building: 2013
Robert Evans

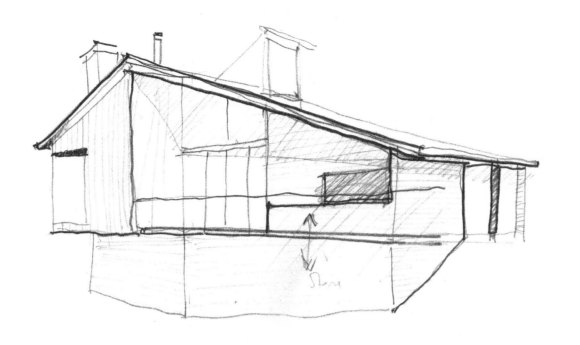

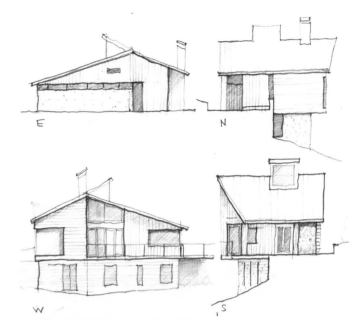

E

N

W

S

High Edge
Derbyshire, United Kingdom
0.9 mm pencil and colored pencil on paper
18 x 16 cm
Sketches: 2011
Building: 2013
Robert Evans

This roof could be a terrace

Timber deck

Timber doors

12·1·07

Sea House
Cornwall, United Kingdom
0.9 mm pencil and colored pencil
on cartridge paper
18 x 17 cm
Sketches: 2007
Building: 2010
Robert Evans

timber deck
on posts

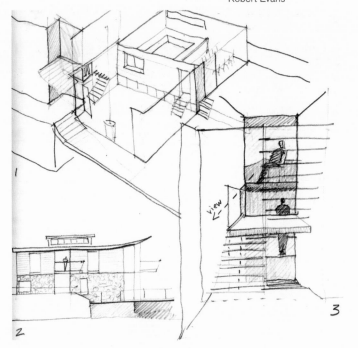

view

1

2

3

The telescope

Arts Center Competition
Kent, United Kingdom
Rotring pen on tracing paper
41 x 20 cm
1988
Robert Evans

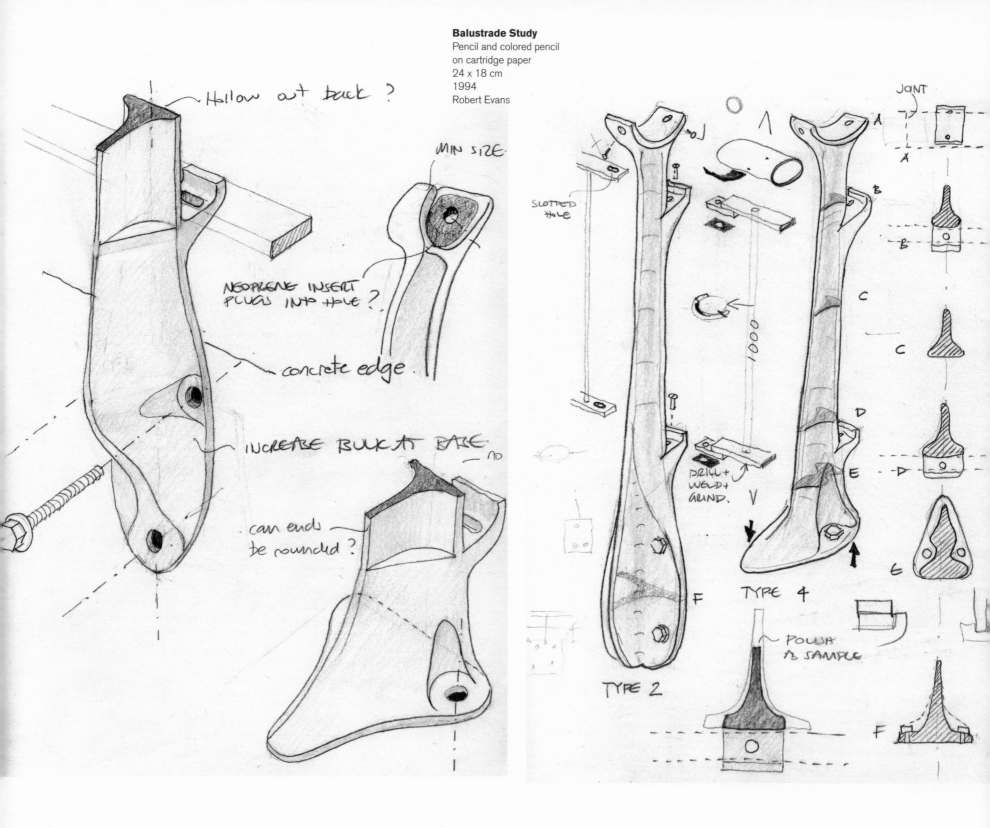

Hollow out back ?

MIN SIZE.

NEOPRENE INSERT PLUGS INTO HOLE ?

concrete edge

INCREASE BULK AT BASE

can ends be rounded ?

SLOTTED HOLE

JOINT

A

A

B

B

C

C

D

D

E

E

F

1000

DRILL + WELD + GRIND.

V

TYPE 4

TYPE 2

POLISH AS SAMPLE

Balustrade Study
Pencil and colored pencil
on cartridge paper
24 x 18 cm
1994
Robert Evans

Arts Centre Halifax
Halifax, United Kingdom
Fiber-tip pen on tracing paper scanned,
with digital color
28 x 14 cm
Sketches: 2011
Building: 2015
Robert Evans

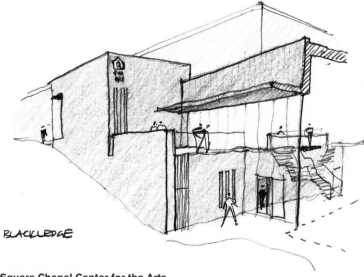

BLACKLEDGE

Square Chapel Center for the Arts
Halifax, United Kingdom
Pencil and colored pencil
on cartridge paper
20 x 19 cm
Sketches: 2009
Building: 2015
Robert Evans

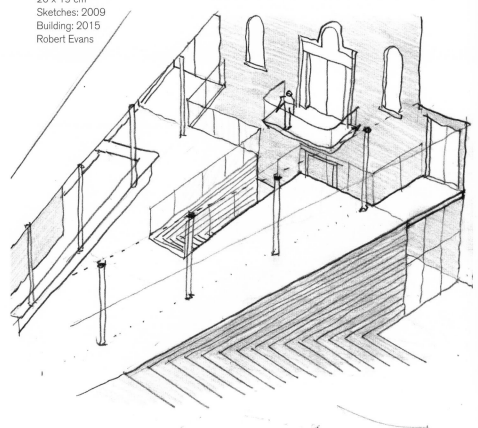

DOUGLAS FENTON

Douglas Fenton (born in Brighton, United Kingdom, 1989) is a London-based creative designer who works with architecture, film, imagination and narrative to produce projects that question the way we conceive of and inhabit spaces. He utilizes digital as well as hand-made techniques and styles to create a unique design aesthetic, and holds a huge interest in methods of architectural drawing and delineation as well as exploratory and investigative design. He gained a First Class Honors degree in architecture from the University of Plymouth, and studied architecture and film at the Bartlett School of Architecture at UCL, London. He has worked on a range of architectural and design schemes from large-scale housing and office developments, town master planning and one-off residences to graphic design, speculative architectural concepts and critiques.

**An Architecture of Solitude:
The City Between Here and There**
Pencil and charcoal
2011
Douglas Fenton

An Architecture of Solitude: The Observation Station
Mixed media: colored pencil, charcoal and Photoshop collage
2011
Douglas Fenton

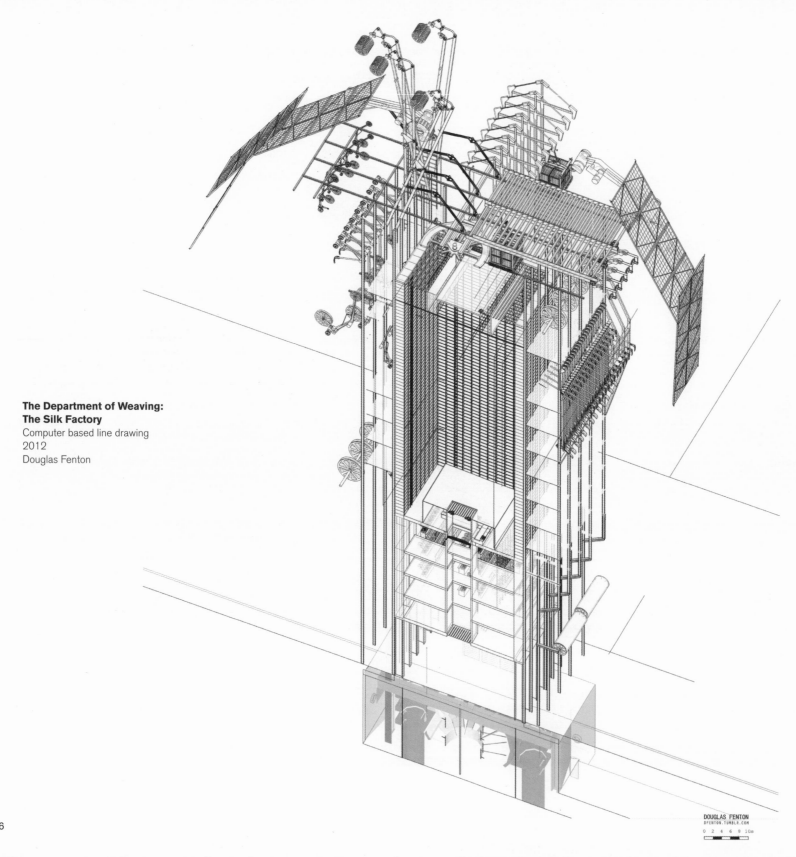

The Department of Weaving:
The Silk Factory
Computer based line drawing
2012
Douglas Fenton

The Department of Weaving:
The Silk Factory
Computer render and Photoshop collage
2012
Douglas Fenton

Speculative Future:
The School of the Hyperreal
Computer based line drawing
2010
Douglas Fenton

Speculative Future:
The School of the Hyperreal
Physical model photograph and Photoshop collage
2010
Douglas Fenton

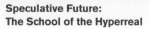

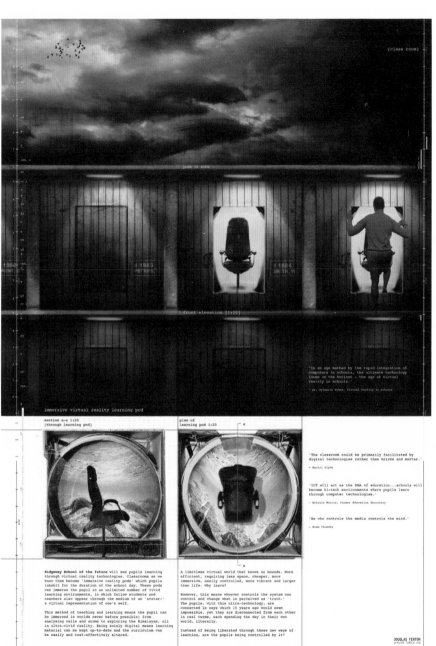

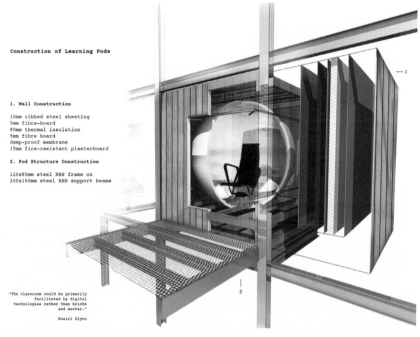

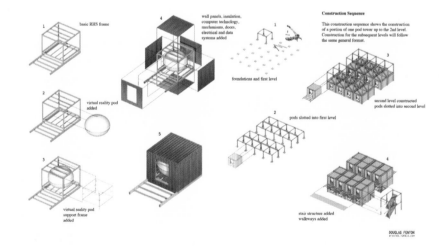

Speculative Future:
The School of the Hyperreal
Physical model photograph and Photoshop collage
2010
Douglas Fenton

Speculative Future:
The School of the Hyperreal
Computer render and Photoshop collage
2010
Douglas Fenton

NORMAN FOSTER

Norman Foster (born in Manchester, United Kingdom, 1935) graduated from Manchester University School of Architecture and City Planning and won a scholarship to attend Yale University in 1961, where he gained a master's in architecture. During his time at Yale Foster met Richard Rogers, and the two worked together with Sue Rogers, Gorgie Wolton and Wendy Foster, as Team 4, until he founded Foster Associates (now Foster + Partners) in 1967. Since its inception the practice has received more than 620 awards and citations for excellence and has won over 100 national and international competitions. Foster was honored with the title Lord Foster of Thames Bank in 1999 and in the same year he was awarded the prestigious Pritzker Architecture Prize. His remarkable buildings and urban projects have transformed cityscapes, revamped transportation systems and restored city centers all over the world. His world-renowned projects include the Reichstag in Berlin, the design of the Great Court at the British Museum in London, the Millennium Bridge, and the new Hong Kong International Airport.

Commerzbank
Frankfurt/Main, Germany
Pencil
29.7 x 21.1 cm
Sketch: 1996
Building: 2007
Norman Foster

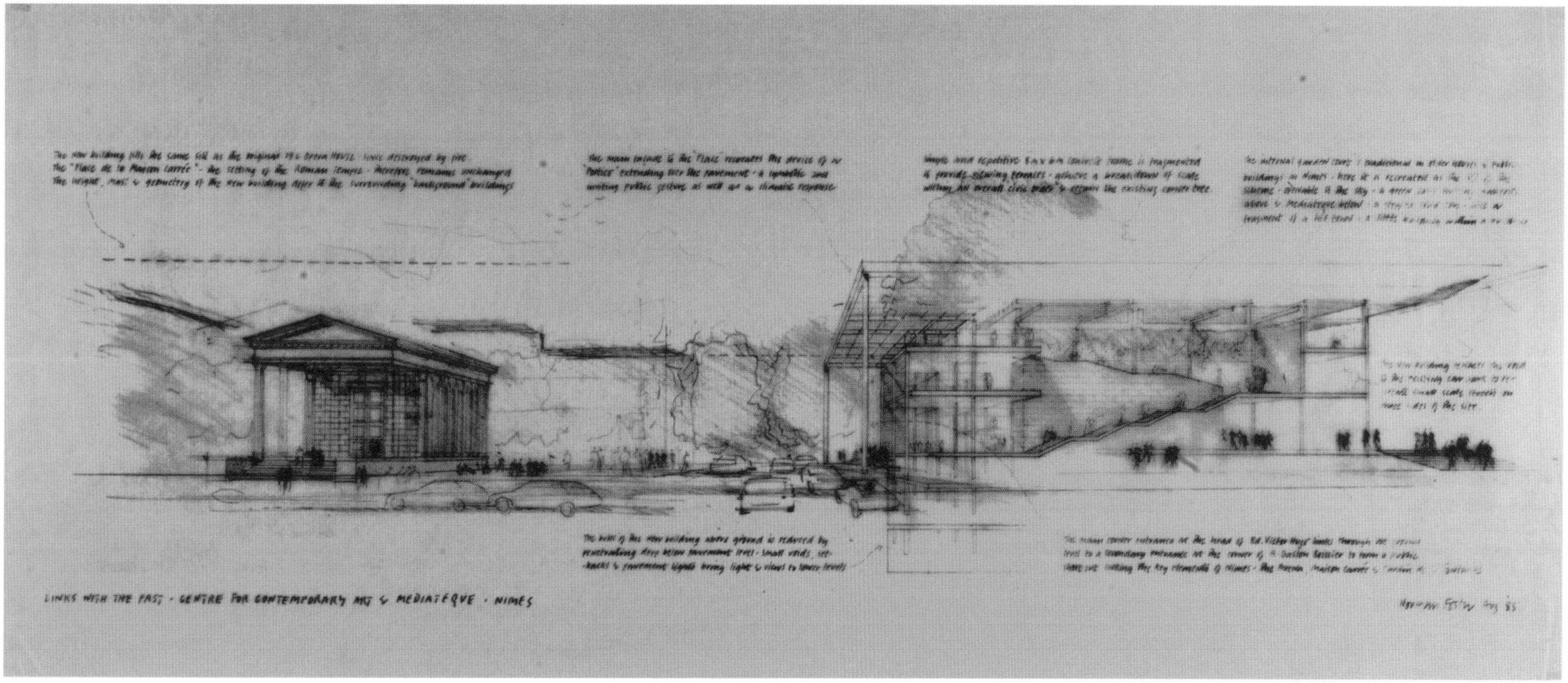
LINKS WITH THE PAST · CENTRE FOR CONTEMPORARY ART & MEDIATEQUE · NIMES

Carre d'Art
Nîmes, France
Pencil and colored pencil
56.9 x 29.7 cm
Sketch: 1993
Building: 1993
Norman Foster

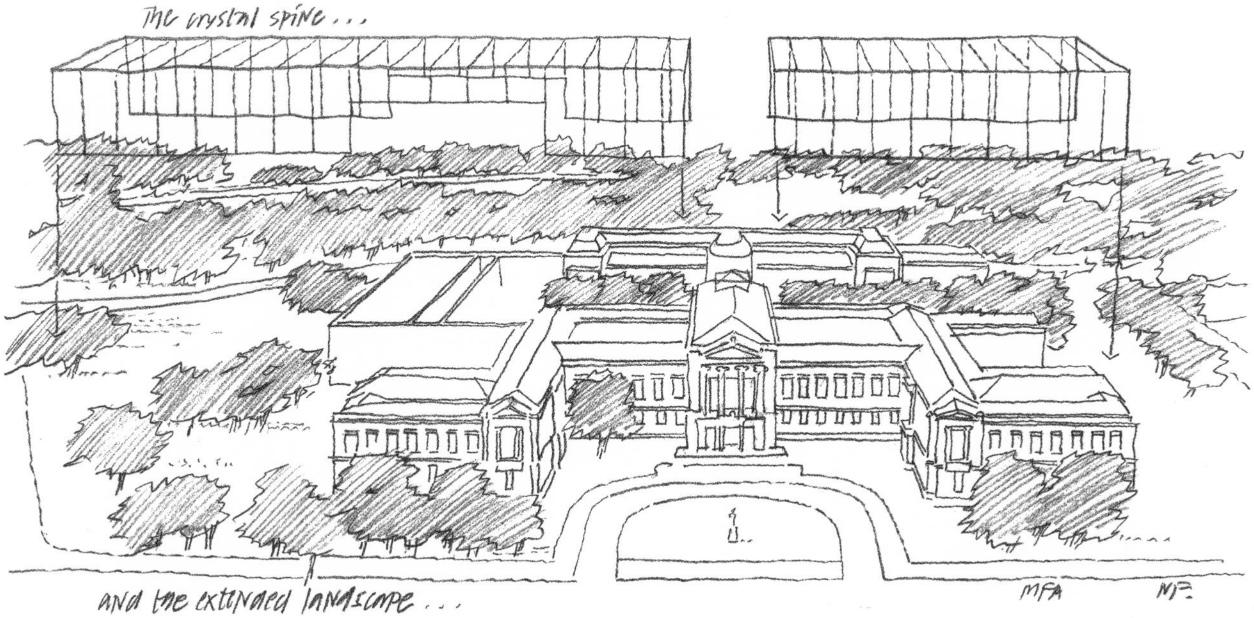
The crystal spine . . .
and the extended landscape . . .
MFA
NF

MFA
Boston, MA, USA
Pencil
41.9 x 29.7 cm
Sketch: 2010
Building: 2010
Norman Foster

**Reichstag, New German Parliament
Berlin, Germany**
Pen
29.8 x 21.1 cm
Sketch: 1995
Building: 1999
Norman Foster

**Great Court at the British Museum
London, United Kingdom**
Pen and pencil
29.8 x 21.1 cm
Sketch: 1996
Building: 2000
Norman Foster

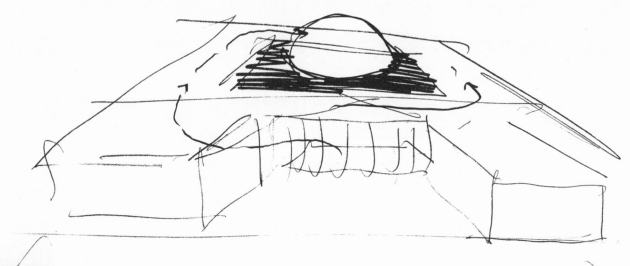

**Hong Kong & Shanghai Bank
Hong Kong, China**
Pencil
29.8 x 21.1 cm
Sketch: 1983
Building: 2004
Norman Foster

**30 St Mary Axe,
London, United Kingdom**
Pen and pencil
41.9 x 29.8 cm
2004
Norman Foster

a reflective splay top · following the ·o· shading··

The 'maypole' effect?

the city grid

4

The "city grid" is really a 4, storey increment, visually

The "city within a city" has always been full of surprises!

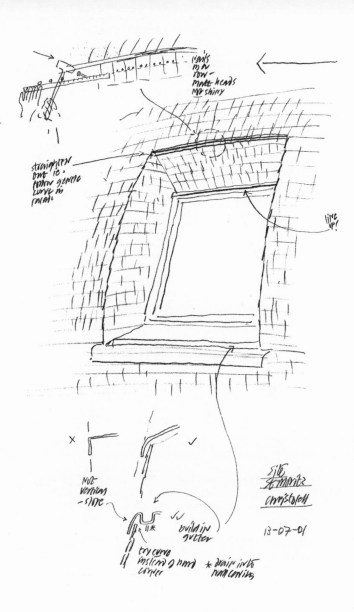

nails in a row - matte heads not shiny

straighten out ie: from genue curve in facial

line up!

Chesa Futura
St. Moritz, Switzerland
Pencil
29.8 x 21.1 cm
Sketch: 2001
Building: 2004
Norman Foster

X

✓

not vertical - slate

build in gutter

try curve instead of hard corner

* drain into rear cavity

site st moritz

christofell

13-07-01

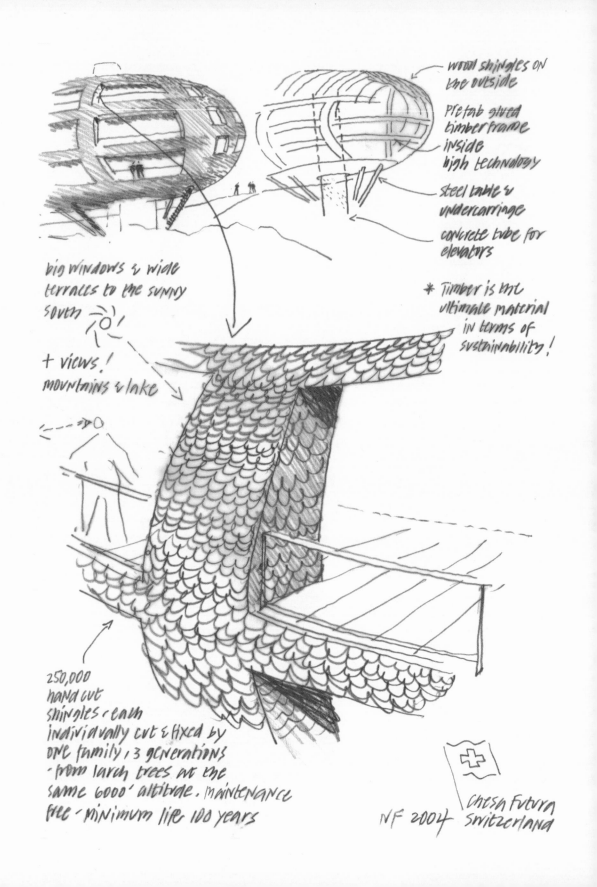

wood shingles on the outside

prefab glued timber frame inside high technology

steel table & undercarriage

concrete tube for elevators

big windows & wide terraces to the sunny south

+ views! mountains & lake

* Timber is the ultimate material in terms of sustainability!

250,000 hand cut shingles each individually cut & fixed by one family, 3 generations - from larch trees at the same 6000' altitude. maintenance free - minimum life 100 years

NF 2004   Chesa Futura Switzerland

School
Sierra Leone
Pencil and colored pencil
41.2 x 29.8 cm
2008
Norman Foster

NF
04/09

A school
for Sierra Leone

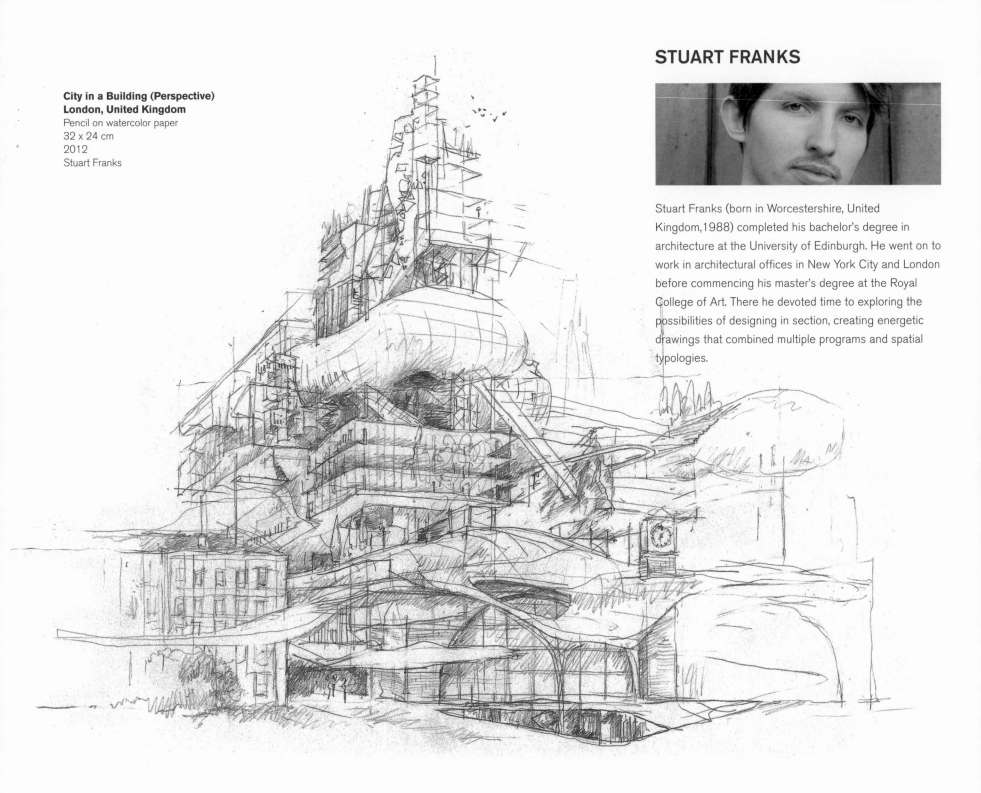

City in a Building (Perspective)
London, United Kingdom
Pencil on watercolor paper
32 x 24 cm
2012
Stuart Franks

STUART FRANKS

Stuart Franks (born in Worcestershire, United Kingdom,1988) completed his bachelor's degree in architecture at the University of Edinburgh. He went on to work in architectural offices in New York City and London before commencing his master's degree at the Royal College of Art. There he devoted time to exploring the possibilities of designing in section, creating energetic drawings that combined multiple programs and spatial typologies.

City in a Building (Section)
London, United Kingdom
Pencil on watercolor paper
58 x 35 cm
2012
Stuart Franks

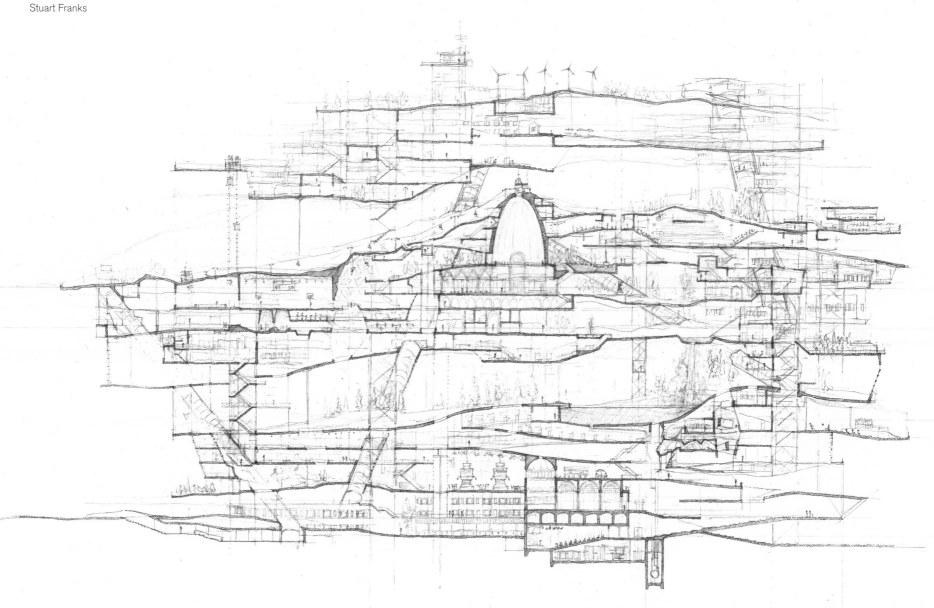

City in a Building (Perspective)
London, United Kingdom
Pencil on watercolor paper
27 x 19 cm
2012
Stuart Franks

Multiplicity (Section)
London, United Kingdom
Ink and pencil on detail paper
63 x 42 cm
2012
Stuart Franks

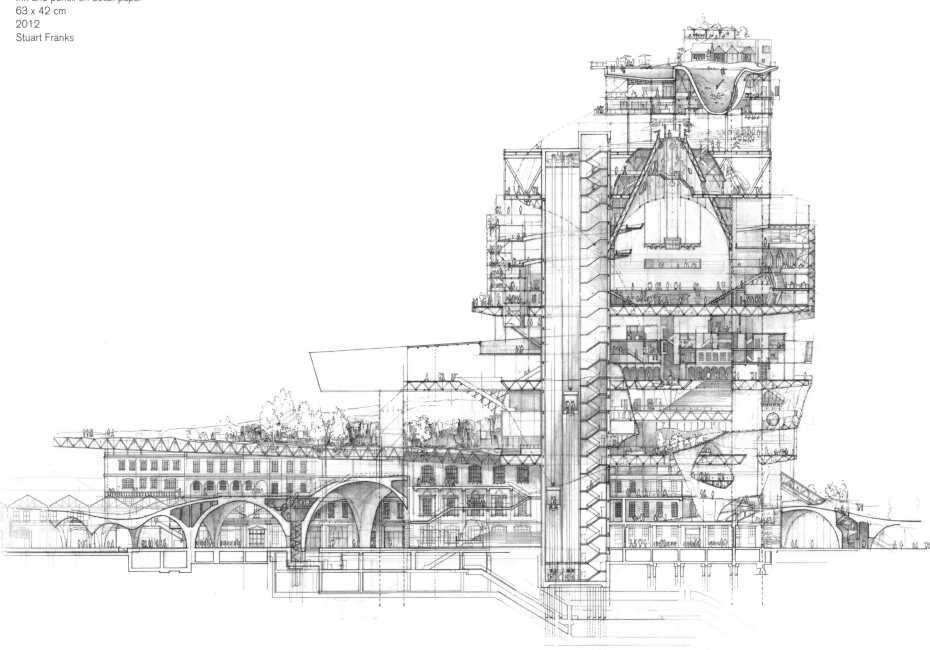

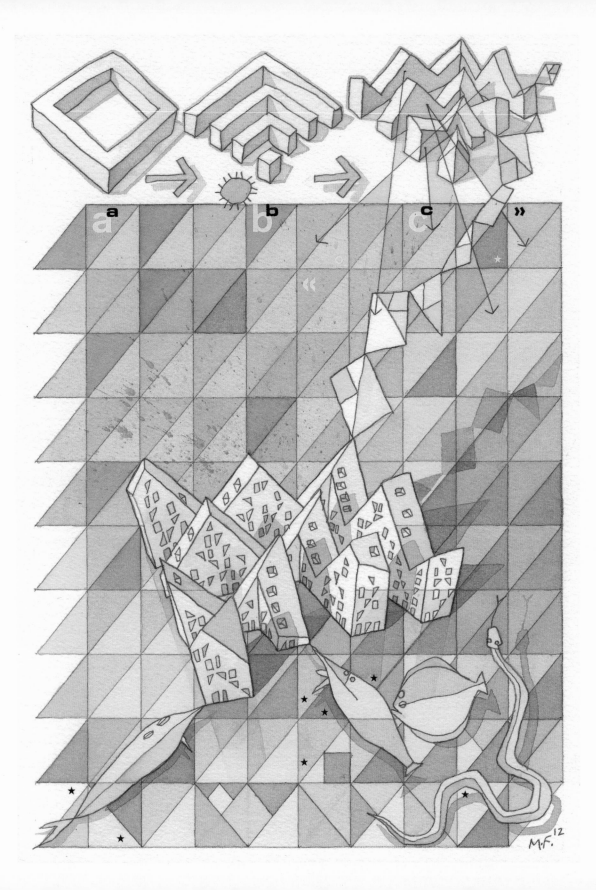

MIKKEL FROST

Mikkel Frost (born in Denmark, 1971) graduated from the Aarhus School of Architecture in 1996. He co-founded CEBRA in 2001. Frost is a skilled and versatile illustrator, with a unique and easily recognizable style. When a project's initial design is completed, Frost draws a cartoonish concept illustration, using watercolors whenever possible. These drawings can be best described as visual summaries that condense the idea of an entire project onto just one piece of paper. In this sense, they serve as playful reminders of what the project is all about.

The Iceberg
Aarhus, Denmark
Watercolor
29.7 x 21 cm
2012/2013
Mikkel Frost/CEBRA together with
JDS Search Louis Palliard

Adult Education Center
Odense, Denmark
Watercolor
29.7 x 21 cm
2012/2014
Mikkel Frost

Rebild Porten
Rebild, Denmark
Watercolor
29.7 x 21 cm
2012
Mikkel Frost

Skate City
Haderslev, Denmark
Watercolor
29.7 x 21 cm
2012/2013
Mikkel Frost

**Office sketch showing several
CEBRA projects**
Watercolor
29.7 x 21 cm
2012
Mikkel Frost

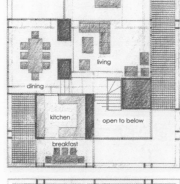

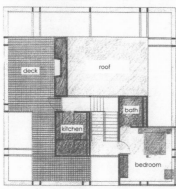

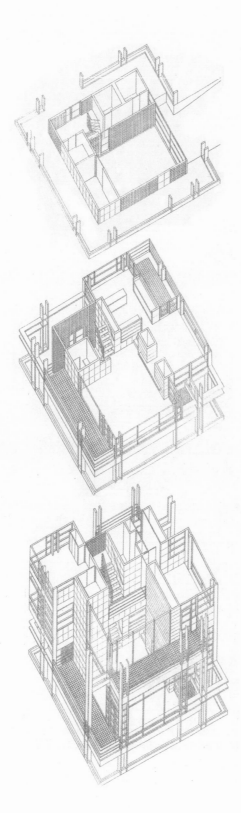

GILBERT GORSKI

Gilbert Gorski (born in Milwakee, WI, USA, 1955) began his career as an associate principal with FCL architects, the successor firm to the office of Mies van der Rohe. He was the project designer on numerous buildings including the world headquarters of the McDonalds Corporation in Oak Brook, and the Oceanarium in Chicago. In 1987, Gorski was designated as the Chicago Architectural Club's Burnham Fellow and received a three-month fellowship to the American Academy in Rome. He founded his own company specializing in design and illustration in 1989. His drawings and paintings have been included in numerous publications and architecture exhibitions. He was awarded the Hugh Ferriss Memorial Prize in 1990 and 2002. He is currently an associate professor at the University of Notre Dame and holds the James A. and Louise F. Nolen Chair in Architecture.

Devon House
Ada, MI, USA
Pencil
30.5 x 46 cm
Sketch: 1988
Building: 1990
Gilbert Gorski

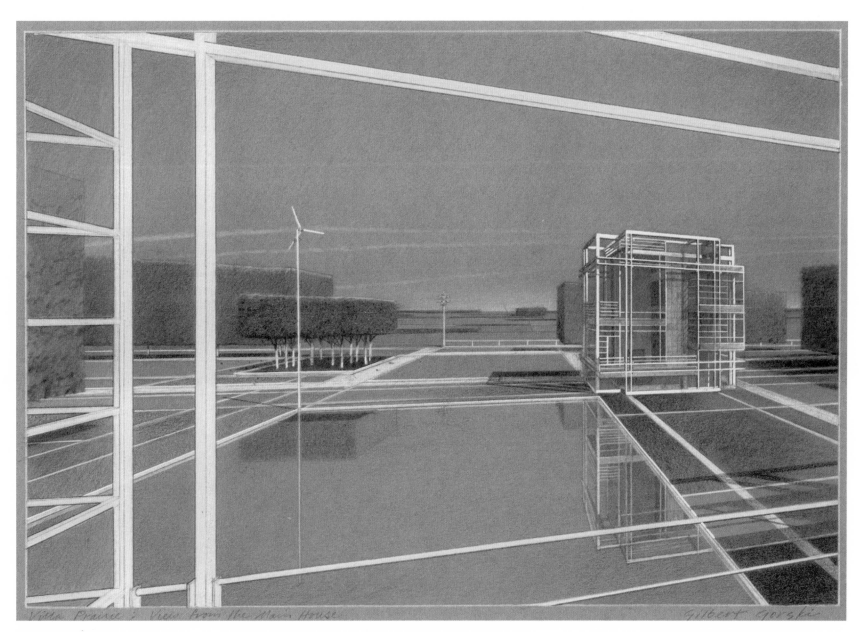

Villa Prairie : View from the Main House   Gilbert Gorski

Devon House
Ada, MI, USA
Colored pencil on gray board
18 x 28 cm
Sketch: 1989
Building: 1990
Gilbert Gorski

420 East Ohio
Chicago, IL, USA
Retro-colored print, airbrush
and colored pencil
Original: pencil on paper
35.5 x 53 cm
Sketch: 1988
Building: 1991
Gilbert Gorski

420 East Ohio
Chicago, IL, USA
Retro-colored print, airbrush
and colored pencil
Original: pencil on paper
46 x 61 cm
Sketch: 1988
Building: 1991
Gilbert Gorski

420 East Ohio
Chicago, IL, USA
Pencil on paper
23 x 14 cm
Sketch: 1988
Building: 1991
Gilbert Gorski

Oceanarium
Chicago, IL, USA
Print colored with colored pencil
20 x 28 cm
Sketch: 1986
Building: 1990
Gilbert Gorski

McDonalds Lodge
Oak Brook, IL, USA
Felt-tip pen on paper, retro-colored print, colored pencil
22 x 28 cm
Sketches: 1982–1983
Building: 1985
Gilber Gorski

McDonalds Training Center
Oak Brook, IL, USA
Felt-tip pen on paper
42 x 28 cm
Sketch: 1978
Building: 1983
Gilbert Gorski

McDonalds Office Building
Retro-colored print
35.5 x 61 cm
Sketch: 1985
Building: 1990
Gilbert Gorski

MARY GRIFFIN, ERIC HAESLOOP

Eric Haesloop received his Masters of Architecture from Yale University. After graduating he worked at Cesar Pelli & Associates in New Haven and later joined William Turnbull Associates in 1985. He worked closely with William Turnbull until his death in 1997. Haesloop has taught architectural design at Yale, Stanford, and UC Berkeley and was the Friedman Visiting Professor of Professional Practice in 2008. Mary Griffin received her Masters of Architecture degree from MIT. After five years in Washington D.C. with Hartman-Cox Architects, she moved to San Francisco to marry William Turnbull and join his architectural practice. She has taught architectural design at UC Berkeley and was the Friedman Visiting Professor of Professional Practice in 2008.

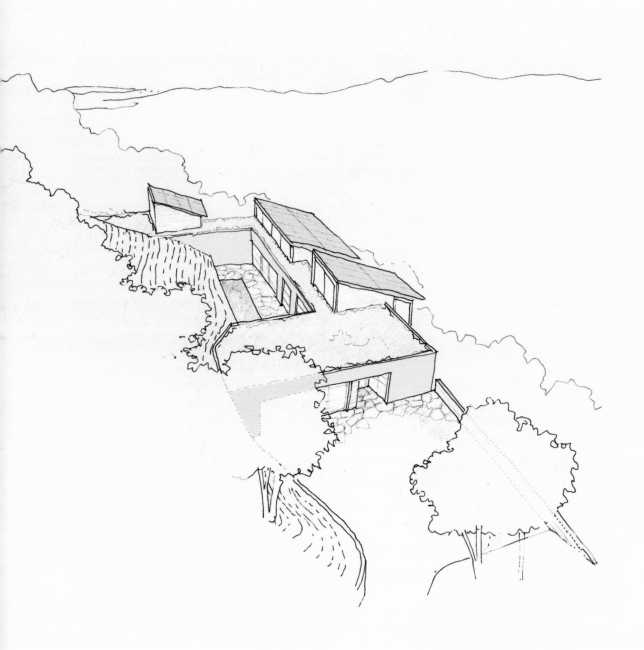

Kentfield Residence
Kentfield, CA, USA
Pen and colored pencil
19.77 x 21.04 cm
Sketch: 2006
Building: 2010
Eric Haesloop and Mary Griffin/Turnbull Griffin Haesloop

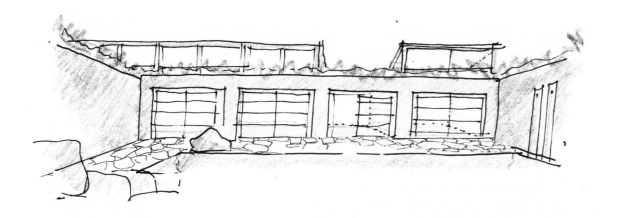

Kentfield Residence
Kentfield, CA, USA
Pen and colored pencil
6.6 x 15.24 cm
Sketch: 2006
Building: 2010
Eric Haesloop and Mary Griffin/Turnbull Griffin Haesloop

Kentfield Residence
Kentfield, CA, USA
Pen and colored pencil
8.517 x 15.24 cm
Sketch: 2006
Building: 2010
Eric Haesloop and Mary Griffin/Turnbull Griffin Haesloop

MAXXI: Museum of XXI Century Arts
Rome, Italy
Acrylic painting on black cartridge paper
62 x 85 cm
Painting: 1998
Building: 2009
Zaha Hadid

ZAHA HADID

Zaha Hadid (born in Baghdad, 1950) consistently pushes the boundaries of architecture and urban design, experimenting with new spatial concepts and developing visionary aesthetics that encompass all fields of design. Hadid studied architecture at the Architectural Association (AA) from 1972 and was awarded the Diploma Prize in 1977. She then became a partner of the Office for Metropolitan Architecture, taught at the AA with OMA collaborators Rem Koolhaas and Elia Zenghelis, and later led her own studio at the AA until 1987. She was made Honorary Member of the American Academy of Arts and Letters, Fellow of the American Institute of Architecture, and Dame Commander of the Order of the British Empire in 2012. She is currently a professor at the University of Applied Arts in Vienna, Austria.

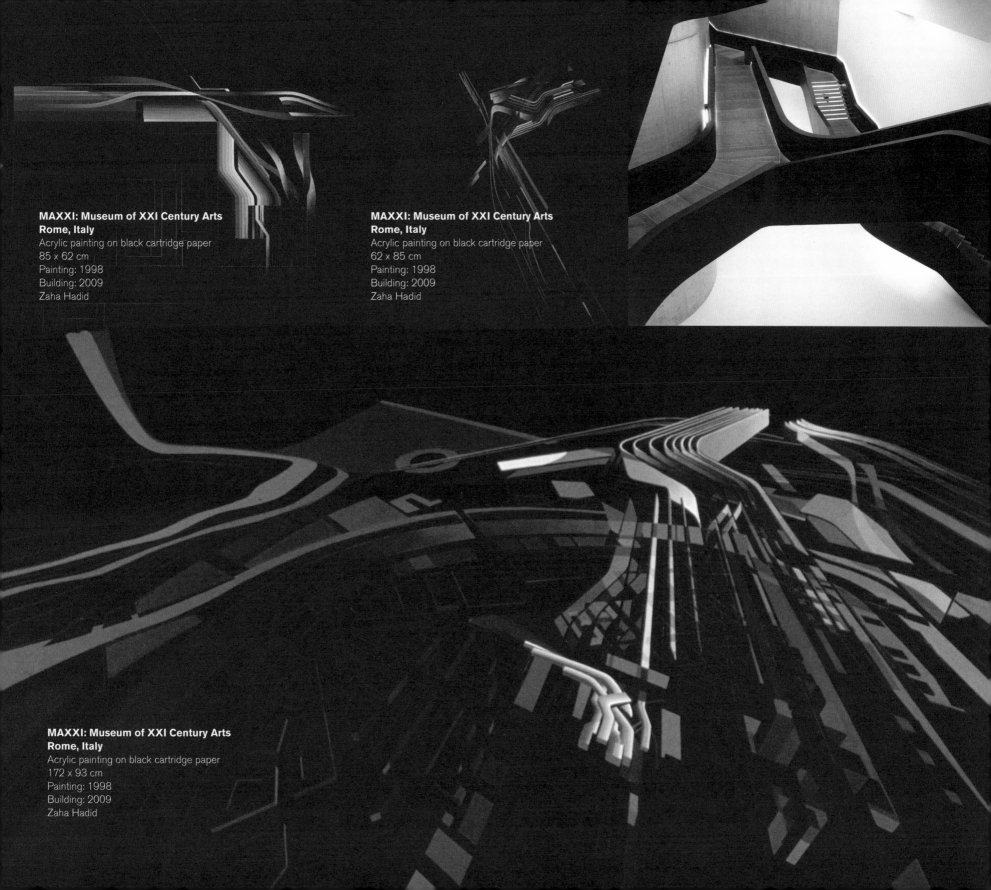

MAXXI: Museum of XXI Century Arts
Rome, Italy
Acrylic painting on black cartridge paper
85 x 62 cm
Painting: 1998
Building: 2009
Zaha Hadid

MAXXI: Museum of XXI Century Arts
Rome, Italy
Acrylic painting on black cartridge paper
62 x 85 cm
Painting: 1998
Building: 2009
Zaha Hadid

MAXXI: Museum of XXI Century Arts
Rome, Italy
Acrylic painting on black cartridge paper
172 x 93 cm
Painting: 1998
Building: 2009
Zaha Hadid

ROLAND HARMER

Roland Harmer (born in Callington, United Kingdom, 1952) completed an arts foundation course at the Cambridge College of Arts and Technology, followed by a degree in Industrial Design at Manchester Polytechnic. Harmer produces visualizations for architects, developers and others who need to know how a building or landscape proposal will look. Most work now takes the form of computer models, usually built in VectorWorks and rendered in Cinema 4D. The renderings are often used as the basis for drawings either freehand or ruled. These add charm, life, emphasis and extra detail. They can also suggest tentativeness, important when a scheme is not finalized. Pencil drawings can be sufficient but watercolor, or pastel are sometimes added.

3 Redcross Street
Bristol, United Kingdom
Pencil and watercolor
Drawing: 2008
Building: 2013
Roland Harmer

Prior Park Junior School,
Prior Park College
Bath, United Kingdom
Pencil and watercolor
30 x 42 cm
Drawing: 2007
Building: 2010
Roland Harmer

Dorothy House Hospice
Pencil and watercolor
30 x 50 cm
Drawing: 2004
Building: 2006
Roland Harmer

North Hill Farm
Somerset, United Kingdom
Pencil
30 x 42 cm
2010
Roland Harmer

North Hill Farm
Somerset, United Kingdom
Pencil
30 x 42 cm
2010
Roland Harmer

Biomaths Building
University of Bristol
Bristol, United Kingdom
Pencil and watercolor
30 x 42 cm
2009
Roland Harmer

Winterbourne Barn
Winterbourne, United Kingdom
Pencil and watercolor
30 x 42 cm
2006
Roland Harmer

Chippenham Riverside
Pencil and watercolor
30 x 42 cm
2012
Roland Harmer

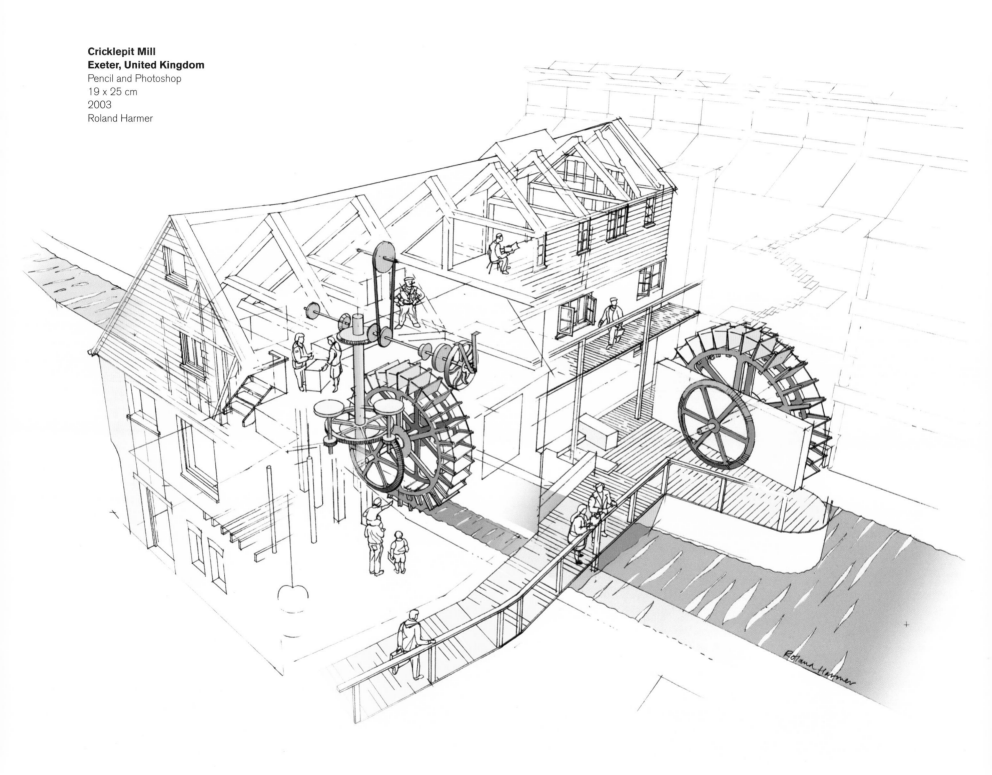

Cricklepit Mill
Exeter, United Kingdom
Pencil and Photoshop
19 x 25 cm
2003
Roland Harmer

heri&salli

Heribert Wolfmayr (born in Grießkirchen, Austria, 1973) and Josef Saller (born in Bischofshofen, Austria, 1971) founded the architecture office heri&salli in 2004, and have since then worked together on architectural, spatial and temporary concepts. The interaction between people and the object is always a key focus of the design process, and the projects are only considered complete when in use as the user is an active component of the design as a whole. The company heri&salli has received a number of awards, including the Salzburg Holzbaupreis in 2003; and a nomination for the Adolf Loos Staatspreis. Exhibitions included in the Künstlerhaus in Vienna, the MAK – Museum für angewandte Kunst Vienna, and the DAC Danish Architecture Centre.

Flederhaus
Vienna, Austria
Rollerball pen
Sketch: 2011
Building: 2011
heri&salli

bodypuzzle
Vienna, Austria
Rollerball pen
Sketch: 2012
Interior: 2012
heri&salli

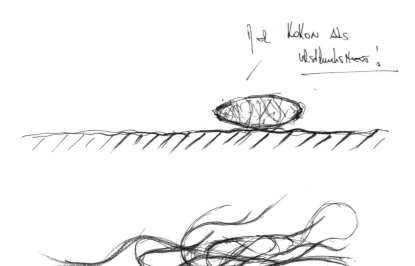

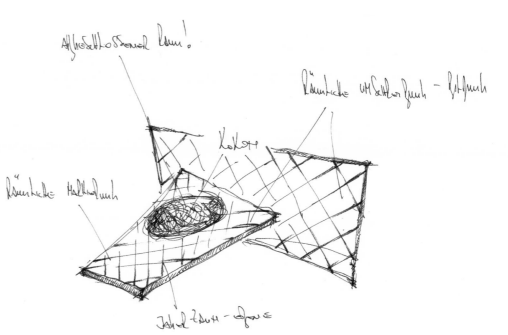

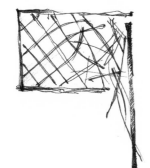

land schaf(f)t zaun
Upper Austria
Rollerball pen
Sketches: 2010
Fence: 2011
heri&salli

153

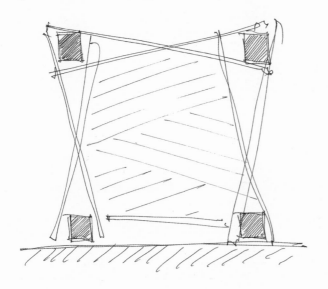

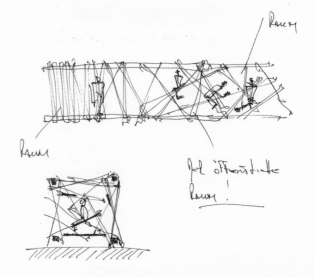

raumverschlag
AFO – Architekturforum
Upper Austria
Rollerball pen
2009
heri&salli

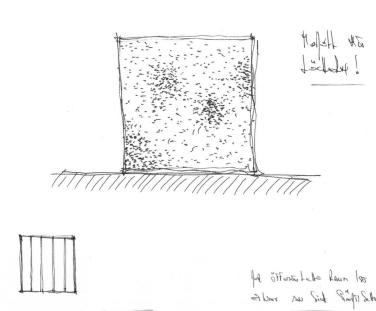

housedress
Charintia, Austria
Rollerball pen
Sketch: 2011
Building: 2011
heri&salli

raumverschlag
AFO – Architekturforum
Upper Austria
Rollerball pen
Sketch: 2009
Building: 2011
heri&salli

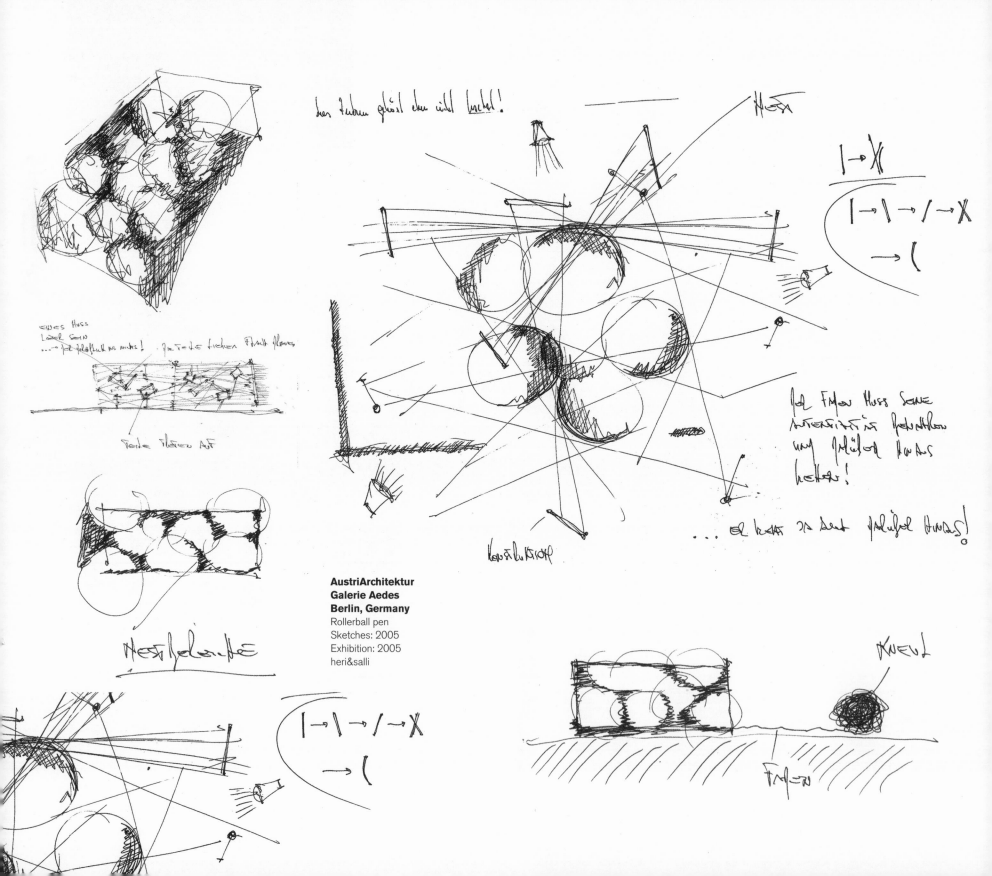

AustriArchitektur
Galerie Aedes
Berlin, Germany
Rollerball pen
Sketches: 2005
Exhibition: 2005
heri&salli

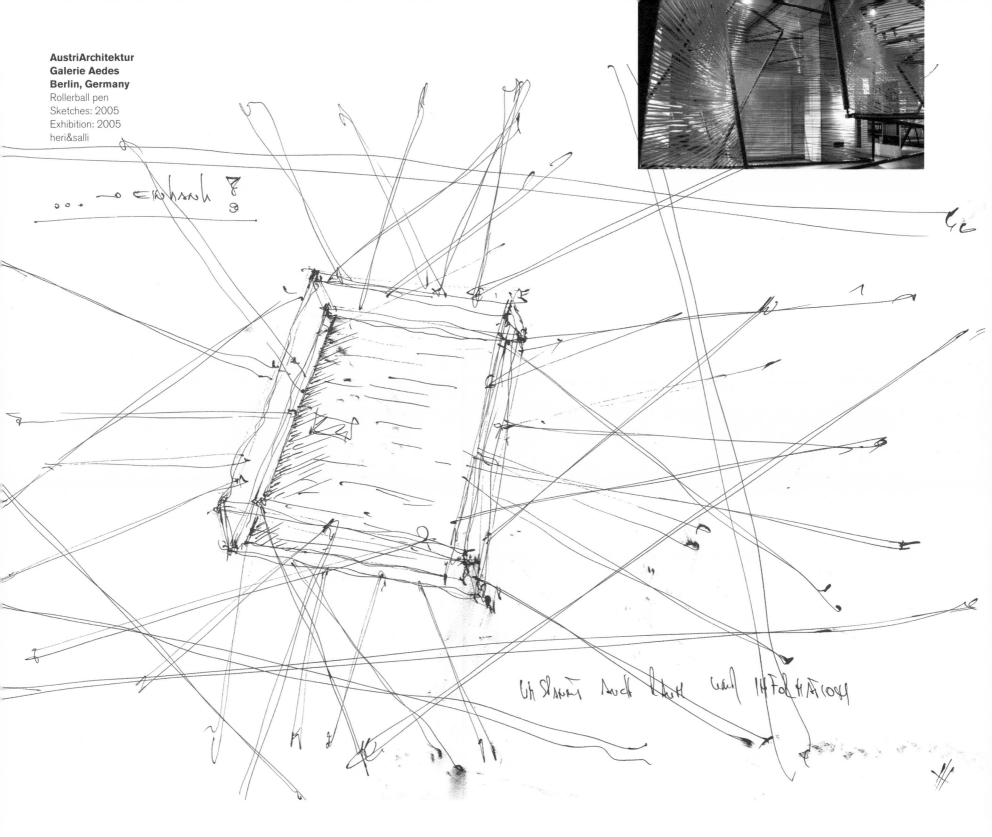

AustriArchitektur
Galerie Aedes
Berlin, Germany
Rollerball pen
Sketches: 2005
Exhibition: 2005
heri&salli

157

**Film Center Esplanade
Berlin, Germany**
Pencil, colored pencil and pen
on tracing paper
42 x 29.7 cm
1995
Herman Hertzberger

HERMAN HERTZBERGER

Dutch architect Herman Hertzberger (born in Amsterdam, the Netherlands, 1932) graduated in 1958 from what is now the Technical University of Delft. His architectural practice, now called Architectuurstudio HH, was established in 1960. His best known designs include those for the Centraal Beheer head office in Apeldoorn, Music Center Vredenburg in Utrecht, The Ministry of Social Affairs and Employment in The Hague and the Chassé Theater in Breda. Herman Hertzberger was recently awarded with the Royal Institute of British Architects (RIBA) Gold Medal 2012. He has lectured at the Academy of Architecture, Amsterdam (1965–1969), and was professor at the Technical University of Delft (1970–1999), visiting professor at the University of Geneva (Switzerland) and chairman of the Postgraduate Berlage Institute (1990–1995). He is and has been presenting lectures in Europe, North, Middle and South America, the Middle East, Asia and Australia.

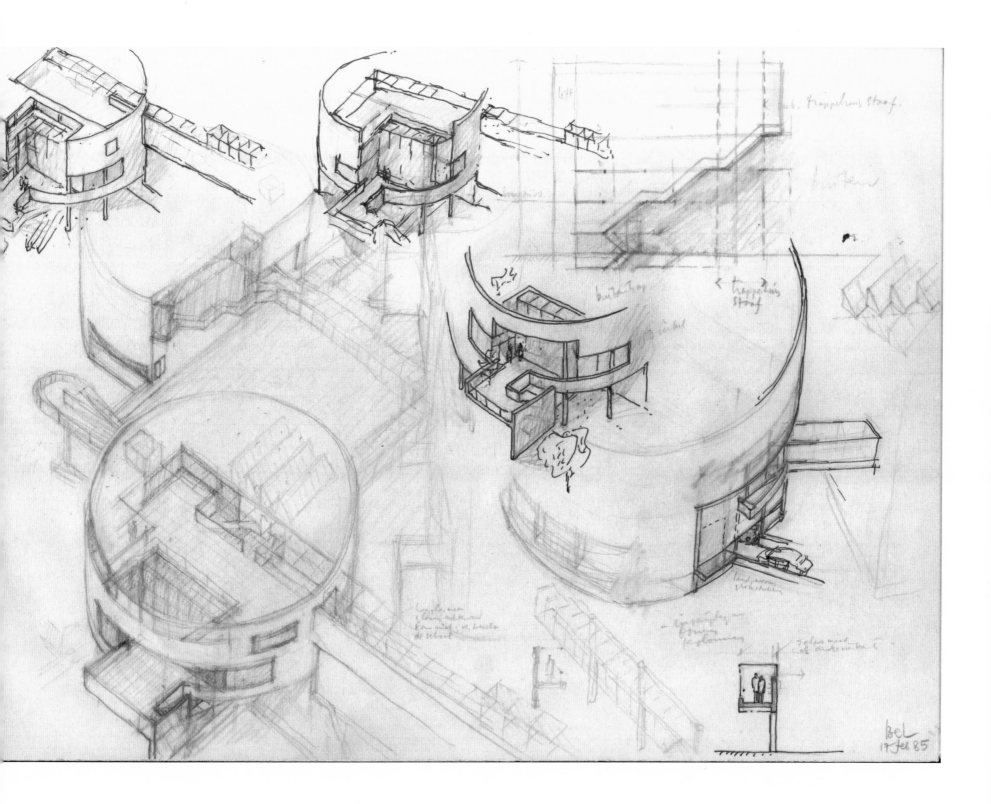

159

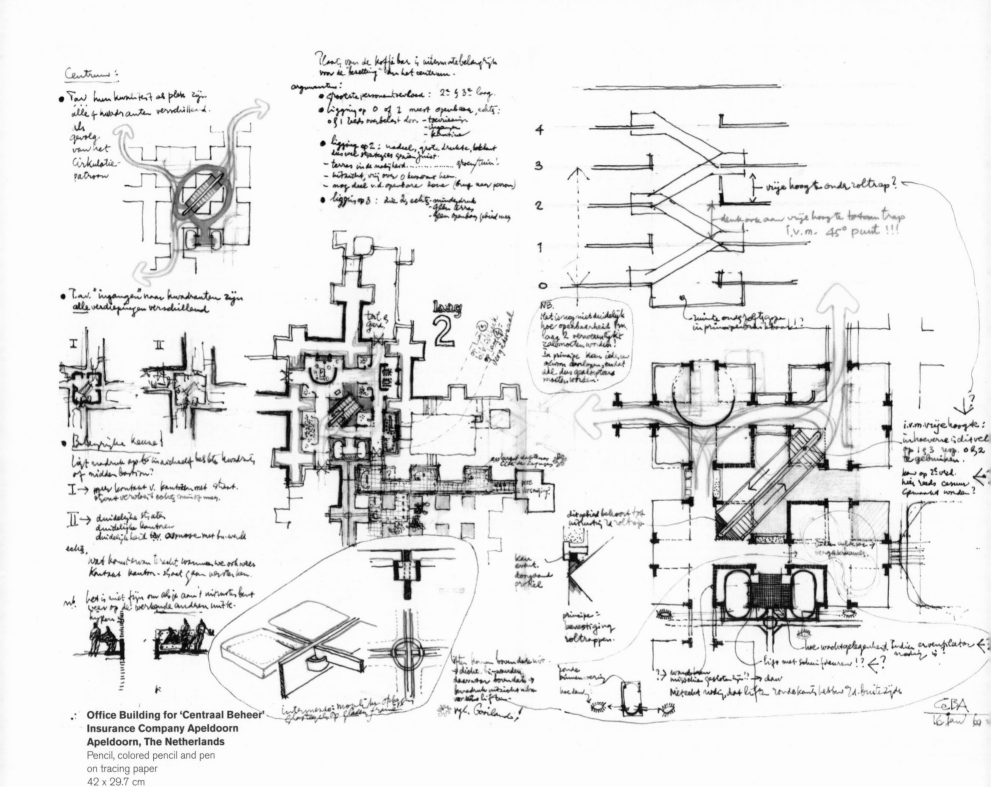

Office Building for 'Centraal Beheer'
Insurance Company Apeldoorn
Apeldoorn, The Netherlands
Pencil, colored pencil and pen
on tracing paper
42 x 29.7 cm
Sketch: 1972
Building: 1972
Herman Hertzberger

160

Office Building for 'Centraal Beheer'
Insurance Company Apeldoorn
Apeldoorn, The Netherlands
Pencil, colored pencil and pen
on tracing paper
42 x 29.7 cm
Sketch: 1972
Building: 1972
Herman Hertzberger

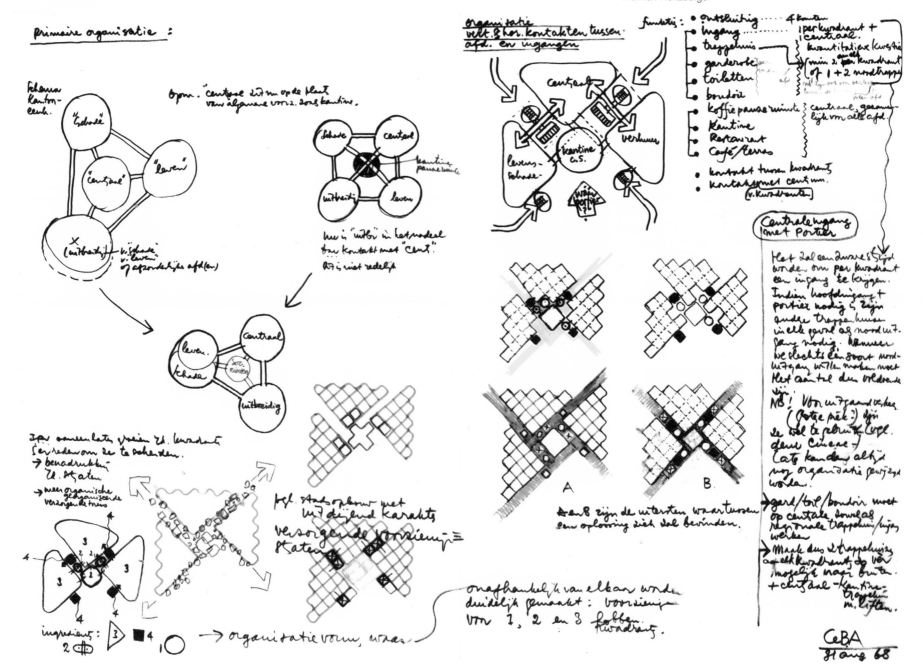

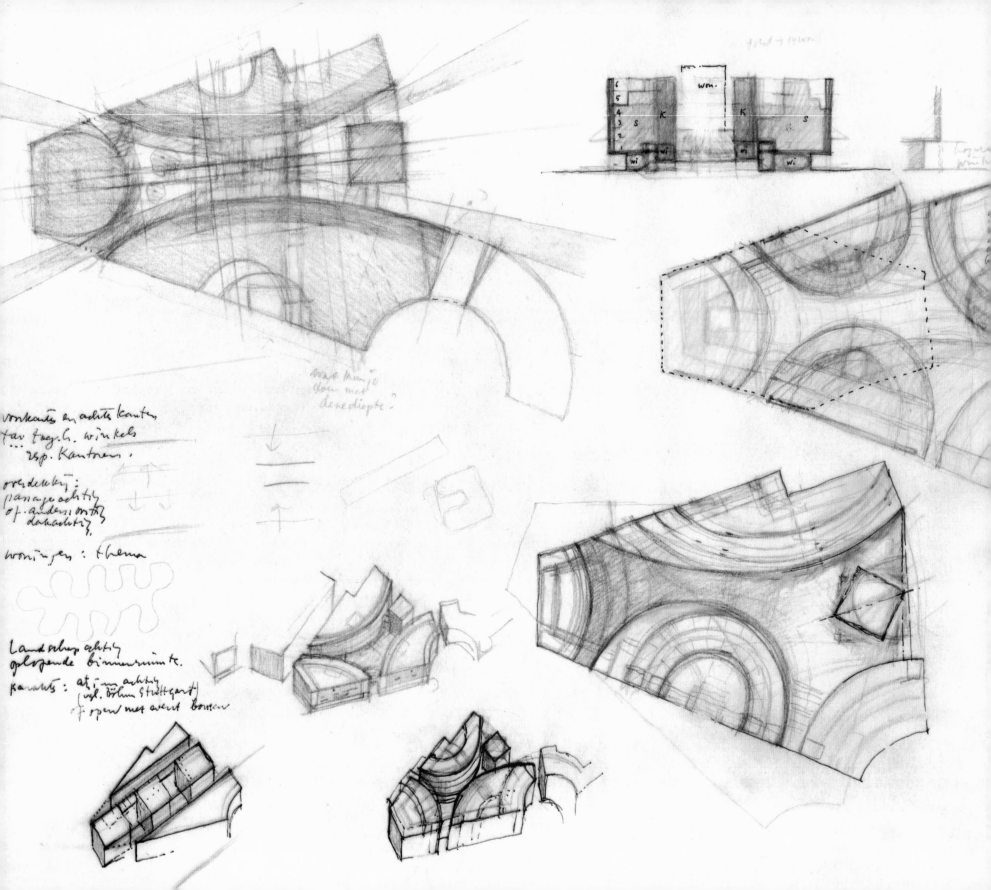

**Office Building MediaPark
Cologne, Germany**
Pencil, colored pencil and pen
on tracing paper
42 x 29.7 cm
Sketches: 2004
Building: 2004
Herman Hertzberger

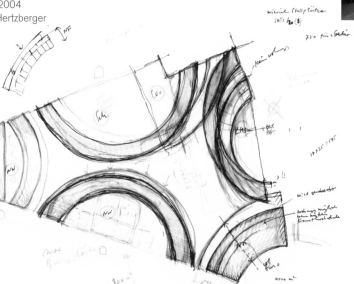

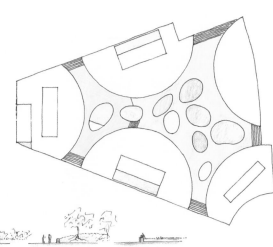

Primary School and
Junior High School
Rome, Italy
Pencil, colored pencil and pen
on tracing paper
42 x 29.7 cm
Drawing: 2012
Building: 2012
Herman Hertzberger

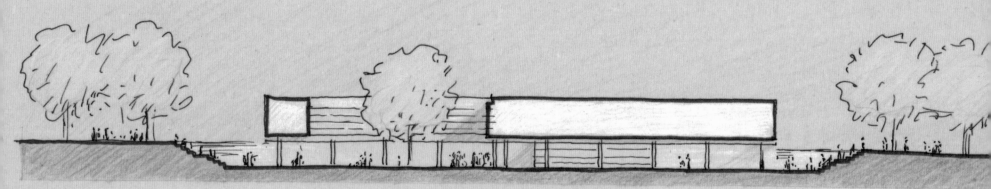

RoRo dron. 17 03 10

**Science Center for the Faculty of Sciences,
Mathematics and Information Science,
Amsterdam University
Amsterdam, The Netherlands**
Pencil, colored pencil and pen on tracing paper
42 x 29.7 cm
Drawing: 2009
Building: 2010
Herman Hertzberger

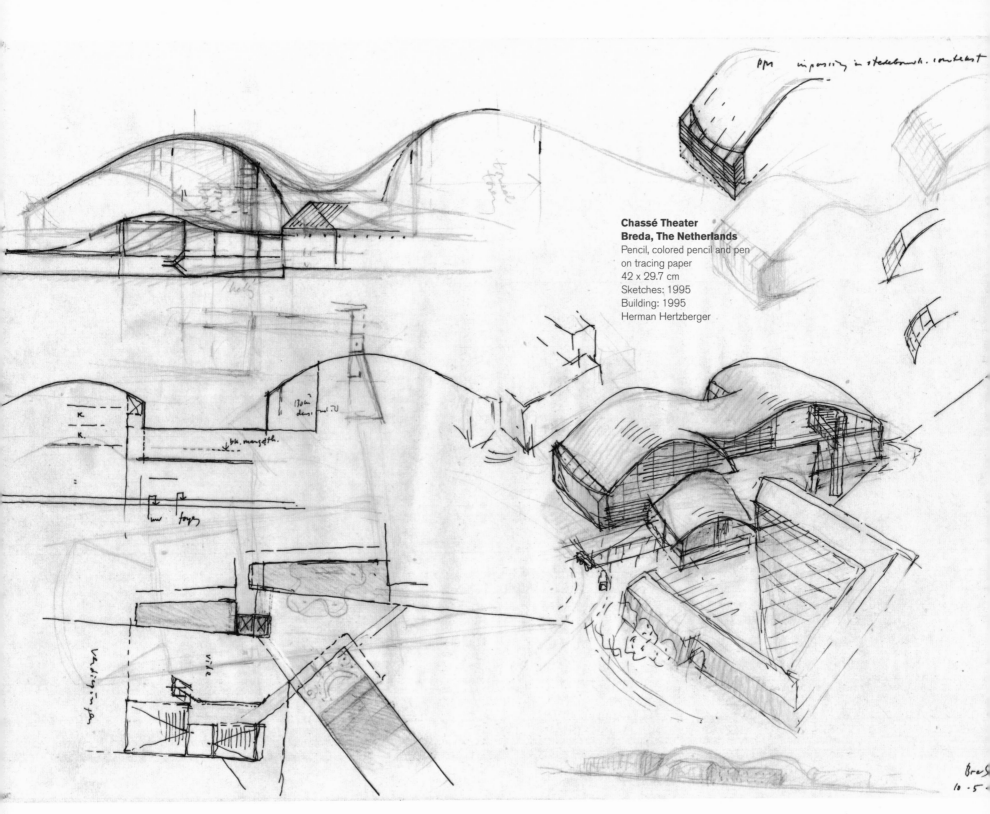

Chassé Theater
Breda, The Netherlands
Pencil, colored pencil and pen
on tracing paper
42 x 29.7 cm
Sketches: 1995
Building: 1995
Herman Hertzberger

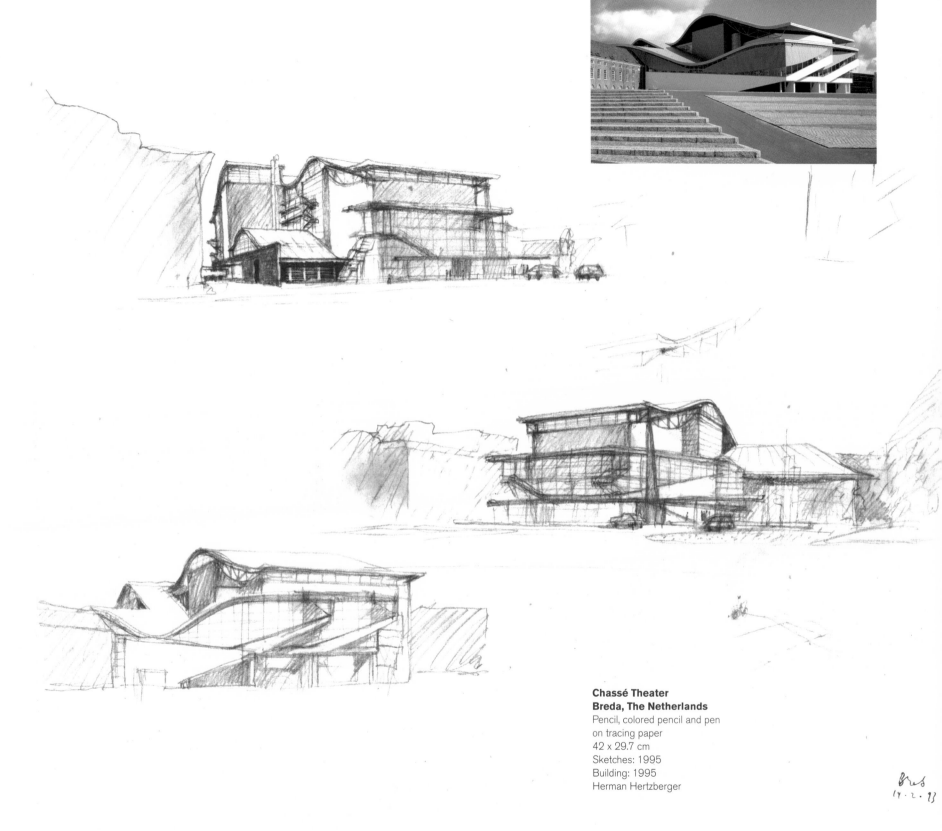

Chassé Theater
Breda, The Netherlands
Pencil, colored pencil and pen
on tracing paper
42 x 29.7 cm
Sketches: 1995
Building: 1995
Herman Hertzberger

Bres
14·2·93

**Gehua Youth and Cultural Center
Qinhuangdao, China**
Pen on sketch paper
30 x 25 cm
Sketch: 2012
Building: 2012
Li Hu

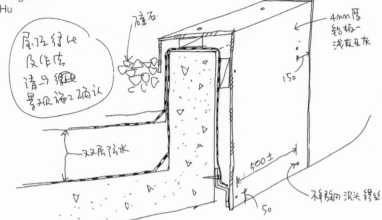

LI HU

Li Hu (born in Fushun, China, 1973) is founding partner of Open Architecture, director of Columbia University GSAPP's Studio-X Beijing, and former partner of Steven Holl Architects. Li Hu received his Bachelor of Architecture from Tsinghua University in Beijing in 1996 and his Master of Architecture from Rice University in 1998. He worked at Steven Holl Architects from 2000 to 2010, and became a partner of the firm in 2005. Li Hu founded the SHA's Beijing Office, and was responsible for the firm's many award winning urban projects in China. He left SHA at the end of 2010 to focus on Open Architecture with partner Huang Wenjing. Li Hu is also actively evolved in academic and cultural activities. In 2012, he was the curator for the Space category of the first China Design Exhibition, initiated and supported by the Ministry of Culture of China.

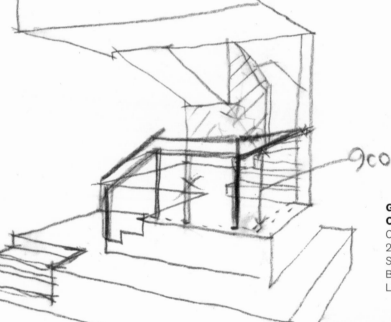

**Gehua Youth and Cultural Center
Qinhuangdao, China**
Charcoal on sketch paper
23 x 23 cm
Sketch: 2012
Building: 2012
Li Hu

Gehua Youth and Cultural Center
Qinhuangdao, China
Crayon on sketch paper
38 x 12 cm
Sketch: 2012
Building: 2012
Li Hu

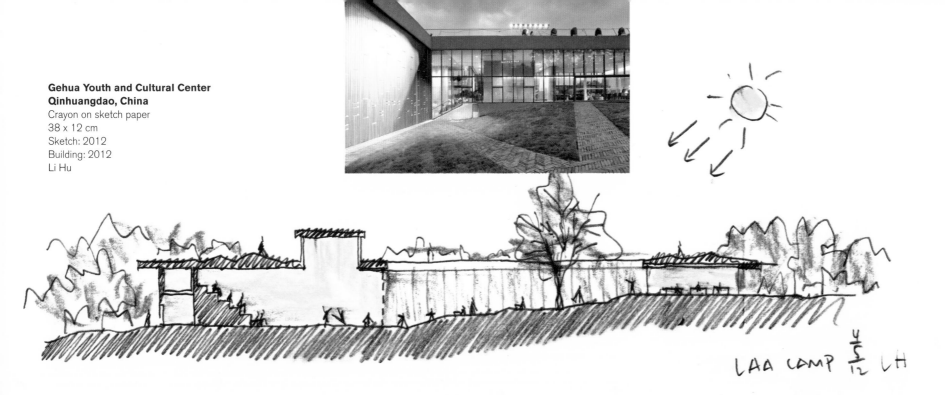

LAA CAMP $\frac{4}{5}$ $\frac{}{12}$ LH

Gehua Youth and Cultural Center
Qinhuangdao, China
Pen on paper
42 x 30 cm
Sketch: 2012
Building: 2012
Li Hu

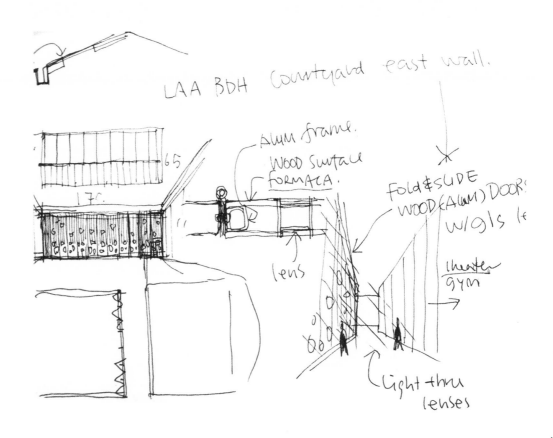

LAA BDH Countyard east wall.

ALUM frame.
WOOD Surface
FORMACA.

65

17C.

lens

FOLD & SLIDE
WOOD (ALUM) DOORS
w/ gls le

theater
gym →

light thru
lenses

MATS JACOBSON

Mats Jacobson (born in Norrbärke, Sweden, 1942) established the firm FOJAB architects, together with English architect Keith Foster, in 1971. He worked for the company as chief architect until 1983. He then went on to work for a number of different companies before establishing Jacobson och Sjögren Arkitekter AB (Josark) together with Magnus Sjögren in 2007. Jacobson studied architecture at Lunds Tekniska Högskola, graduating in 1968. He has been awarded prizes in several architecture competitions – and has also worked as a competition judge on a number of occasions. Hand drawings and sketches are an important part of his design process.

Hinseblick
Karlshamn, Sweden
Pencil
21 x 30 cm
Sketch: 2002
Building: 2004
Mats Jacobson

HINSEBLICK

BOSTÄDER MED HAVSUTSIKT

CENTRALT   I KARLSHAMN

Hinseblick
Karlshamn, Sweden
Pencil and watercolor
42 x 30 cm
Sketch: 2002
Building: 2004
Mats Jacobson

PERSPEKTIV
Västergötland 7
Karlshamn, Karlshamns kommun, Blekinge län
Upprättad av Ja-Arkitekten AB 2004-02-25

Mats Jacobson
Arkitekt SAR/MSA

Jonas Ronsby
Arkitekt SAR/MSA

Glasbruket
Malmö, Sweden
Pencil and watercolor
21 x 30 cm
2001
Mats Jacobson

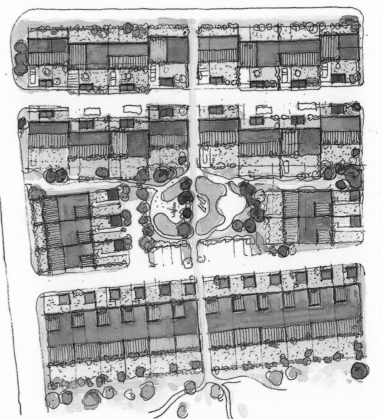

Glasbruket
Malmö, Sweden
Pencil and watercolor
30 x 21 cm
2001
Mats Jacobson

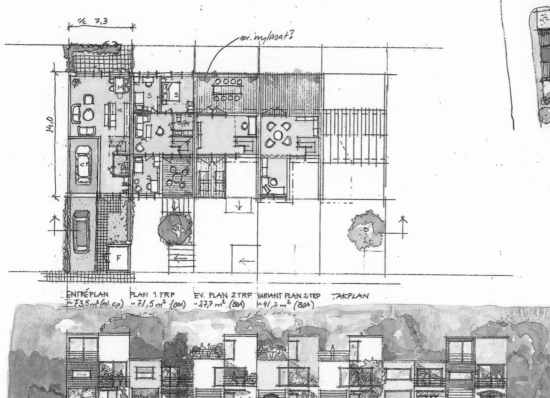

IDÉER TILL FASADVARIATIONER MOT GÅRD

Glasbruket
Malmö, Sweden
Pencil
42 x 30 cm
2004
Mats Jacobson

Kv. Måsen
Lund-Lund Väster, Sweden
Pencil and watercolor
21 x 30 cm
Sketches: 2007–2008
Building: 2010–2013
Mats Jacobson

Kv. Måsen
Lund-Lund Väster, Sweden
Pencil and watercolor
21 x 30 cm
Sketches: 2007–2008
Building: 2010–2013
Mats Jacobson

Kv. Måsen
Lund-Lund Väster, Sweden
Pencil and watercolor
42 x 30 cm
Sketches: 2007–2008
Building: 2010–2013
Mats Jacobson

Sockerbruket
Lund, Sweden
Pencil and watercolor
30 x 21 cm
Sketches: 2008–2011
Building: 2012–2014
Mats Jacobson

Sockerbruket
Lund, Sweden
Pencil and watercolor
30 x 21 cm
Sketches: 2008–2011
Building: 2012–2014
Mats Jacobson

Sockerbruket
Lund, Sweden
Pencil and watercolor
42 x 30 cm
Sketches: 2008–2011
Building: 2012–2014
Mats Jacobson

177

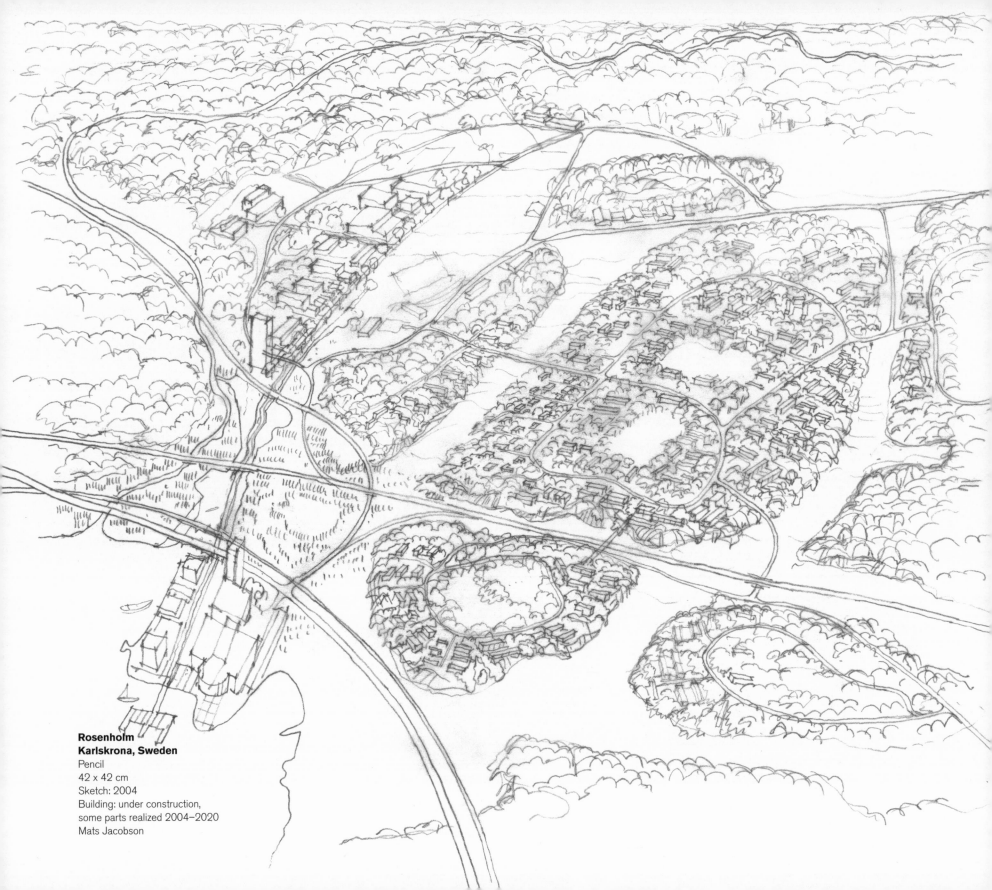

Rosenholm
Karlskrona, Sweden
Pencil
42 x 42 cm
Sketch: 2004
Building: under construction,
some parts realized 2004–2020
Mats Jacobson

Kv, Elefanten
Malmö, Sweden
Pencil
21 x 30 cm
Sketch: 1988
Building: 1989
Mats Jacobson

HELMUT JAHN

Helmut Jahn (born in Nuremberg, Germany, 1940) has earned a reputation for his progressive architecture. His buildings have received numerous design awards and have been represented in architectural exhibitions around the world. Jahn graduated from the Technische Hochschule in Munich. He came to the USA for graduate studies in architecture at the Illinois Institute of Technology (IIT). He joined the firm, at the time named C. F. Murphy Associates, in 1967 and worked under Gene Summers, designing the new McCormick Place. He has taught at the University of Illinois Chicago Campus, was the Elliot Noyes Professor of Architectural Design at Harvard University, the Davenport Visiting Professor of Architectural Design at Yale University, and Thesis Professor at IIT.

James R. Thompson Center
Chicago, IL, USA
Felt-tip pen
Sketch: 1979
Building: 1985
Helmut Jahn

Sony Center
Berlin, Germany
Felt-tip pen
Sketch: 1993
Building: 2000
Helmut Jahn

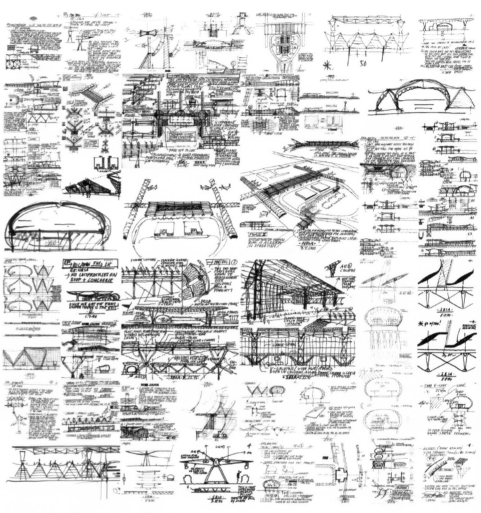

Suvarnabhumi International Airport
Bangkok, Thailand
Felt-tip pen
Sketch: 1995
Building: 2006
Helmut Jahn

181

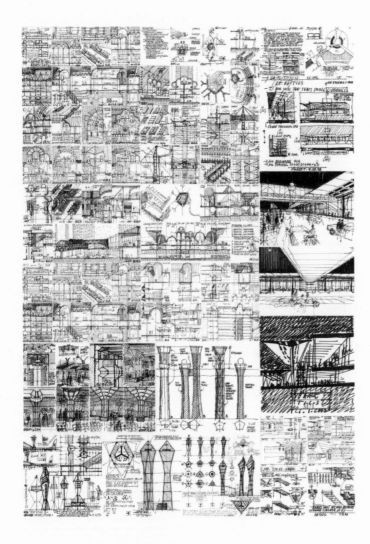

Veer Tower
Las Vegas, NV, USA
Felt-tip pen
Sketch: 2006
Building: 2010
Helmut Jahn

United Airlines Terminal
O'Hare International Airport
Chicago, IL, USA
Felt-tip pen
Sketch: 2001
Building: 2007
Helmut Jahn

Veer Tower
Las Vegas, NV, USA
Felt-tip pen
Sketch: 2006
Building: 2010
Helmut Jahn

VEER·TOWERS·

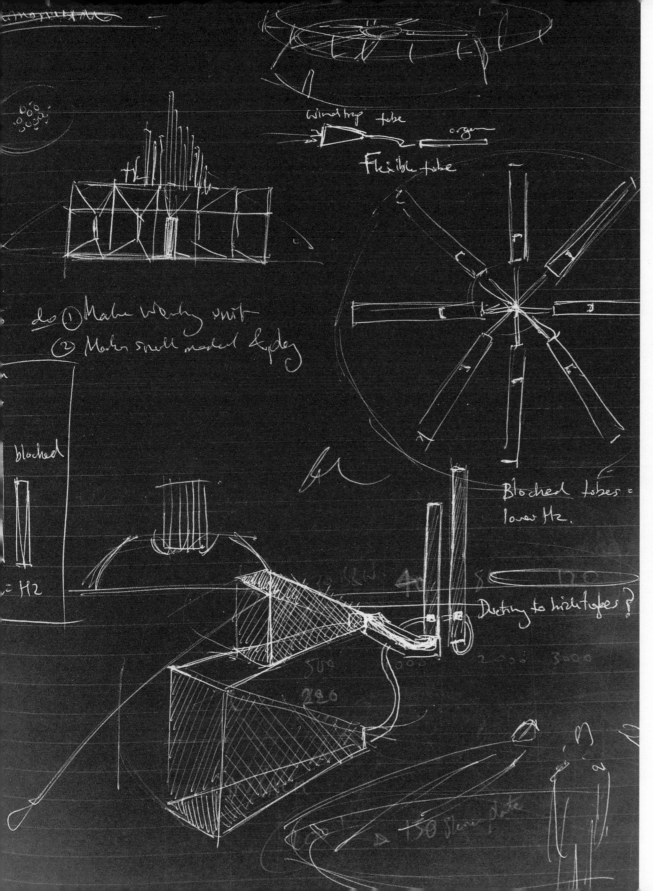

LUKE JERRAM

Luke Jerram (born in Bristol, United Kingdom, 1974) graduated with a First Class degree in architecture in 1997
and is currently a Visiting Senior Research Fellow at CFPR,
University of West of England. His multidisciplinary art
practice involves the creation of sculpture, installations and
live-art projects. Jerram currently lives in the United Kingdom, but has been working internationally since his career
began in 1997. He has created a number of extraordinary
art projects which have excited and inspired people around
the globe. Working with the ISVR (Institute of Sound and
Vibration Research), University of Southampton the team
were awarded a major grant from EPSRC and a further
grant from the Arts Council England to design, build and
tour his artwork Aeolus. The giant ten-ton artwork is an
aeolian wind harp and optical pavilion and has just finished
its tour of the United Kingdom.

Aeolus
Biro on white lined paper, image inverted
using Photoshop
20 x 30 cm
2009
Luke Jerram

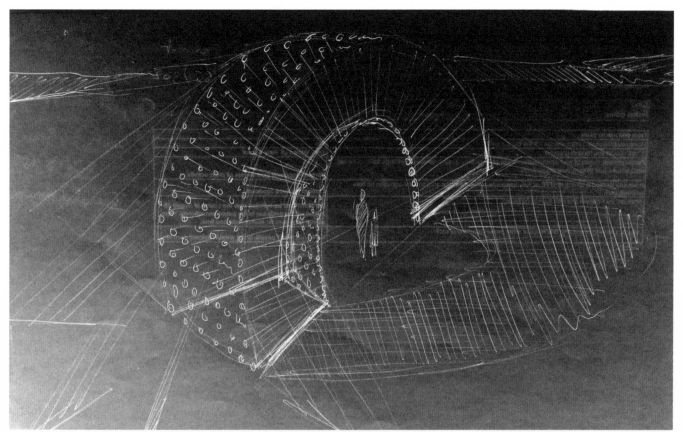

Aeolus
Biro on white lined paper, image inverted
using Photoshop
20 x 30 cm
2009
Luke Jerram

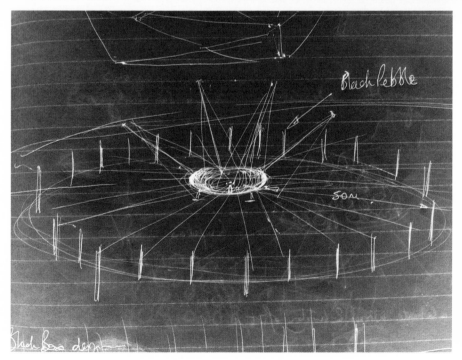

Black Pebble

Som.

Black Box de...

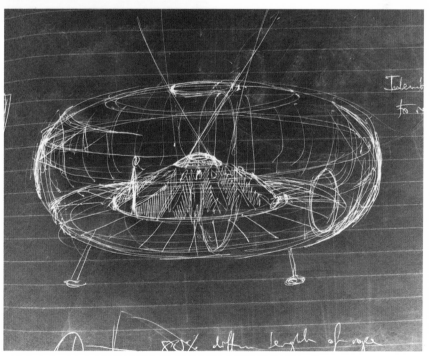

Internal
to ...

...different length of rope

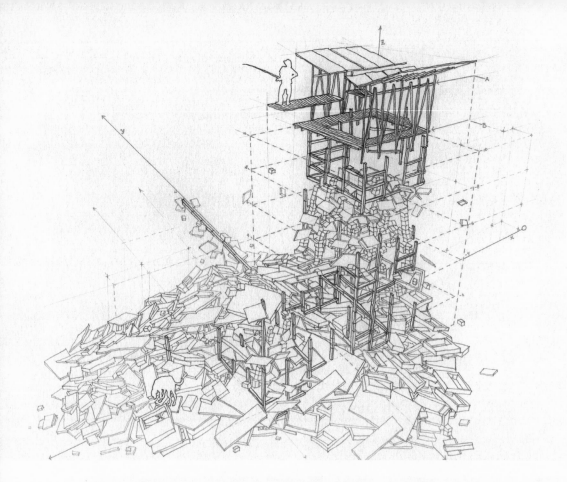

OLALEKAN JEYIFOUS

Olalekan Jeyifous (born in Nigeria, 1977) is a Brooklyn-based artist and designer. He received his bachelor's degree in Architecture from Cornell University in May 2000, where his studies focused on investigating the relevant potential for a variety of computer software within the fields of art, design and architecture. After graduating he enjoyed a four year tenure as a senior designer at the inimitable dbox before continuing on to pursue his creative compulsions full-time. Since then Jeyifous has been fortunate enough to exhibit his artwork in venues throughout the world as well as create beautiful visuals for a variety of clients.

Political Impermanence
Pencil
22.86 x 30.48 cm
2013
Olalekan Jeyifous

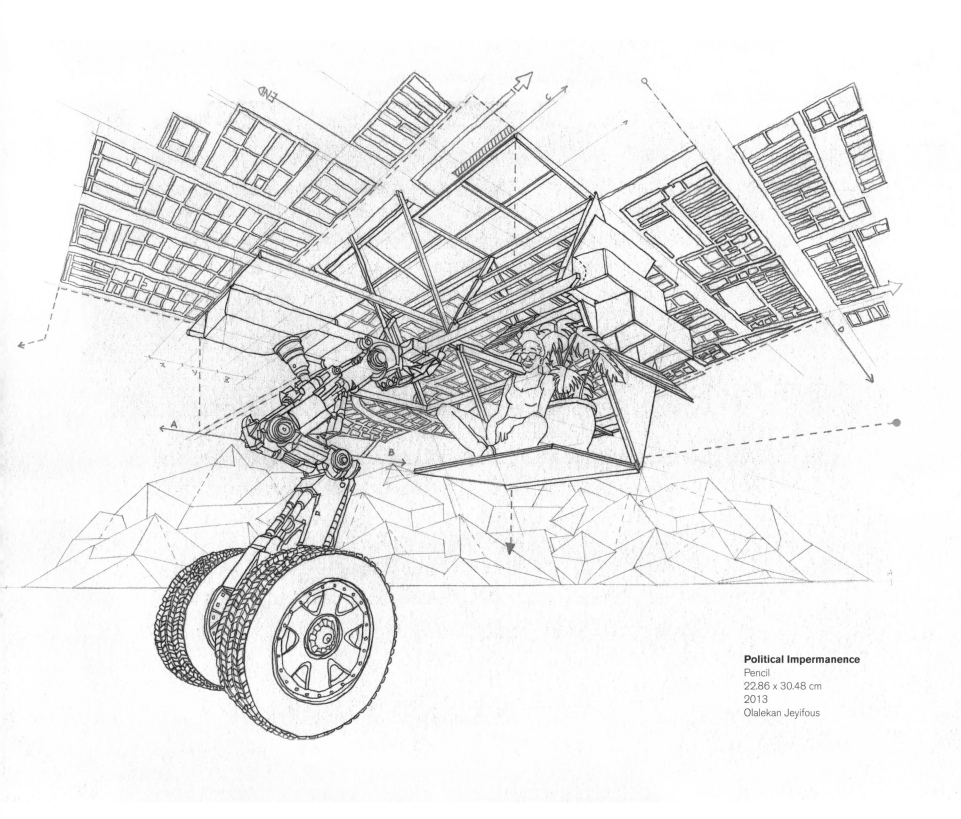

Political Impermanence
Pencil
22.86 x 30.48 cm
2013
Olalekan Jeyifous

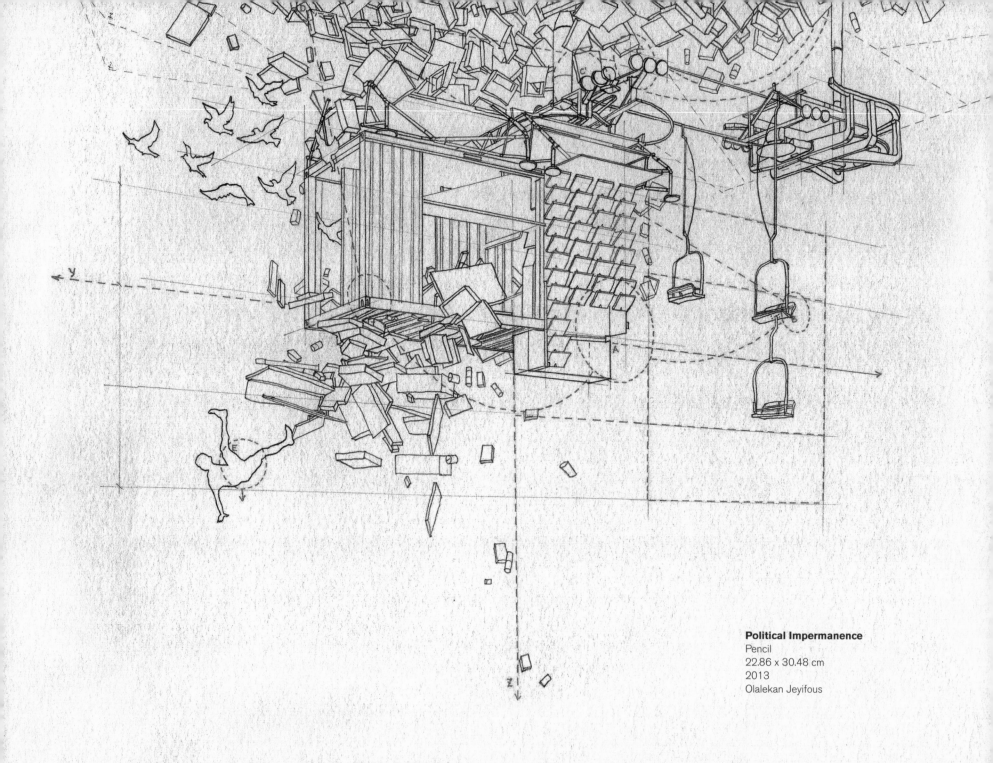

Political Impermanence
Pencil
22.86 x 30.48 cm
2013
Olalekan Jeyifous

Political Impermanence
Pencil
22.86 x 30.48 cm
2013
Olalekan Jeyifous

CH'NG KIAH KIEAN

Ch'ng Kiah Kiean (born in George Town, Malaysia, 1974) studied architecture at the Universiti Sains Malaysia and loves art, design and photography. He is a blog correspondent for Urban Sketchers and also one of the founding members of Urban Sketchers Penang. He published Sketchers of Pulo Pinang in 2009 and Line-line Journey in 2011.

Interior Air Well of Ching Lotus
Humanist Space
George Town, Malaysia
38 x 28 cm
2002
Ch'ng Kiah Kiean

Wesley Methodist Church
Georgetown, Pulau Pinang, Malaysia
Chinese ink on paper
28 x 76 cm
2013
Ch'ng Kiah Kiean

Exterior of Ching Lotus Humanist Space
George Town, Malaysia
Chinese ink on paper
28 x 76 cm
2011
Ch'ng Kiah Kiean

191

Prangin Lane
George Town, Malaysia
Chinese ink and watercolor on paper
28 x 76 cm
2012
Ch'ng Kiah Kiean

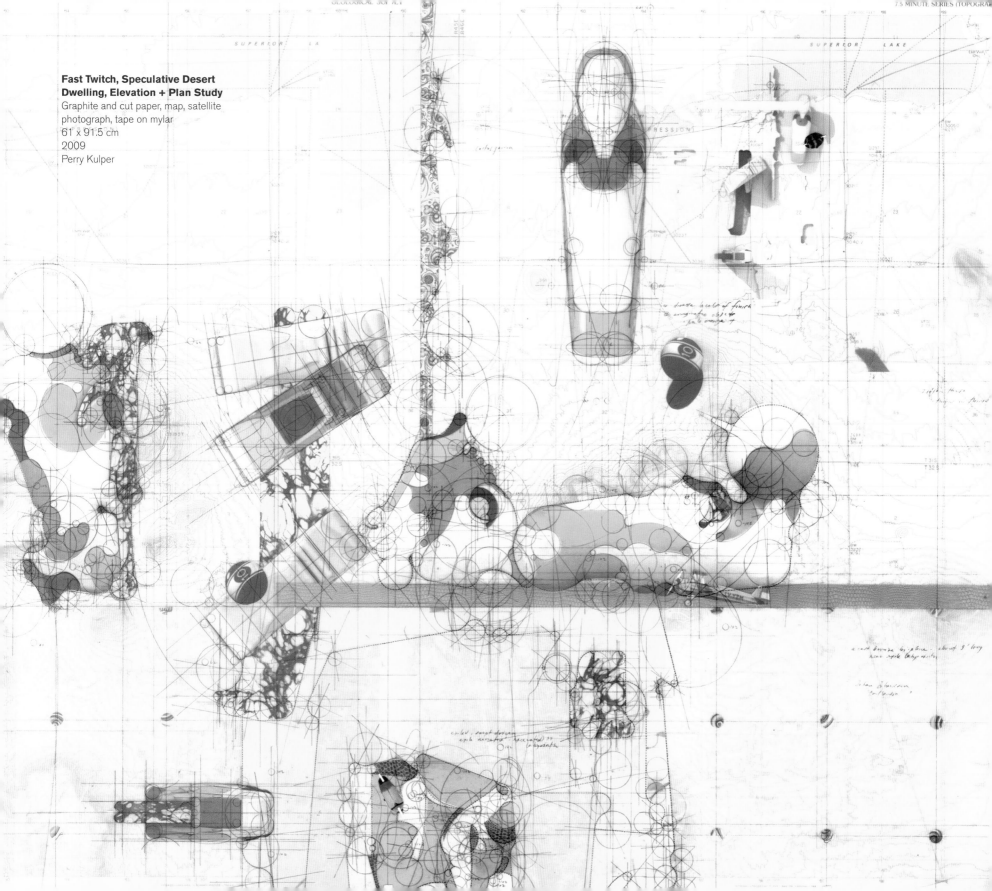

**Fast Twitch, Speculative Desert
Dwelling, Elevation + Plan Study**
Graphite and cut paper, map, satellite
photograph, tape on mylar
61 x 91.5 cm
2009
Perry Kulper

Perspective Central California History Museum
Digital print
22.5 x 25.5 cm
2009
Perry Kulper

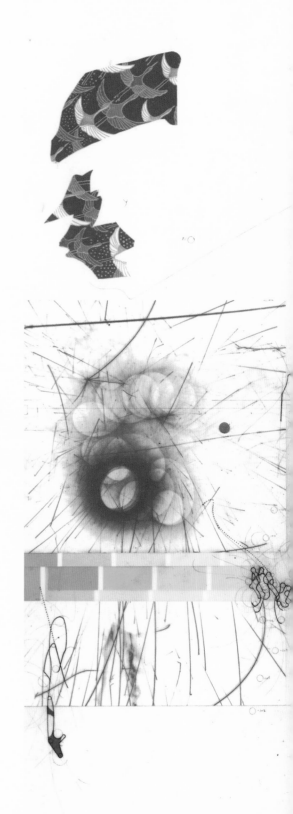

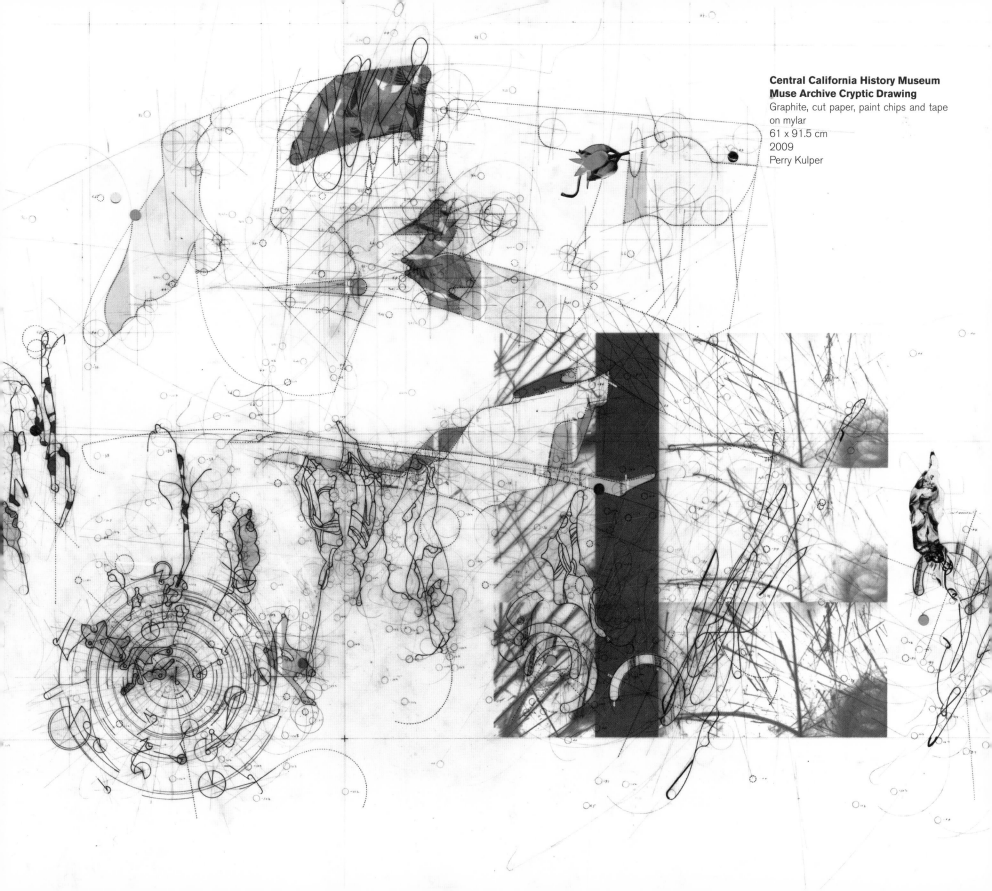

Central California History Museum
Muse Archive Cryptic Drawing
Graphite, cut paper, paint chips and tape
on mylar
61 x 91.5 cm
2009
Perry Kulper

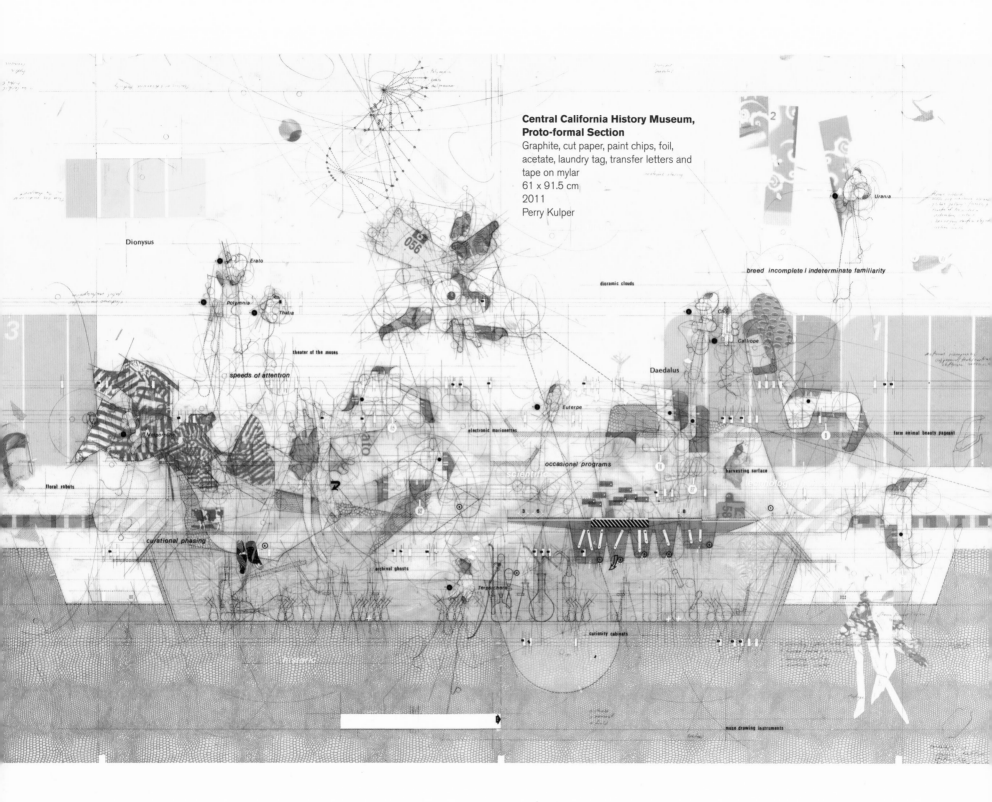

Central California History Museum, Proto-formal Section
Graphite, cut paper, paint chips, foil, acetate, laundry tag, transfer letters and tape on mylar
61 x 91.5 cm
2011
Perry Kulper

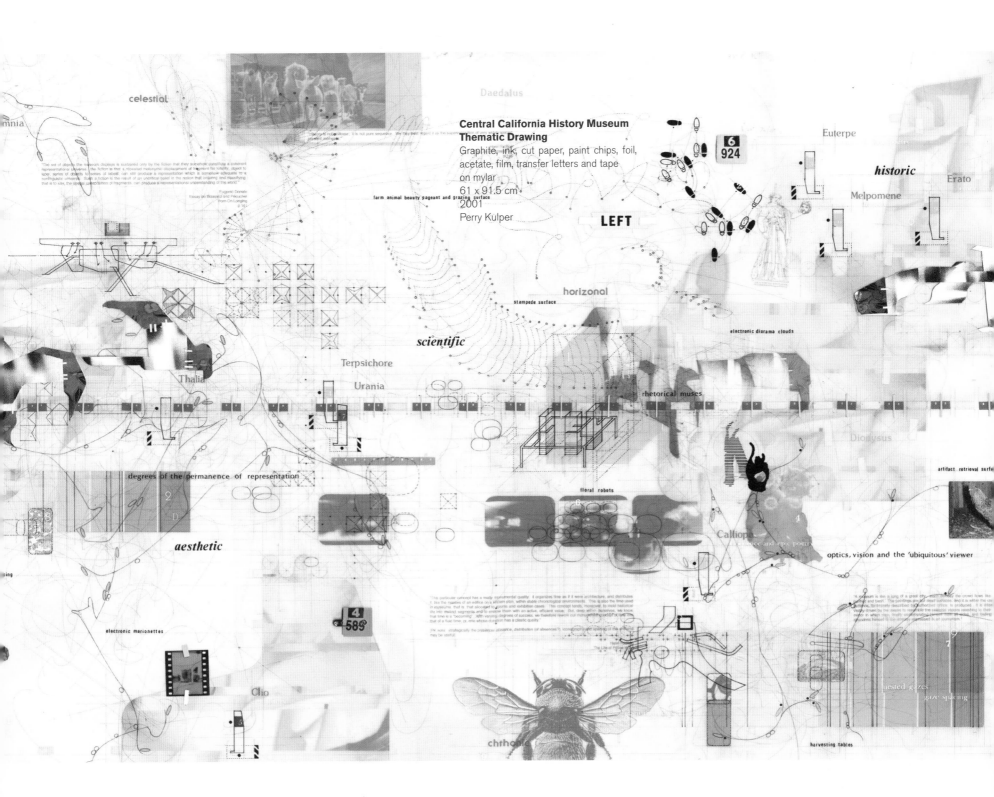

**Central California History Museum
Thematic Drawing**
Graphite, ink, cut paper, paint chips, foil,
acetate, film, transfer letters and tape
on mylar
61 x 91.5 cm
2001
Perry Kulper

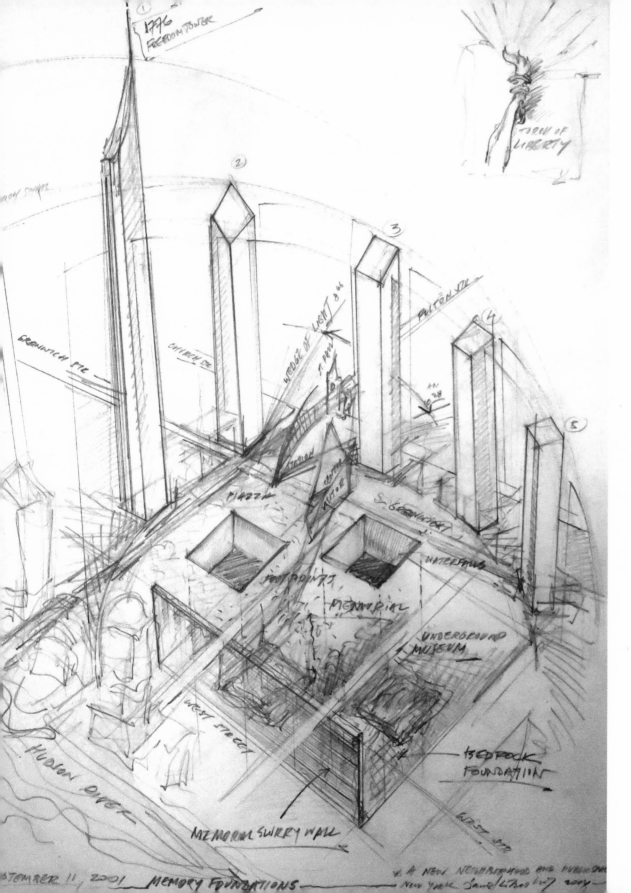

DANIEL LIBESKIND

Daniel Libeskind (born in Lodz, Poland, 1946) is an international architect and designer. His practice extends worldwide from museums and concert halls to convention centers, universities, hotels, and residential projects. Libeskind was a virtuoso musician at a young age before giving up music to become an architect. He has received numerous awards and designed world-renowned projects including: the Jewish Museum in Berlin, the Denver Art Museum, the Royal Ontario Museum in Toronto, the Military History Museum in Dresden, and the master plan for Ground Zero. His work reflects his profound interest and involvement in philosophy, art, literature and music. Fundamental to Libeskind's philosophy is the notion that buildings are crafted with the perceptible human energy, and that they address the greater cultural context in which they are built. Libeskind teaches and lectures at universities across the world.

World Trade Center Master Plan
New York City, NY, USA
Pencil on parchment
57.2 x 76.2 cm
2003
Daniel Libeskind/Studio Daniel Libeskind

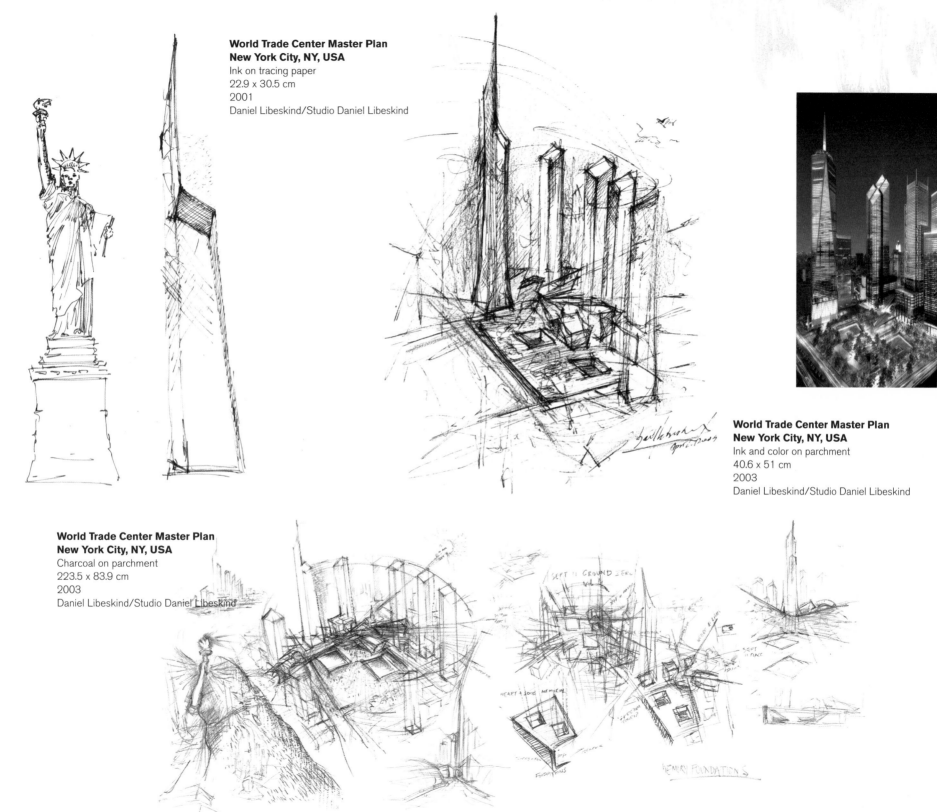

**World Trade Center Master Plan
New York City, NY, USA**
Ink on tracing paper
22.9 x 30.5 cm
2001
Daniel Libeskind/Studio Daniel Libeskind

**World Trade Center Master Plan
New York City, NY, USA**
Ink and color on parchment
40.6 x 51 cm
2003
Daniel Libeskind/Studio Daniel Libeskind

**World Trade Center Master Plan
New York City, NY, USA**
Charcoal on parchment
223.5 x 83.9 cm
2003
Daniel Libeskind/Studio Daniel Libeskind

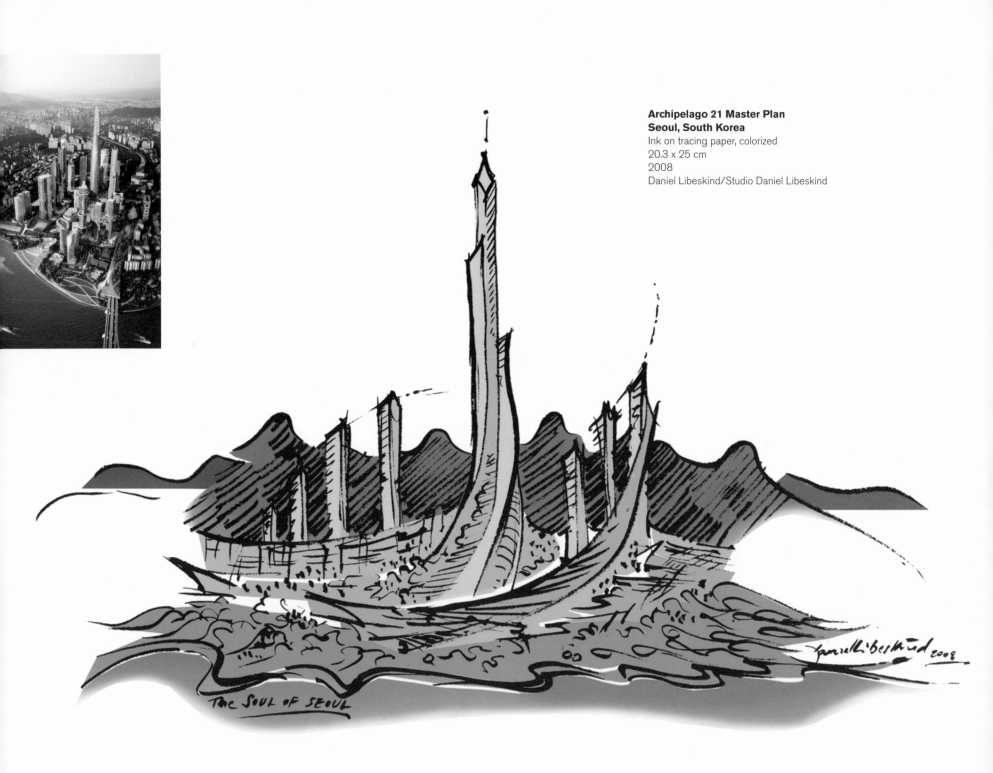

Archipelago 21 Master Plan
Seoul, South Korea
Ink on tracing paper, colorized
20.3 x 25 cm
2008
Daniel Libeskind/Studio Daniel Libeskind

THE SOUL OF SEOUL

214

**Archipelago 21 Master Plan
Seoul, South Korea**
Ink on tracing paper, inverted
20.3 x 25.4 cm
2008
Daniel Libeskind/Studio Daniel Libeskind

HOMOGENEOUS URBAN STRUCTURE (IDEAL/ABSTRACT)

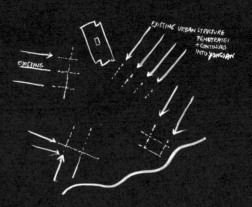

EXISTING URBAN STRUCTURE PENETRATES + CONTINUES INTO YONGSAN

EXISTING

BUSINESS DOWNTOWN
LUXURY RESIDENTIAL
STATION
FASHION DISTRICT
TRENDY LIFESTYLE
PARK
ARCHIPELAGO 21 SEOUL KOREA

URBAN STRUCTURE DEFINED BY URBAN FLOW OF ACTIVITY OF ARCHIPELAGOES

RIVER OF RETAIL CENTERING OPEN PUBLIC SPACE FLOWING INTO THE —HAN

**Archipelago 21 Master Plan
Seoul, South Korea**
Ink on tracing paper, inverted
40.6 x 50.8 cm
2008
Daniel Libeskind/Studio Daniel Libeskind

GATHERING SCALES

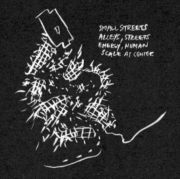

SMALL STREETS ALLEYS, STREETS ENERGY, HUMAN SCALE AT CENTER

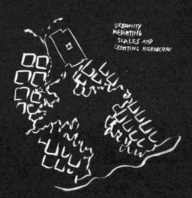

URBANITY MEDIATING SCALES AND CREATING HIERARCHIES

ARCHIPELAGO 21 SEOUL

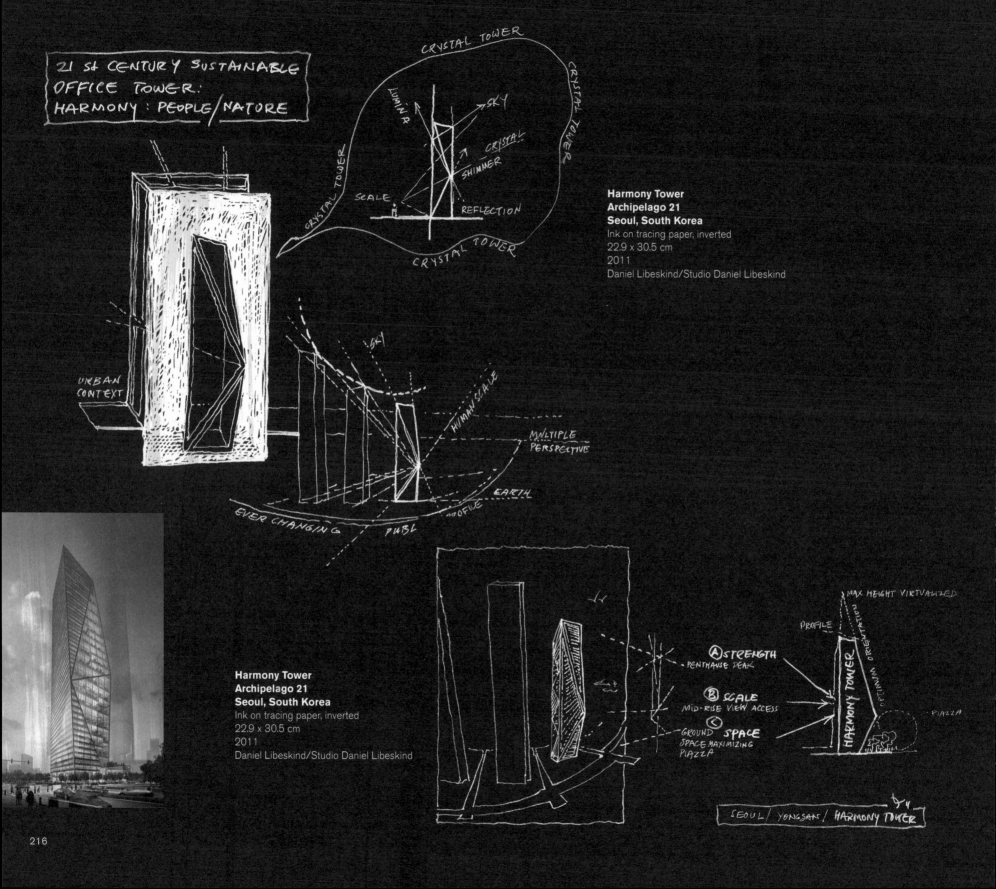

21 st CENTURY SUSTAINABLE
OFFICE TOWER:
HARMONY : PEOPLE/NATURE

CRYSTAL TOWER
CRYSTAL TOWER
CRYSTAL TOWER
CRYSTAL TOWER
CRYSTAL TOWER

LUMINA
SKY
CRYSTAL
SHIMMER
SCALE
REFLECTION

Harmony Tower
Archipelago 21
Seoul, South Korea
Ink on tracing paper, inverted
22.9 x 30.5 cm
2011
Daniel Libeskind/Studio Daniel Libeskind

URBAN CONTEXT

SKY
HUMAN SCALE
MULTIPLE PERSPECTIVE
EARTH
PROFILE
EVER CHANGING
PUBL

Harmony Tower
Archipelago 21
Seoul, South Korea
Ink on tracing paper, inverted
22.9 x 30.5 cm
2011
Daniel Libeskind/Studio Daniel Libeskind

MAX HEIGHT VIRTUALIZED
PROFILE
(A) STRENGTH
PENTHOUSE PEAK
(B) SCALE
MID-RISE VIEW ACCESS
(C) GROUND SPACE
SPACE MAXIMIZING PIAZZA
OPTIMUM ORIENTATION
HARMONY TOWER
PIAZZA

SEOUL / YONGSAN / HARMONY TOWER

216

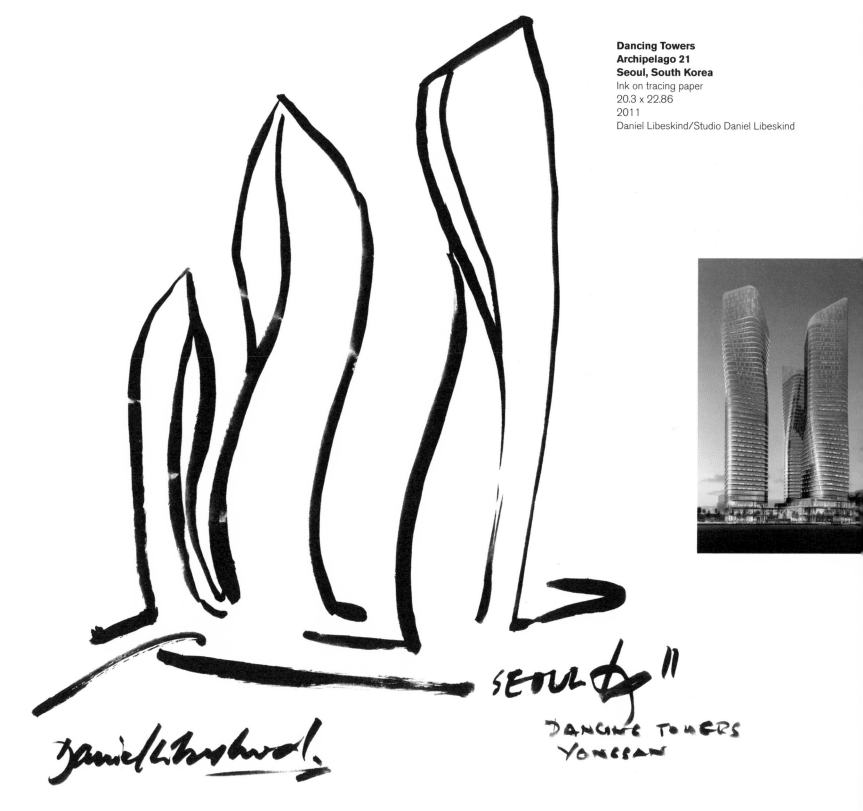

Dancing Towers
Archipelago 21
Seoul, South Korea
Ink on tracing paper
20.3 x 22.86
2011
Daniel Libeskind/Studio Daniel Libeskind

SEOUL 11
DANCING TOWERS
YONGSAN

**Jewish Museum
Berlin, Germany**
Charcoal on parchment
50.8 x 76.2 cm
Sketch: 1989
Building: 1999
Daniel Libeskind/Studio Daniel Libeskind

218

Jewish Museum
Berlin, Germany
Color and pencil on parchment
24.1 x 30.5 cm
Sketch: 1989
Building: 1999
Daniel Libeskind/Studio Daniel Libeskind

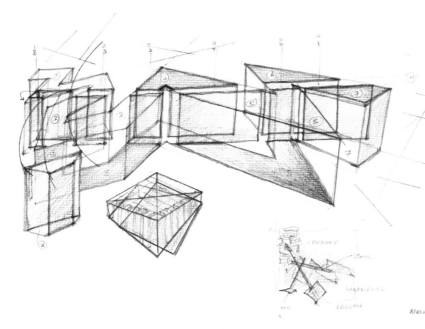

Jewish Museum
Berlin, Germany
Pencil on parchment
24.13 x 30.5 cm
Sketch: 1990
Building: 1999
Daniel Libeskind/Studio Daniel Libeskind

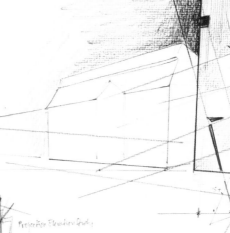

Jewish Museum
Berlin, Germany
Color and pencil on parchment
24.13 x 30.5 cm
Sketch: 1990
Building: 1999
Daniel Libeskind/Studio Daniel Libeskind

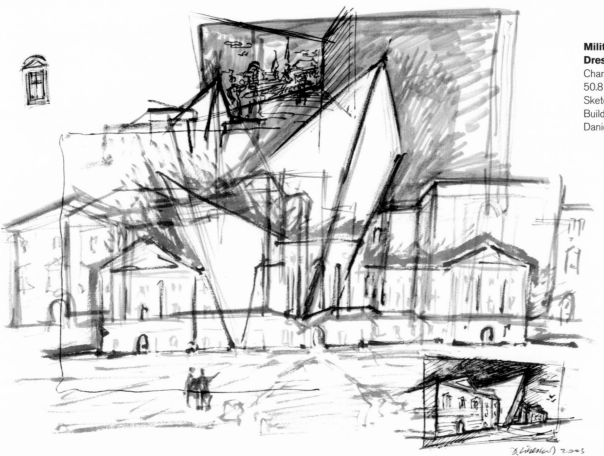

Military History Museum
Dresden, Germany
Charcoal on parchment
50.8 x 76.2 cm
Sketch: 1989
Building: 2011
Daniel Libeskind/Studio Daniel Libeskind

Military History Museum
Dresden, Germany
Charcoal on parchment
50.8 x 76.2 cm
Sketch: 1989
Building: 2011
Daniel Libeskind/Studio Daniel Libeskind

Military History Museum
Dresden, Germany
Charcoal on parchment
50.8 x 76.2 cm
Sketch: 1989
Building: 2011
Daniel Libeskind/Studio Daniel Libeskind

Military History Museum
Dresden, Germany
Ink on parchment
50.8 x 76.2 cm
Sketch: 2009
Building: 2011
Daniel Libeskind/Studio Daniel Libeskind

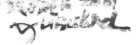

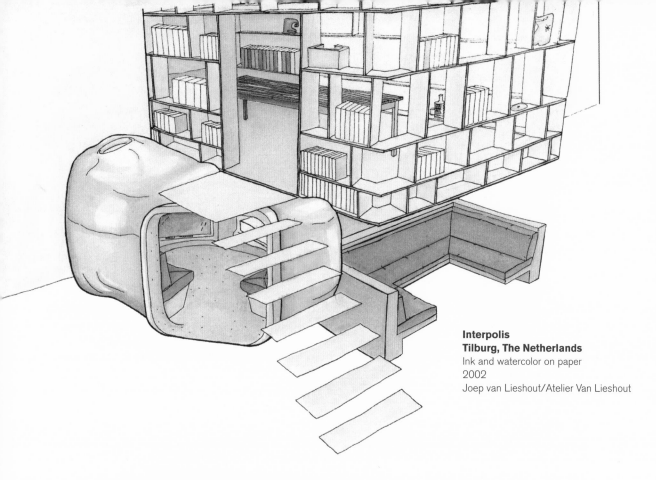

Interpolis
Tilburg, The Netherlands
Ink and watercolor on paper
2002
Joep van Lieshout/Atelier Van Lieshout

ATELIER VAN LIESHOUT

Joep van Lieshout (born in Ravenstein, the Netherlands, 1963) is the founder of the internationally recognized workshop Atelier Van Lieshout (AVL). Initially working as a solo artist, he started out producing objects in bright colored polyester – the material that would become his trademark. In 1995 he founded Atelier Van Lieshout. AVL produces objects that balance on the boundary between art, architecture and design, encompassing sculpture and installations, buildings and furniture, utopias and dystopias. Recurring themes in the work of AVL are power, politics and autarky, as well as a fascination for life and death. Over the past 25 years, AVL has had exhibitions at major art institutions and collections worldwide.

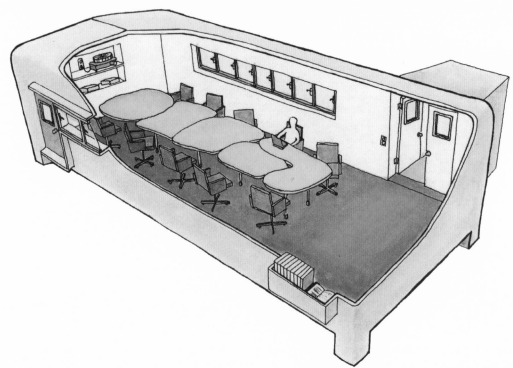

Interpolis
Tilburg, The Netherlands
Ink and watercolor on paper
2002
Joep van Lieshout/Atelier Van Lieshout

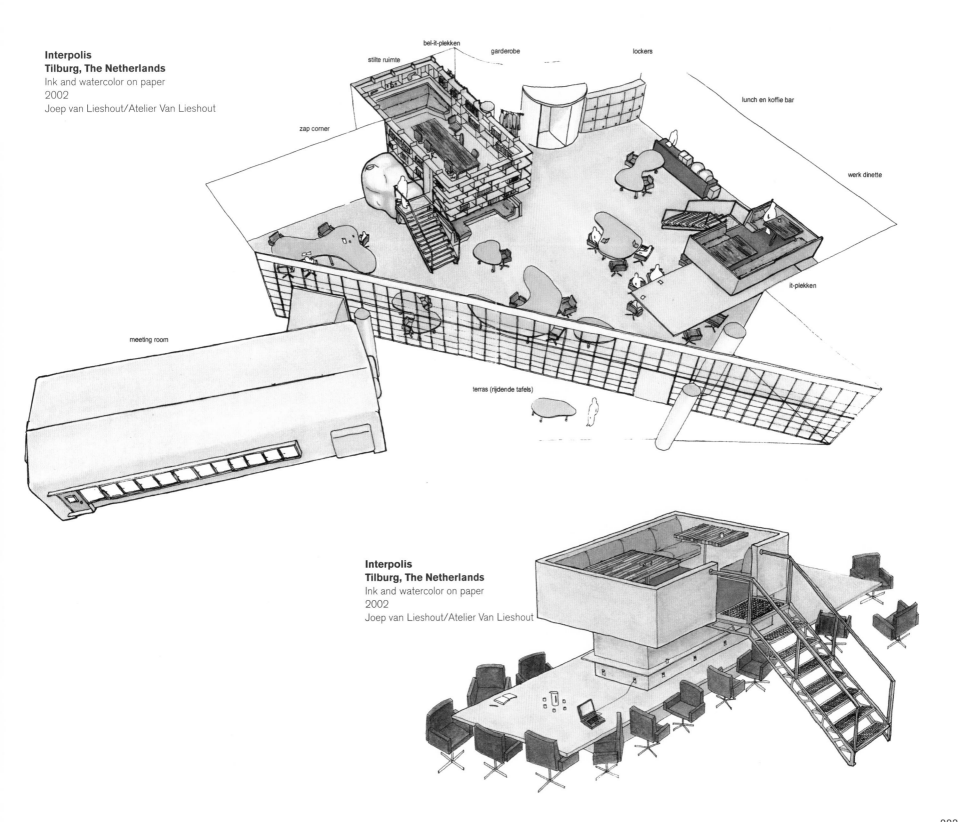

Interpolis
Tilburg, The Netherlands
Ink and watercolor on paper
2002
Joep van Lieshout/Atelier Van Lieshout

bel-it-plekken

stilte ruimte

garderobe

lockers

lunch en koffie bar

zap corner

werk dinette

it-plekken

meeting room

terras (rijdende tafels)

Interpolis
Tilburg, The Netherlands
Ink and watercolor on paper
2002
Joep van Lieshout/Atelier Van Lieshout

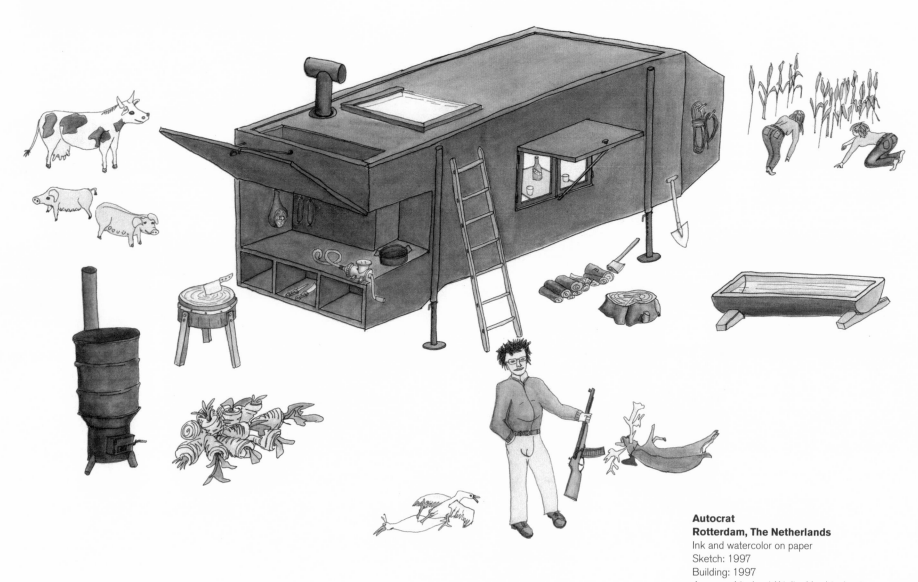

Autocrat
Rotterdam, The Netherlands
Ink and watercolor on paper
Sketch: 1997
Building: 1997
Joep van Lieshout/Atelier Van Lieshout

224

Junior Slave Manager House
Hook of Holland, The Netherlands
Ink and watercolor on paper
2008
Joep van Lieshout/Atelier Van Lieshout

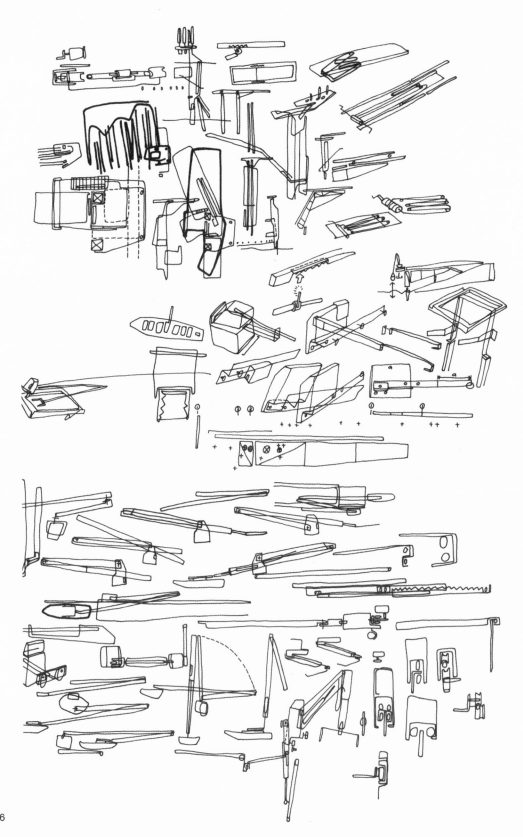

CJ LIM

CJ Lim (born in Perak, Malaysia, 1964) is the founding director of Studio 8 Architects, an international award-winning practice specializing in architecture, landscape and urban planning. He is also the Professor of Architecture and Urbanism at the Bartlett UCL. He was awarded the Grand Architecture Prize by the Royal Academy of Arts London in 2006. His drawings and models are part of the permanent architectural collection of the Victoria + Albert Museum London, and Fonds Regional d'Art Contemporain du Centre [FRAC] France. His celebrated 'Virtually Venice', architecture as 'built cultural assemblage' for the Venice Architecture Biennale, is an investigation of East-West cultures and identities.

Dusable Park
Chicago, IL, USA
Pen on detail paper
29.7 x 21 cm
2008
CJ Lim

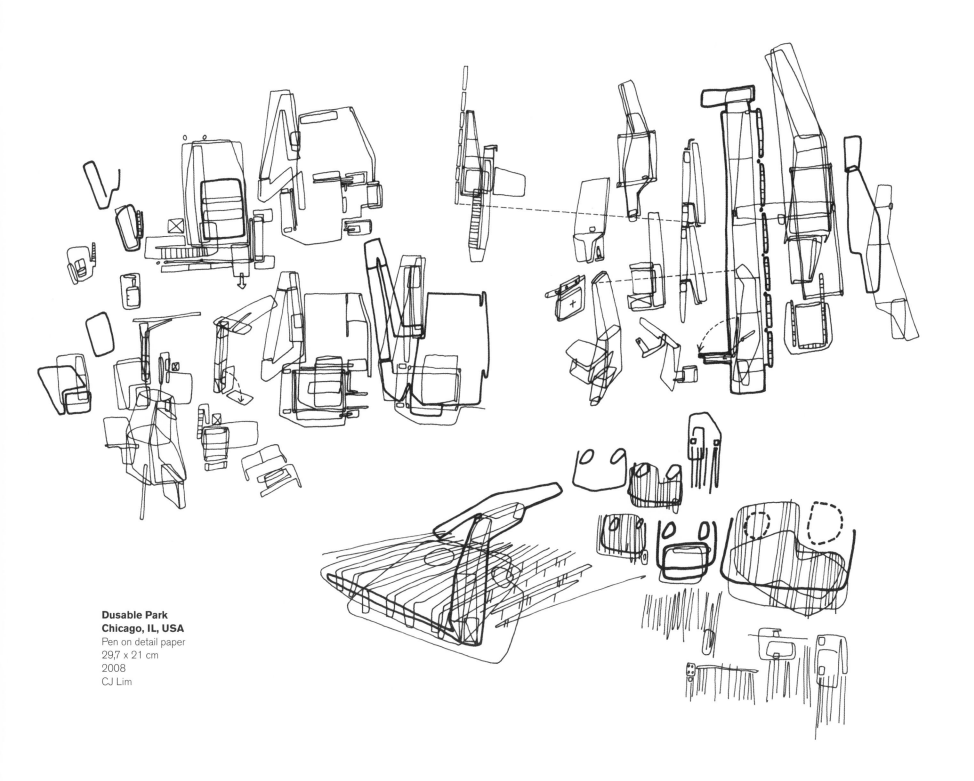

Dusable Park
Chicago, IL, USA
Pen on detail paper
29,7 x 21 cm
2008
CJ Lim

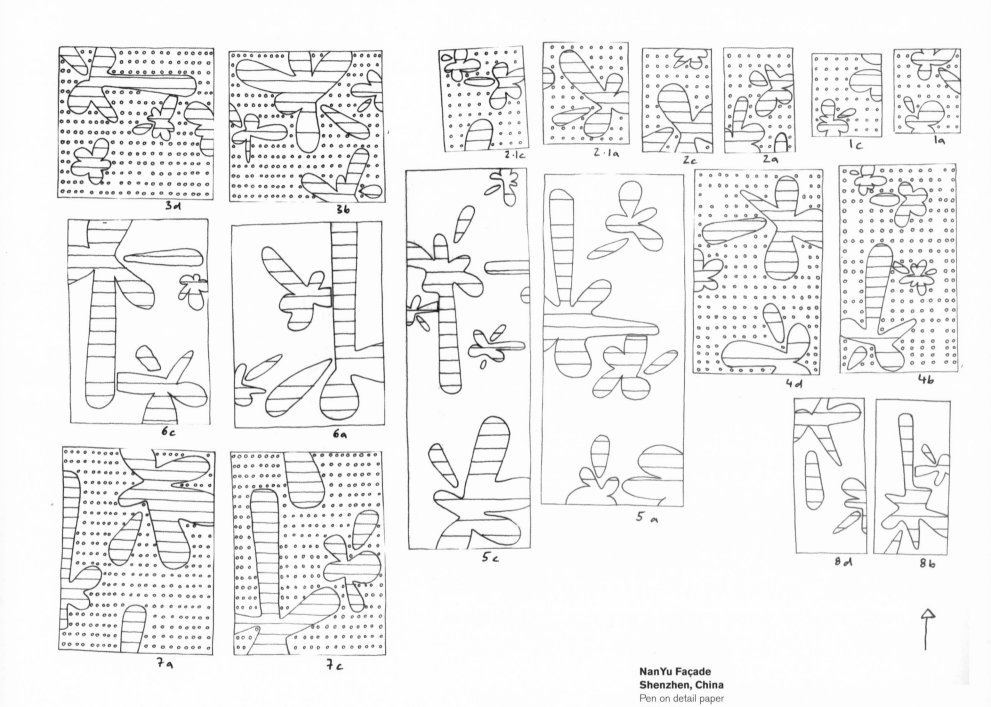

NanYu Façade
Shenzhen, China
Pen on detail paper
29.7 x 21 cm
2008
CJ Lim

Seasons Through the Looking Glass
V&A Museum
London, United Kingdom
Pen on detail paper
29.7 x 21 cm
2008
CJ Lim

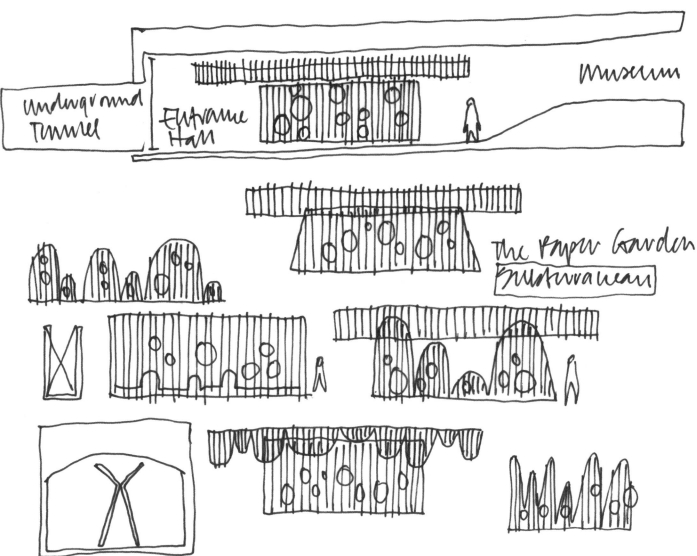

Bloom House
Southern California, USA
Pen
28 x 36 cm
Sketch: 2004
Building: 2010
Greg Lynn

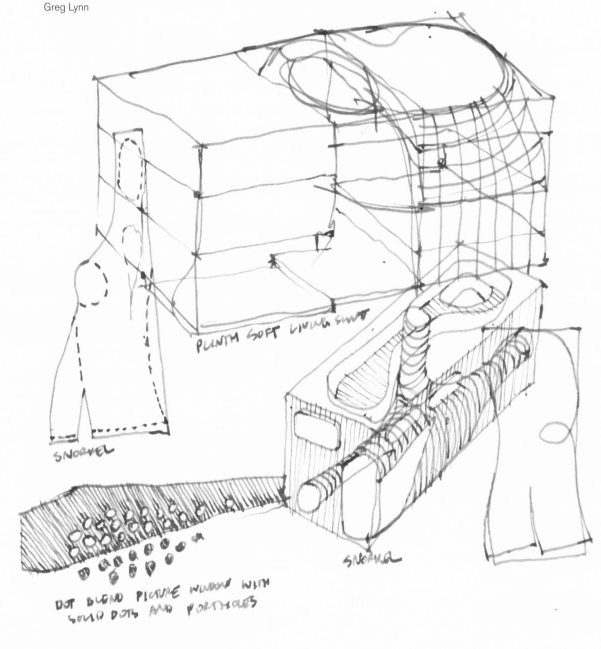

SNORKEL

PLINTH SOFT LIVING SLAB

SNORKEL

DOT BLEND PICTURE WINDOW WITH
SOLID DOTS AND PORTHOLES

GREG LYNN

Greg Lynn (born in North Olmsted, Ohio, USA, 1964) graduated from Miami University of Ohio with Bachelor of Environmental Design and Bachelor of Philosophy degrees and from Princeton University with a Master of Architecture degree. He won a Golden Lion at the Venice Biennale of Architecture, received the American Academy of Arts & Letters Architecture Award and was awarded a fellowship from United States Artists. Time Magazine named him one of 100 of the most innovative people in the world for the 21st century and Forbes Magazine named him one of the ten most influential living architects.

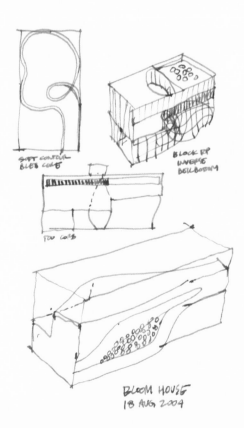

SOFT CONTOUR
BLEB CORE

BLOCK RP
WVERSE
BELLBOTTOM

POD CORE

BLOOM HOUSE
18 AUG 2004

230

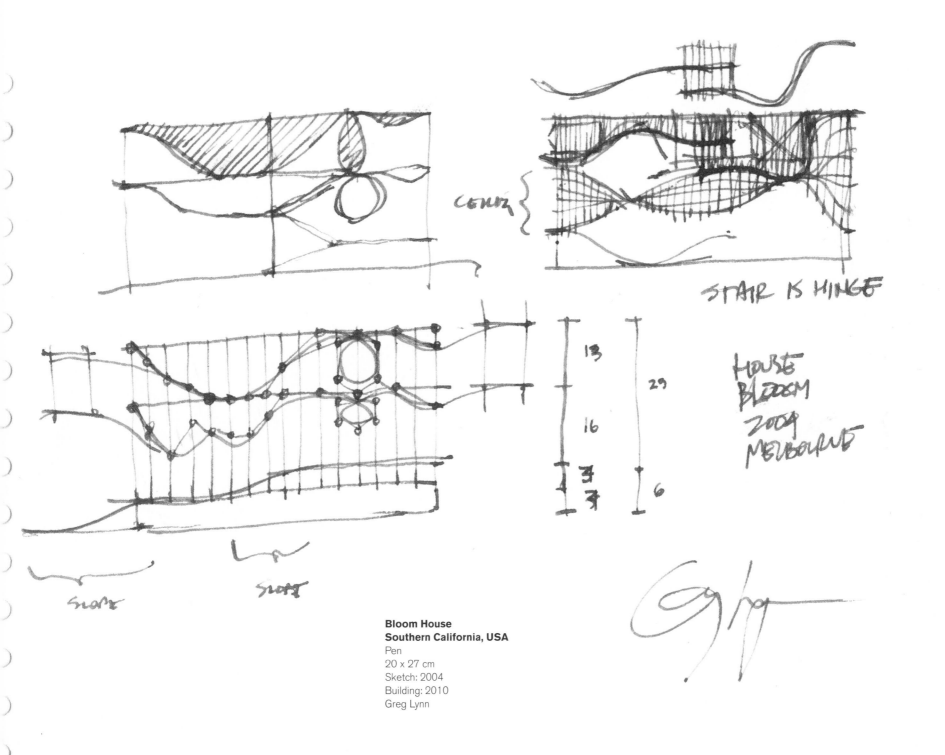

CENTER {

STAIR IS HINGE

13

29

16

7
7

6

SLOPE

SLOPE

HOUSE
BLOOM
2004
MELBOURNE

Bloom House
Southern California, USA
Pen
20 x 27 cm
Sketch: 2004
Building: 2010
Greg Lynn

231

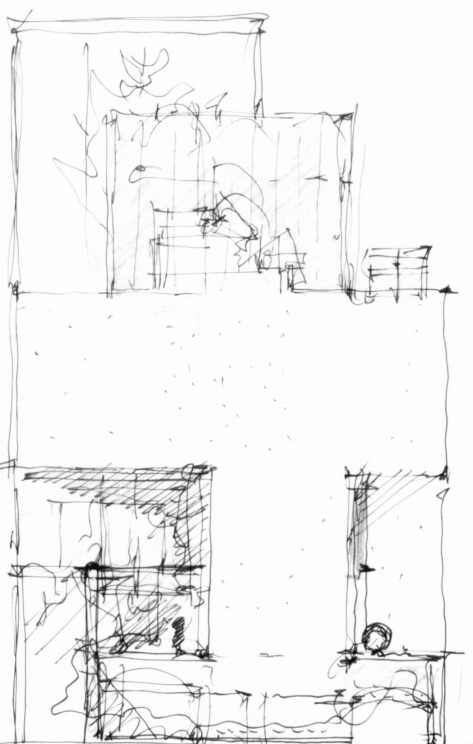

FUMIHIKO MAKI

Fumihiko Maki (born in Japan, 1928) studied and taught at the University of Tokyo and Graduate School of Design, Harvard University. Since establishing Maki and Associates in 1965, Maki has played an active role in many international projects. Completed projects include the Yerba Buena Center for the Arts, 1993, University of Pennsylvania Annenberg Public Policy Center, 2009, Massachusetts Institute of Technology Media Arts and Sciences Building, 2009. He is currently working on the World Trade Center Tower 4, scheduled to be completed in 2013. Maki has been widely published and recognized with many domestic and international awards, including the Wolf Prize, 1988, Union of International Architects Gold Medal, 1993, Praemium Imperiale, 1999 and the Pritzker Prize, 1993. Maki was the recipient of the 2011 American Institute of Architects Gold Medal.

Spiral
Tokyo, Japan
Ink and color on parchment
Sketch:1985
Building: 1985
Fumihiko Maki/Maki and Associates

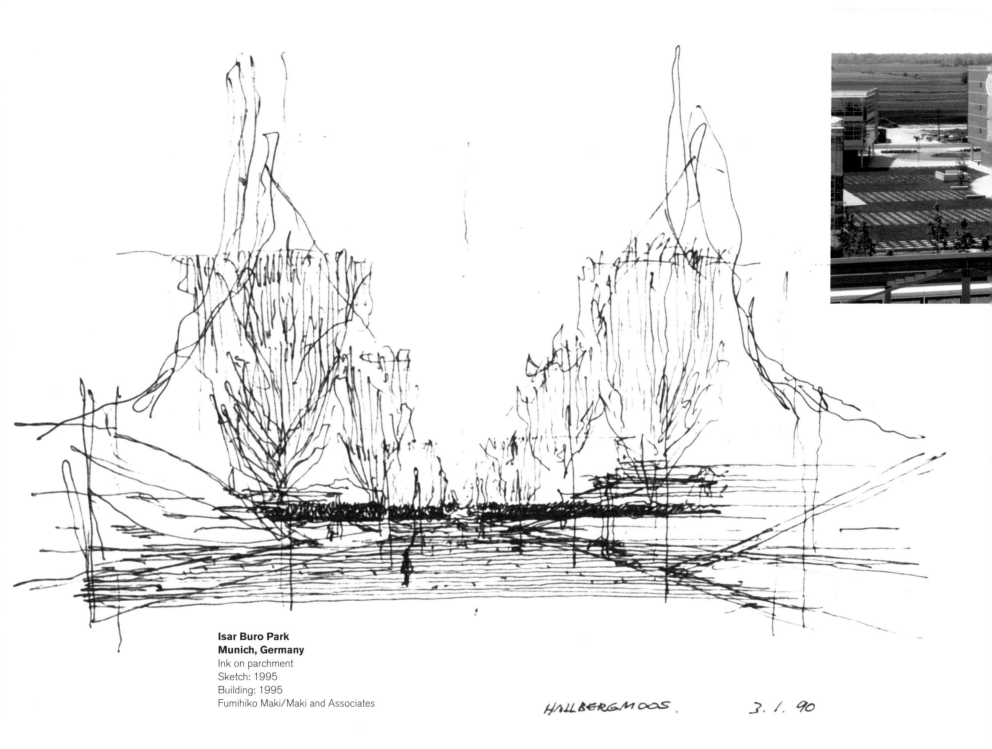

Isar Buro Park
Munich, Germany
Ink on parchment
Sketch: 1995
Building: 1995
Fumihiko Maki/Maki and Associates

HALLBERGMOOS.   3. 1. 90

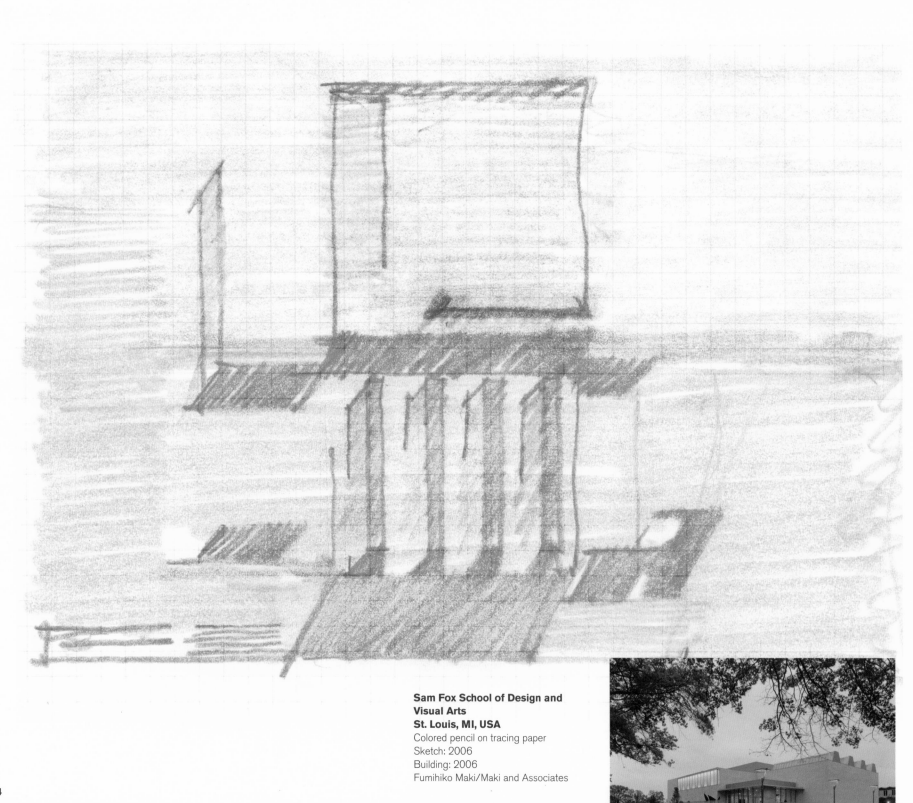

Sam Fox School of Design and Visual Arts
St. Louis, MI, USA
Colored pencil on tracing paper
Sketch: 2006
Building: 2006
Fumihiko Maki/Maki and Associates

234

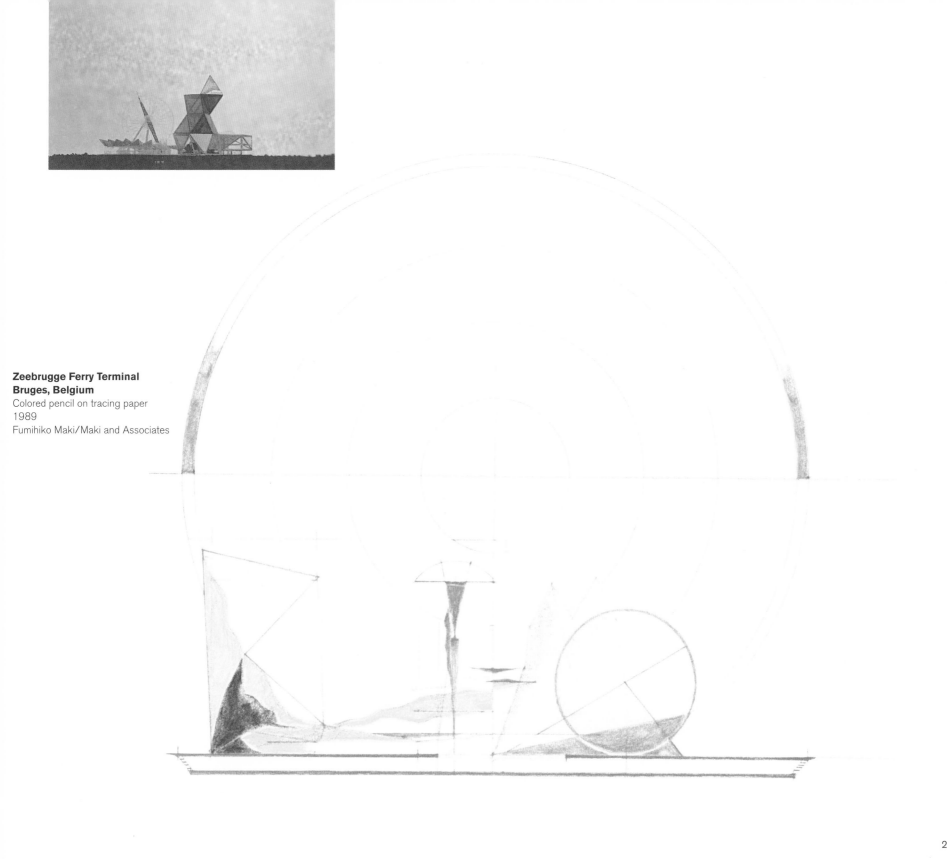

**Zeebrugge Ferry Terminal
Bruges, Belgium**
Colored pencil on tracing paper
1989
Fumihiko Maki/Maki and Associates

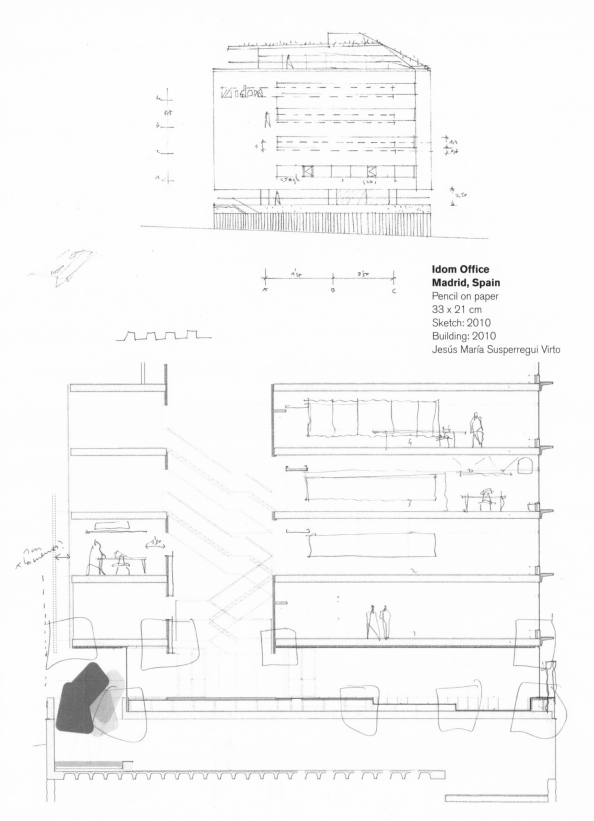

Idom Office
Madrid, Spain
Pencil on paper
33 x 21 cm
Sketch: 2010
Building: 2010
Jesús María Susperregui Virto

JORGE MARTÍNEZ BERMEJO, JESÚS MARÍA SUSPERREGUI VIRTO, ANTONIO VILLANUEVA PEÑALVER

Jorge Martínez Bermejo (born in Madrid, Spain, 1976), is project manager at ACXT. His recent works include the new Idom headquarters in Madrid, the Technology Center Knorr-Bremsey and a residential building in Verger (Alicante) for Llanera real estate. Jesús María Susperregui Virto (born in Hondarribia, Spain, 1961) is both a partner and member of Idom's Board of Directors, as well as director of the department of architecture and construction. The Higher Council of architects of Spain awarded him a special mention at "Modes of Professional Exercise" in 2009. He has worked as a professor and speaker at numerous universities, as well as national and international institutions. Antonio Villanueva Peñalver (born in Madrid, Spain, 1965), is an Industrial Engineer and has a Masters in bioclimatic architecture and environment. He has worked as a project manager at group Idom since 1997 as a team coordinator of industrial engineers in electrical and mechanical installations in the area of architecture and coordinator of the Group of specialty of air conditioning.

Idom Office
Madrid, Spain
Pen on paper with ink jet print
40 x 29.7 cm
Sketch: 2009
Building: 2010
Jesús María Susperregui Virto

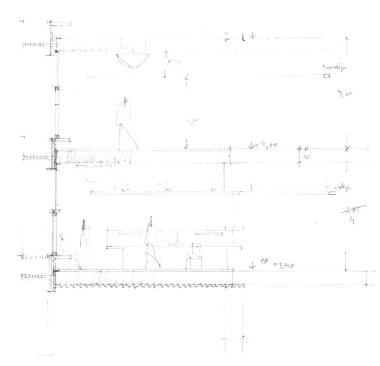

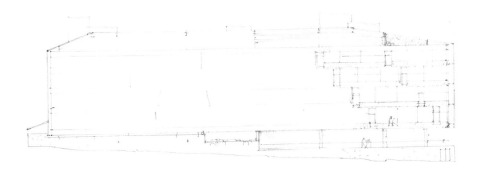

Idom Office
Madrid, Spain
Pen and pencil on tracing paper
41 x 23 cm
Sketch: 2010
Building: 2010
Jesús María Susperregui Virto

Idom Office
Madrid, Spain
Pen and pencil on tracing paper
34 x 24 cm
Sketch: 2010
Building: 2010
Jesús María Susperregui Virto

Idom Office
Madrid, Spain
Pen on tracing paper
42 x 26 cm
Sketch: 2010
Building: 2010
Jesús María Susperregui Virto

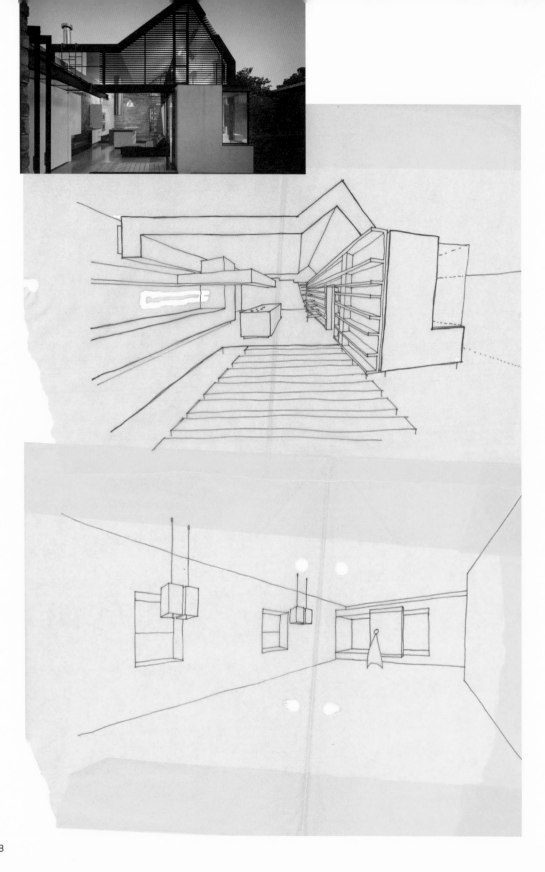

ANDREW MAYNARD

Andrew Maynard graduated from the University of Tasmania, with a bachelors degree in Environmental Design and Architecture with honors. During his time at university, Andrew won the Graphisoft international award, allowing him travel extensively while working in the offices of Allom Lovell, Six Degrees and Richard Rogers. Andrew Maynard Architects was established in 2002, and seeks to operate by balancing between built work and broad polemical design studies. Maynard's work is characterized by energetic, original and playful projects. He continues to be recognized for questioning current practices while proposing a more thoughtful and sustainable future. In 2012 Hill House was winner of the Victorian Architecture and overall vision awards.

Vader House
Melbourne, Australia
Pen on tracing paper
21 x 29.7 cm
Sketch: 2007
Building: 2008
Andrew Maynard

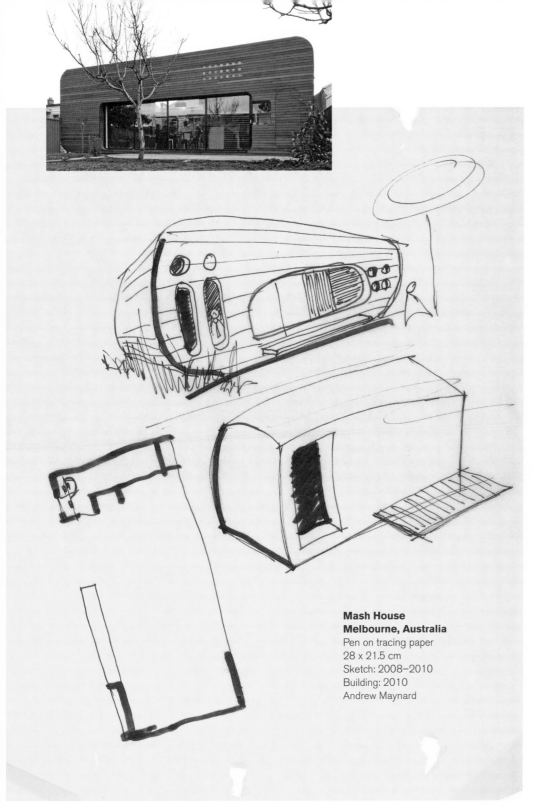

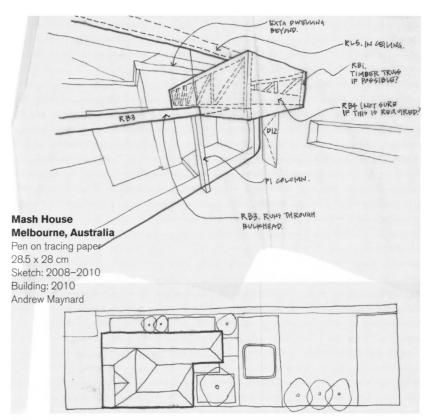

Mash House
Melbourne, Australia
Pen on tracing paper
28.5 x 28 cm
Sketch: 2008–2010
Building: 2010
Andrew Maynard

Mash House
Melbourne, Australia
Pen on tracing paper
28 x 21.5 cm
Sketch: 2008–2010
Building: 2010
Andrew Maynard

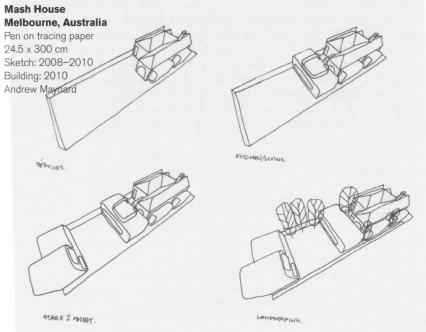

Mash House
Melbourne, Australia
Pen on tracing paper
24.5 x 300 cm
Sketch: 2008–2010
Building: 2010
Andrew Maynard

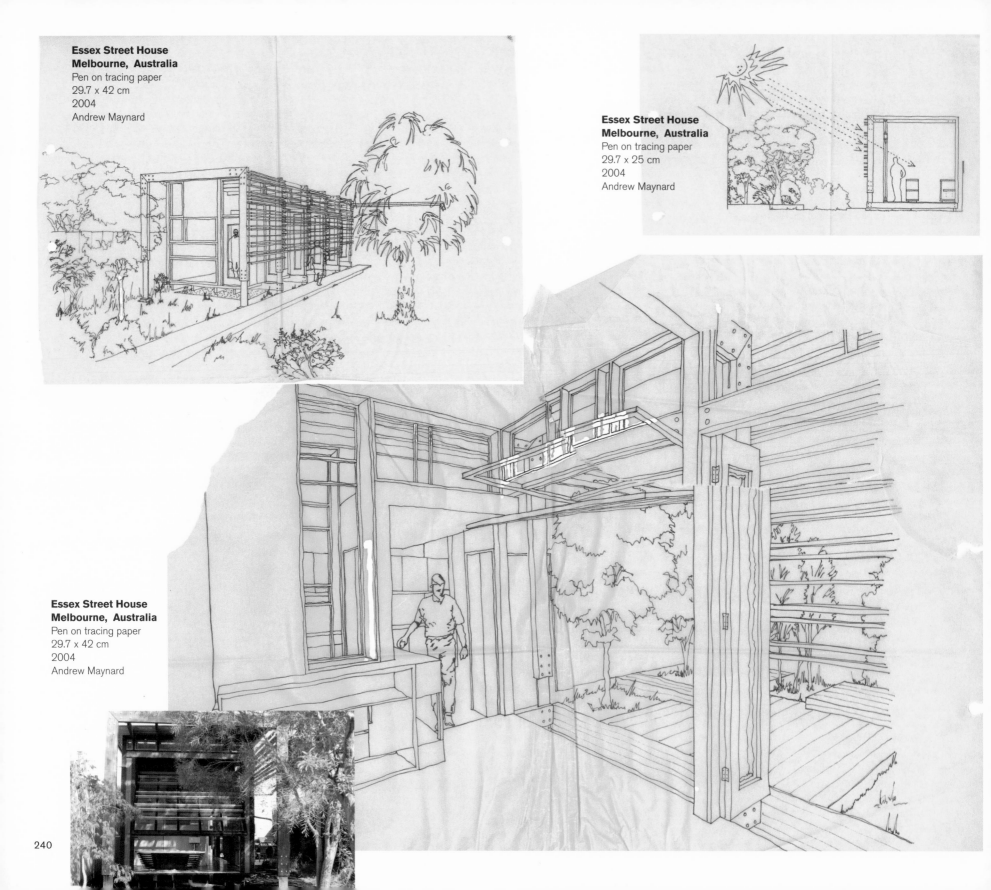

Essex Street House
Melbourne, Australia
Pen on tracing paper
29.7 x 42 cm
2004
Andrew Maynard

Essex Street House
Melbourne, Australia
Pen on tracing paper
29.7 x 25 cm
2004
Andrew Maynard

Essex Street House
Melbourne, Australia
Pen on tracing paper
29.7 x 42 cm
2004
Andrew Maynard

240

Anglesea House
Anglesea, Australia
Pen on trace paper
9 x 25 cm
2007
Mark Austin

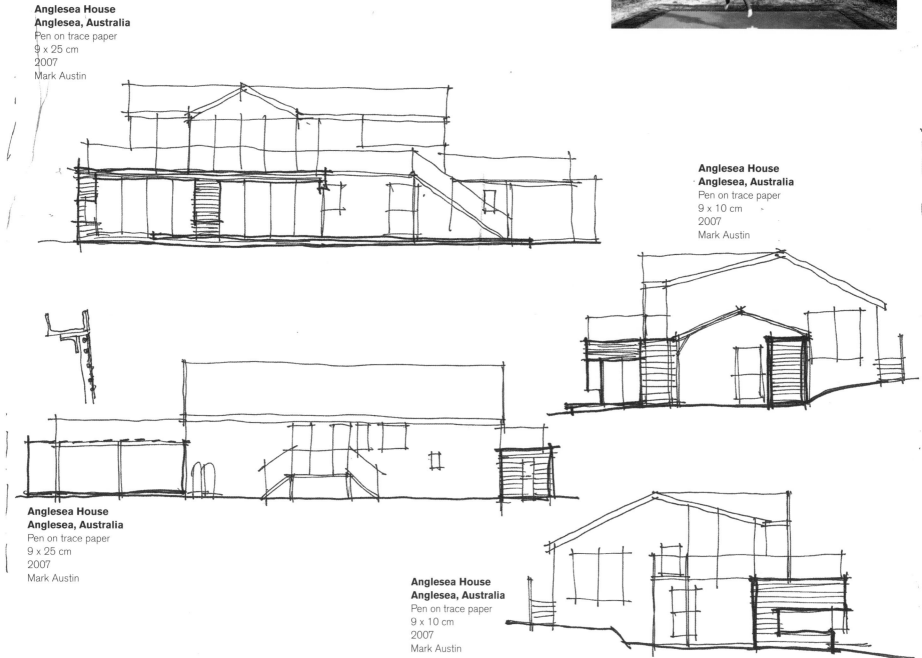

Anglesea House
Anglesea, Australia
Pen on trace paper
9 x 10 cm
2007
Mark Austin

Anglesea House
Anglesea, Australia
Pen on trace paper
9 x 25 cm
2007
Mark Austin

Anglesea House
Anglesea, Australia
Pen on trace paper
9 x 10 cm
2007
Mark Austin

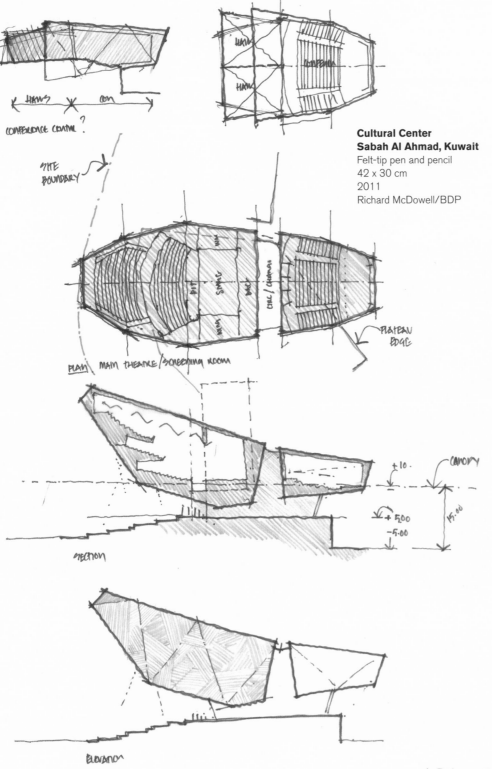

**Cultural Center
Sabah Al Ahmad, Kuwait**
Felt-tip pen and pencil
42 x 30 cm
2011
Richard McDowell/BDP

RICHARD MCDOWELL, GARY WILDE

Richard McDowell (born in London, United Kingdom, 1968) studied architecture at Liverpool John Moore's University, punctuated by a year out in practice and a term at the Technical University of Dresden. On completion of his diploma Richard began his Masters in Site Specific Sculpture at Wimbledon School of Art. During this time he won a number of awards including a Royal Academy award for sculpture. In 1997 he started his architectural career at Pringle Brandon Architects and then FaulknerBrowns where he worked on a wide variety of projects. He began at BDP's Sheffield studio in 2004 and led the design team on the RIBA award winning campus for the University of York. Richard manages a variety of projects including the Sabah Al Ahmad Cultural Center in Kuwait. Gary Wilde (born in Buxton, United Kingdom, 1972) leads the workplace team at BDP's Manchester studio. He has worked as design team leader on 16 built office projects including Birchwood Park, Magnus, Bruntwood, ASK and Town Centre Securities. He has experience in higher education and schools projects, including a new IT Complex for the University of Wolverhampton.

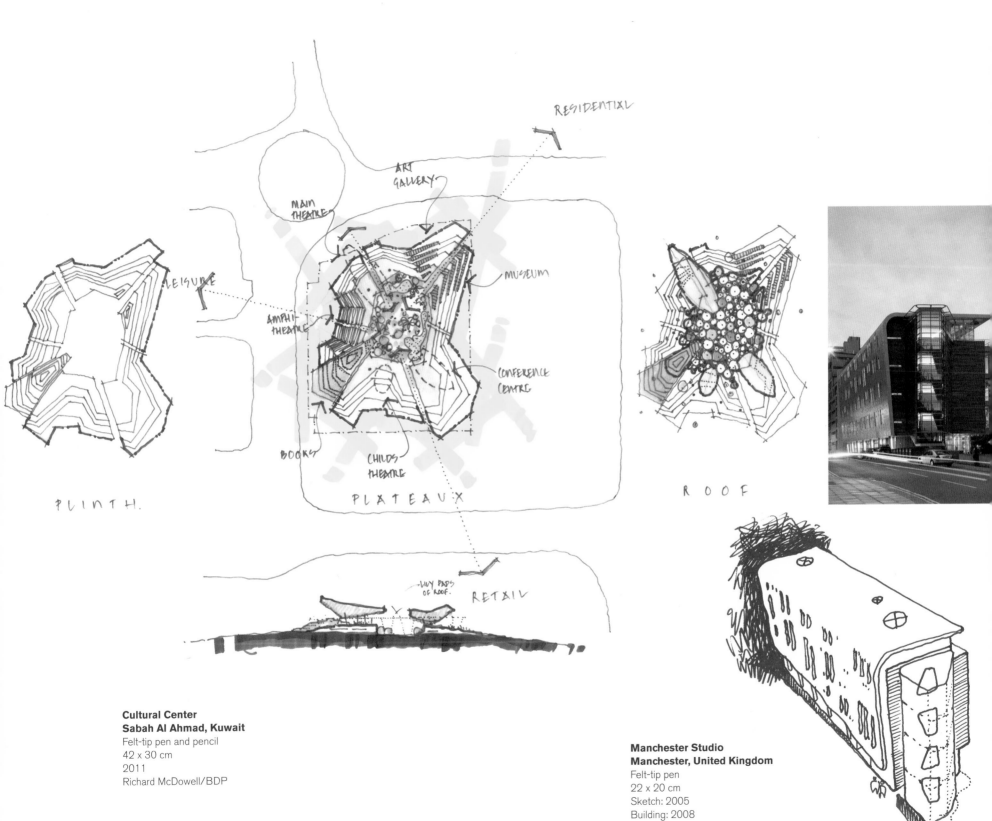

PLINTH.

RESIDENTIAL

ART GALLERY

MAIN THEATRE

MUSEUM

LEISURE

AMPHI-THEATRE

CONFERENCE CENTRE

BOOKS

CHILDS THEATRE

PLATEAUX

ROOF

LILY PADS OF ROOF.

RETAIL

Cultural Center
Sabah Al Ahmad, Kuwait
Felt-tip pen and pencil
42 x 30 cm
2011
Richard McDowell/BDP

Manchester Studio
Manchester, United Kingdom
Felt-tip pen
22 x 20 cm
Sketch: 2005
Building: 2008
Gary Wilde

ENRIC MIRALLES

Enric Miralles (born in Barcelona, Spain, 1953) studied at Escuela Técnica Superior de Arquitectura de Barcelona (ETSAB), graduating in 1974. Between 1973 and 1983 he collaborated with Albert Viaplana and Helio Piñon and in 1985 founded the architectural practice Enric Miralles and Carme Pinós. In 1990 he set up practice with his wife and partner Benedetta Tagliabue. He has taught at the ETSAB since 1985. Two of his most recent projects are The New Scottish Parliament in Edinburgh and The New Headquarters of Gas Natural in Barcelona. He has received numerous awards, including the National Prize of Spanish Architecture, 1995; The European ITALSTAD (Italy), 1991; and the Leone d'Oro Prize at the Biennale di Venezia, 1996.

Diagonal Mar Park
Colored pencil
53 x 31cm
1997
Enric Miralles

Gas Natural
Pencil
29 x 21cm
1999
Enric Miralles

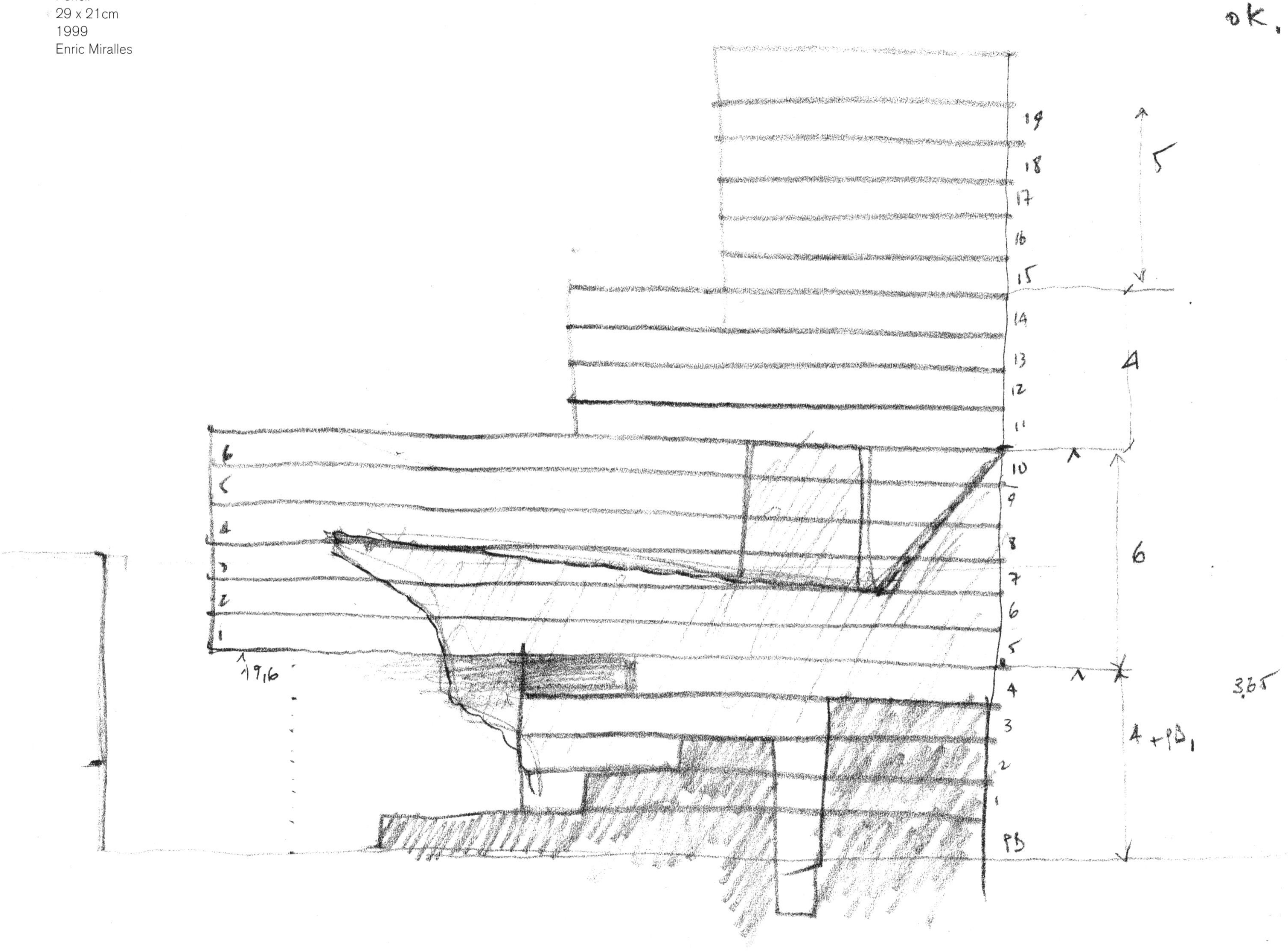

245

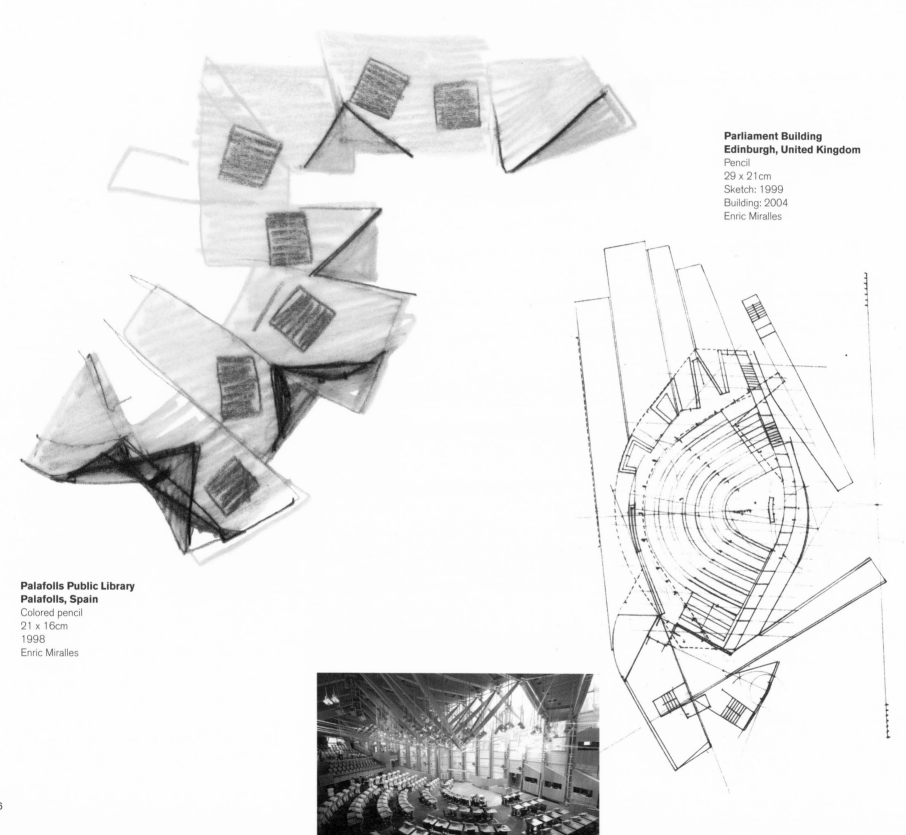

**Parliament Building
Edinburgh, United Kingdom**
Pencil
29 x 21cm
Sketch: 1999
Building: 2004
Enric Miralles

**Palafolls Public Library
Palafolls, Spain**
Colored pencil
21 x 16cm
1998
Enric Miralles

246

Vigo University Campus
Vigo, Spain
Colored pencil
29 x 21cm
1999
Enric Miralles

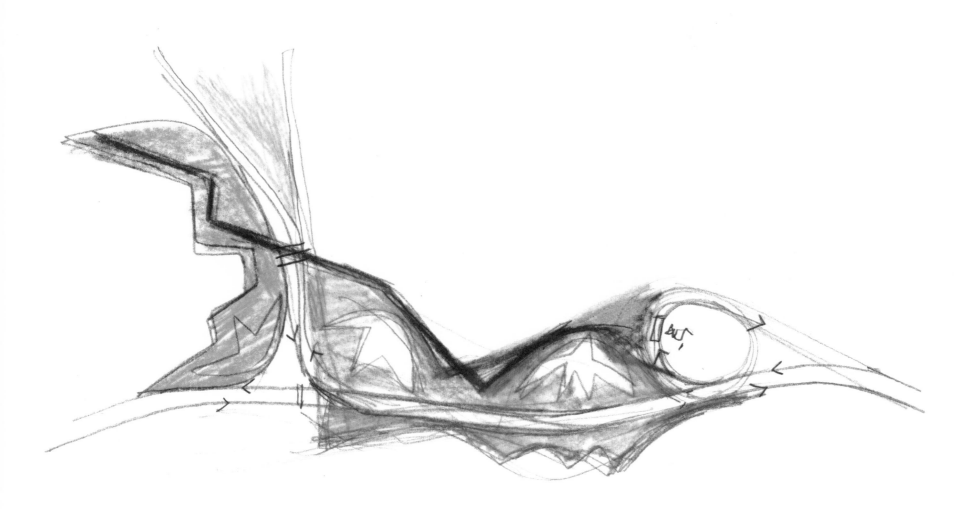

C.F. MØLLER ARCHITECTS

C.F. Møller Architects creates buildings primarily through close co-operation within the practice as well as with clients and fellow design consultants. It is not a question of individual achievement, but rather a process where everyone involved strives for a common architectural goal. The sketch is one of the main tools in this process. Mads Mandrup Hansen (born in Aalborg, Denmark, 1967) graduated from the Royal Academy of Fine Arts in 1999. He was employed at Henning Larsen Architects from 1995–1998 and became a partner at C.F. Møller Architects in 2008. He has received various awards, including His Royal Highness Prince Henrik's Medal in 2012. Klaus Toustrup (born in Tarm, Denmark, 1972) studied at the Aarhus School of Architecture, graduating in 1995. He became a partner at C.F. Møller Architects in 2004 and has received various awards, including Nykredit's Architecture Prize, and His Royal Highness Prince Henrik's Medal in 2012. Peter Dolf (Swiss/American, born 1969) and Mette Heide (born in Denmark, 1971) were both dedicated to the Darwin competition and afterwards worked for a number of years on the project in C.F. Møller's London office.

Darwin Centre
London, United Kingdom
Felt-tip pen and watercolors
Sketch: 2001
Building: 2009
Peter Dolf/C.F. Møller Architects

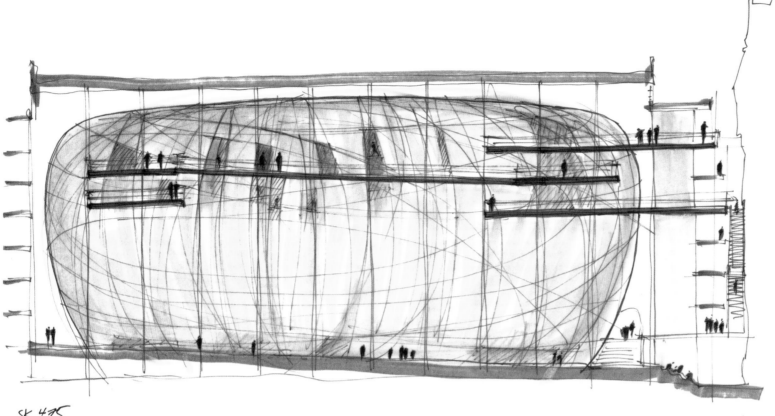

SK 475
5/5-03
CF. MØLLER

INTERIOR ELEVATION
WEST 1:200

Darwin Centre
London, United Kingdom
Felt-tip pen and markers
Sketch: 2003
Building: 2009
Mette Heide/C.F. Møller Architects

Darwin Centre
London, United Kingdom
Felt-tip pen and markers
Sketch: 2003
Building: 2009
Mette Heide/C.F. Møller Architects

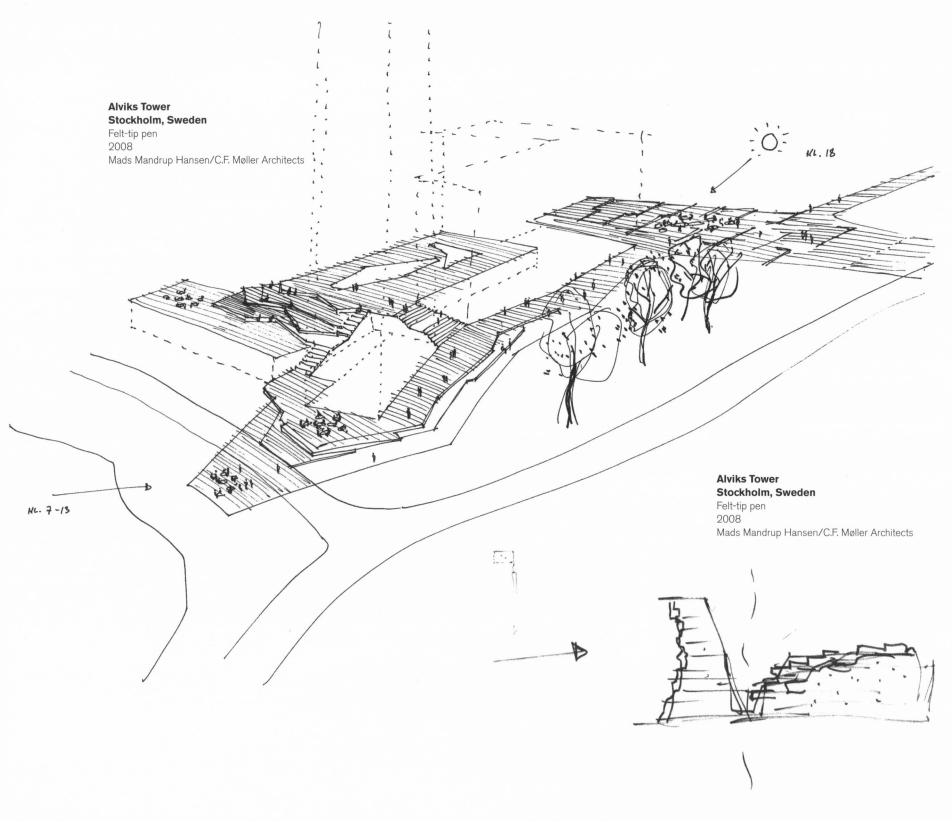

Alviks Tower
Stockholm, Sweden
Felt-tip pen
2008
Mads Mandrup Hansen/C.F. Møller Architects

kl. 18

kl. 7 -13

Alviks Tower
Stockholm, Sweden
Felt-tip pen
2008
Mads Mandrup Hansen/C.F. Møller Architects

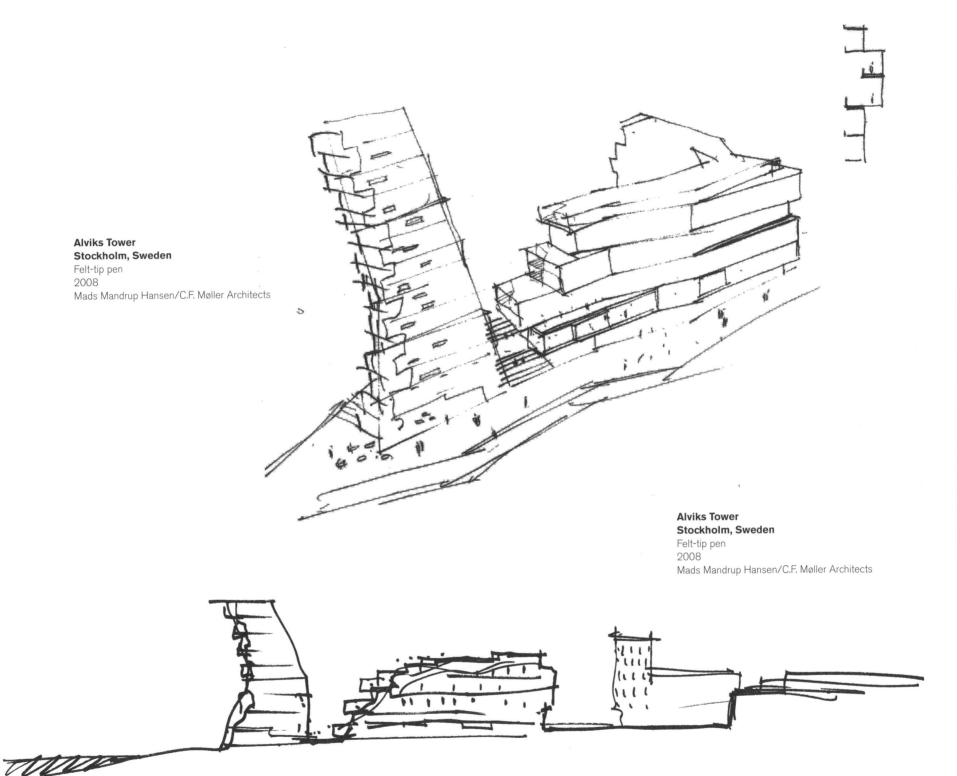

Alviks Tower
Stockholm, Sweden
Felt-tip pen
2008
Mads Mandrup Hansen/C.F. Møller Architects

Alviks Tower
Stockholm, Sweden
Felt-tip pen
2008
Mads Mandrup Hansen/C.F. Møller Architects

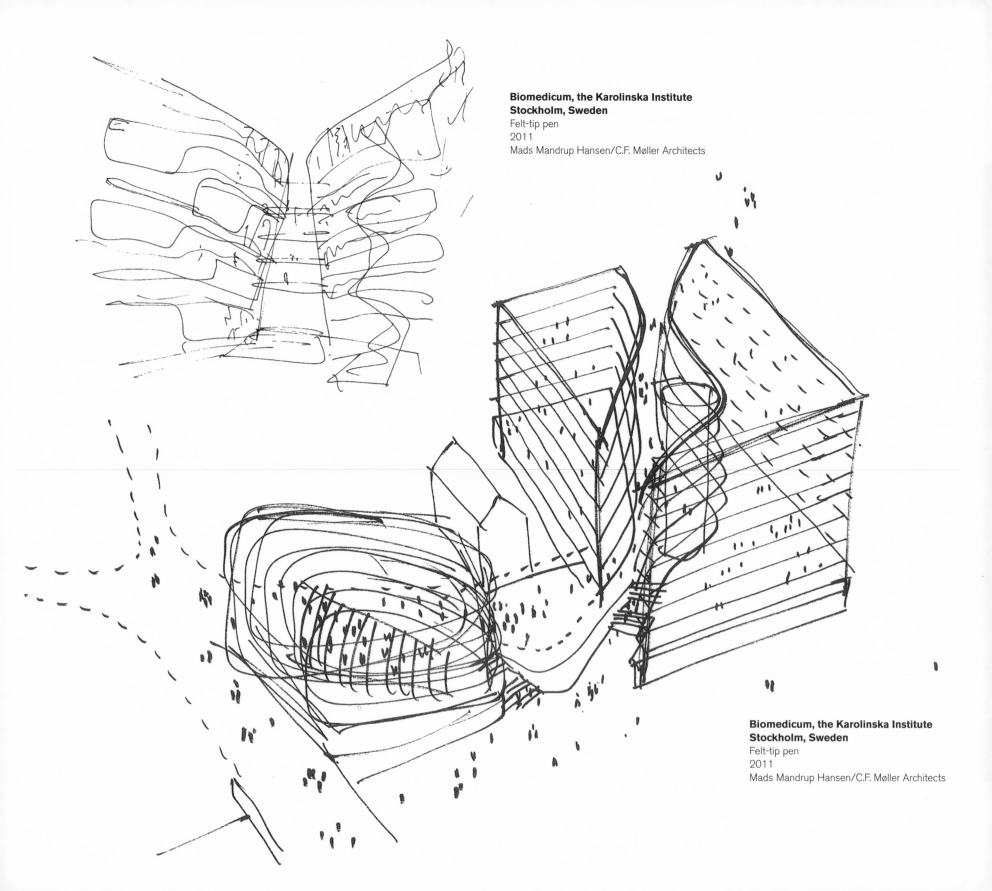

Biomedicum, the Karolinska Institute
Stockholm, Sweden
Felt-tip pen
2011
Mads Mandrup Hansen/C.F. Møller Architects

Biomedicum, the Karolinska Institute
Stockholm, Sweden
Felt-tip pen
2011
Mads Mandrup Hansen/C.F. Møller Architects

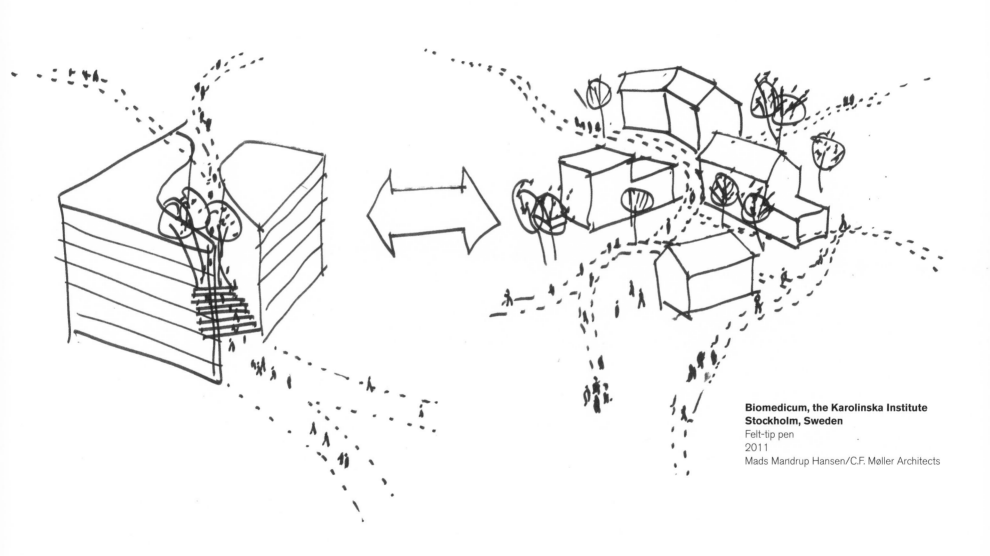

**Biomedicum, the Karolinska Institute
Stockholm, Sweden**
Felt-tip pen
2011
Mads Mandrup Hansen/C.F. Møller Architects

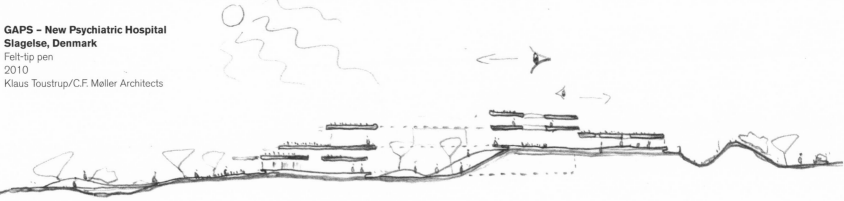

**GAPS – New Psychiatric Hospital
Slagelse, Denmark**
Felt-tip pen
2010
Klaus Toustrup/C.F. Møller Architects

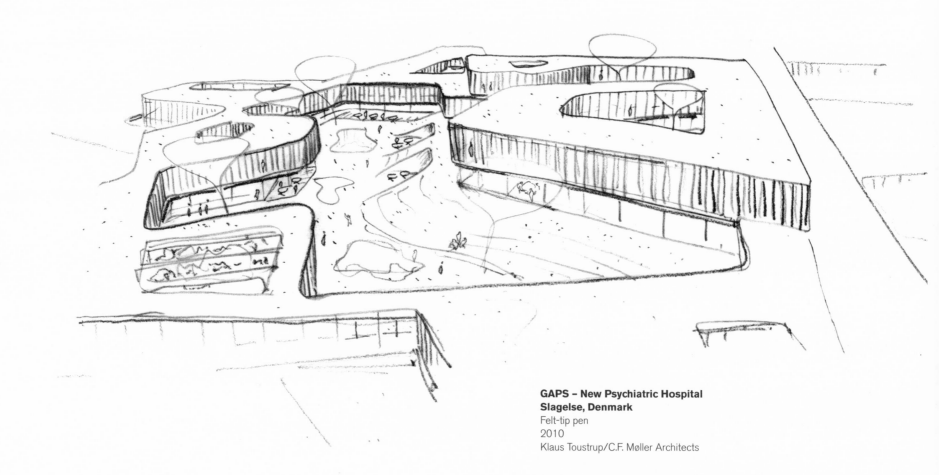

**GAPS – New Psychiatric Hospital
Slagelse, Denmark**
Felt-tip pen
2010
Klaus Toustrup/C.F. Møller Architects

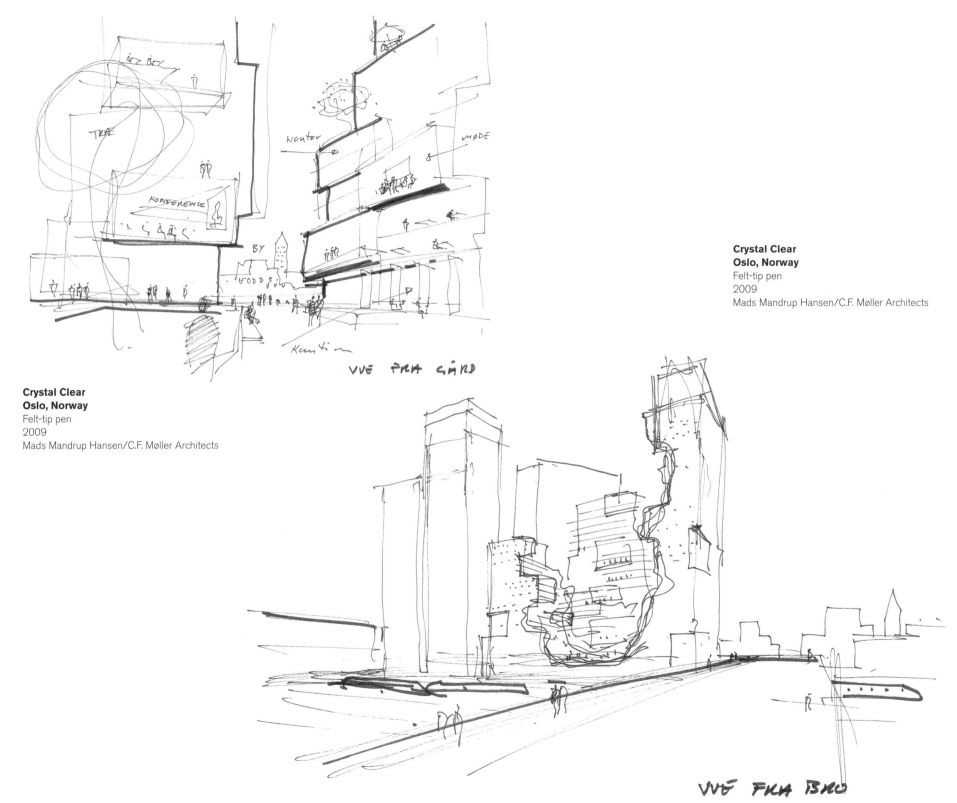

Crystal Clear
Oslo, Norway
Felt-tip pen
2009
Mads Mandrup Hansen/C.F. Møller Architects

Crystal Clear
Oslo, Norway
Felt-tip pen
2009
Mads Mandrup Hansen/C.F. Møller Architects

255

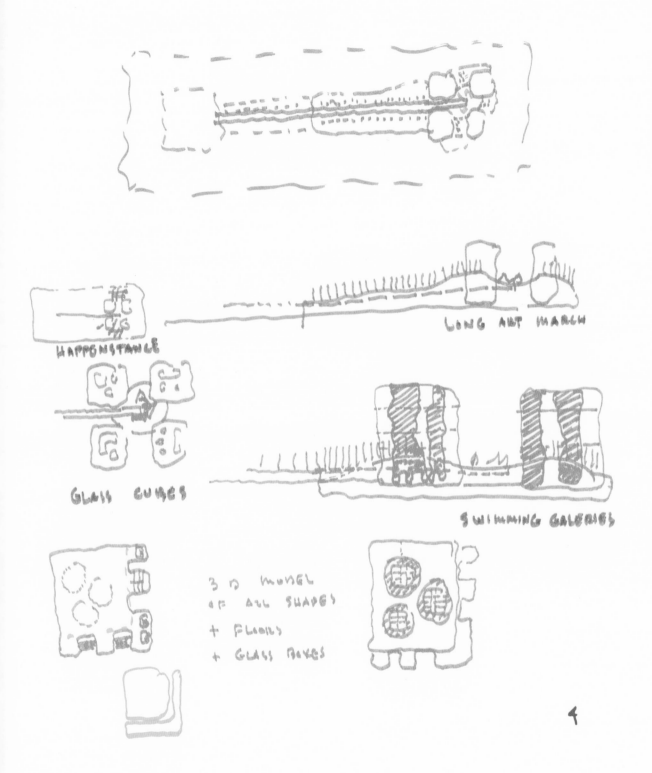

HAPPENSTANCE

LONG ART MARCH

GLASS CUBES

SWIMMING GALERIES

3 D MODEL
OF ALL SHAPES
+ FLOORS
+ GLASS BOXES

ERIC OWEN MOSS

Eric Moss (born in Los Angeles, USA, 1943) received his Bachelor of Arts degree from the University of California in Los Angeles in 1965; his Masters of Architecture from the University of California at Berkeley in 1968; and a second Masters of Architecture from Harvard University Graduate School of Design in 1972. Eric Owen Moss Architects (EOMA) has been the recipient of over 100 local, national, and international design awards. Eric Owen Moss has held teaching positions at major universities around the world including Harvard, Yale, Columbia, University of Applied Arts in Vienna, and the Royal Academy in Copenhagen. Moss has also been a longtime professor at the Southern California Institute of Architecture (SCI-Arc), and has served as its director since 2003.

**Guangdong Provincial Museum
Guangzhou, China**
Marker pen
11 x 8.5 cm
2004
Eric Owen Moss/Eric Owen Moss Architects

Jose Vasconcelos Library
Mexico City, Mexico
Marker pen
8.5 x 11 cm
2003
Eric Owen Moss/Eric Owen Moss Architects

Beehive
Culver City, CA, USA
Marker pen
6 x 6.5 cm
Sketch: 1995
Building: 2001
Eric Owen Moss/Eric Owen Moss Architects

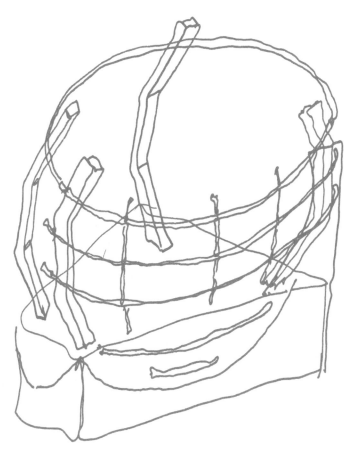

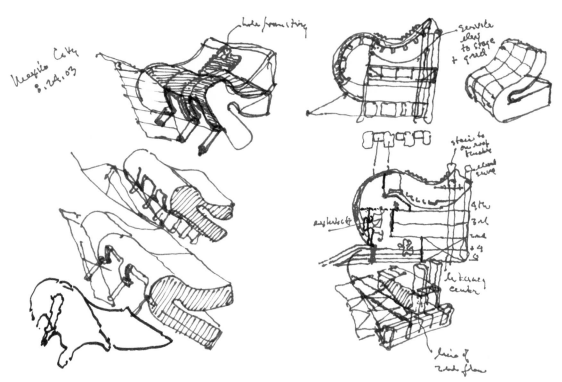

Gasometer
Vienna, Austria
Marker pen
6 x 4.5 cm
1995
Eric Owen Moss/Eric Owen Moss Architects

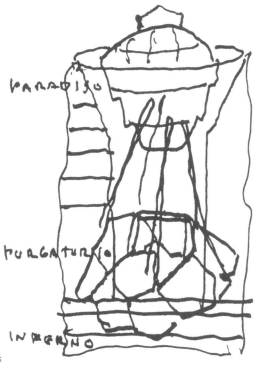

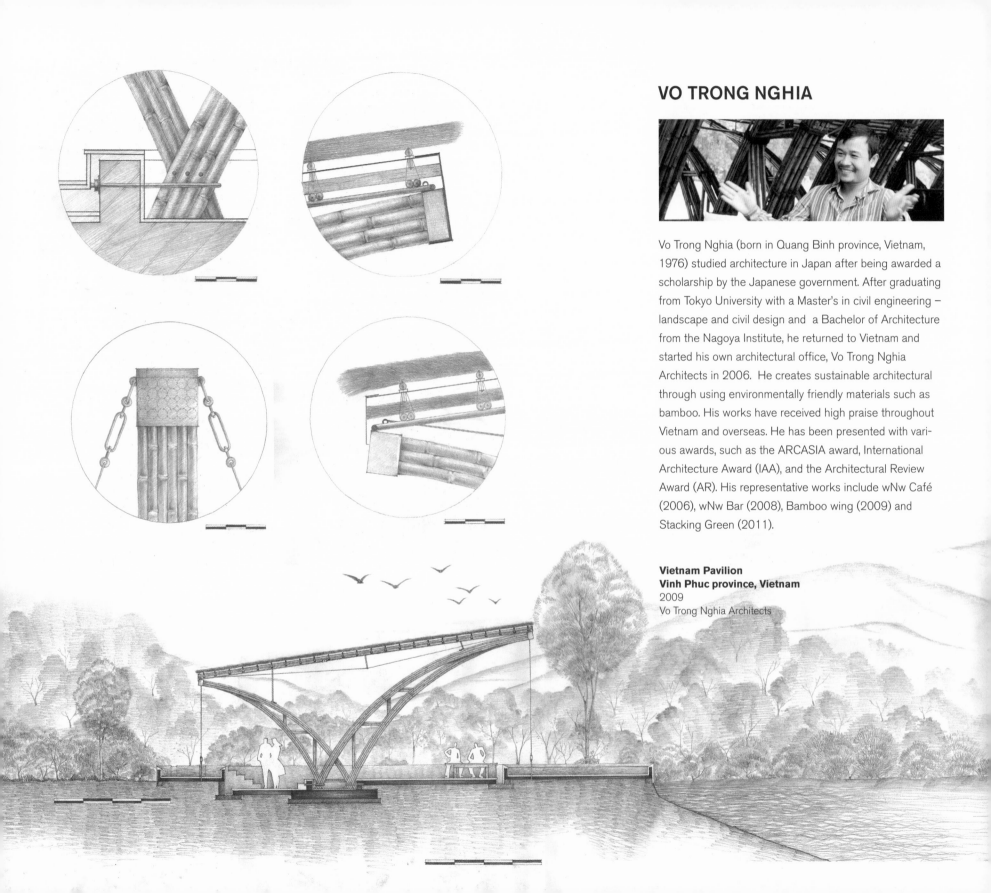

VO TRONG NGHIA

Vo Trong Nghia (born in Quang Binh province, Vietnam, 1976) studied architecture in Japan after being awarded a scholarship by the Japanese government. After graduating from Tokyo University with a Master's in civil engineering – landscape and civil design and a Bachelor of Architecture from the Nagoya Institute, he returned to Vietnam and started his own architectural office, Vo Trong Nghia Architects in 2006. He creates sustainable architectural through using environmentally friendly materials such as bamboo. His works have received high praise throughout Vietnam and overseas. He has been presented with various awards, such as the ARCASIA award, International Architecture Award (IAA), and the Architectural Review Award (AR). His representative works include wNw Café (2006), wNw Bar (2008), Bamboo wing (2009) and Stacking Green (2011).

Vietnam Pavilion
Vinh Phuc province, Vietnam
2009
Vo Trong Nghia Architects

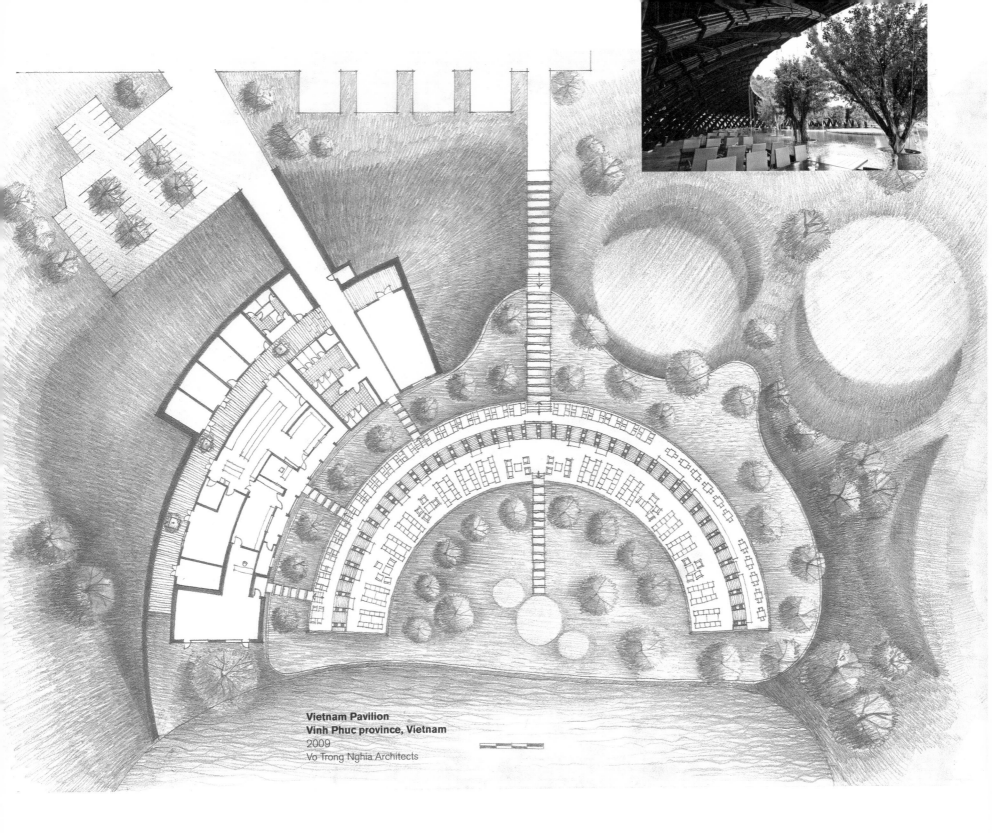

Vietnam Pavilion
Vinh Phuc province, Vietnam
2009
Vo Trong Nghia Architects

259

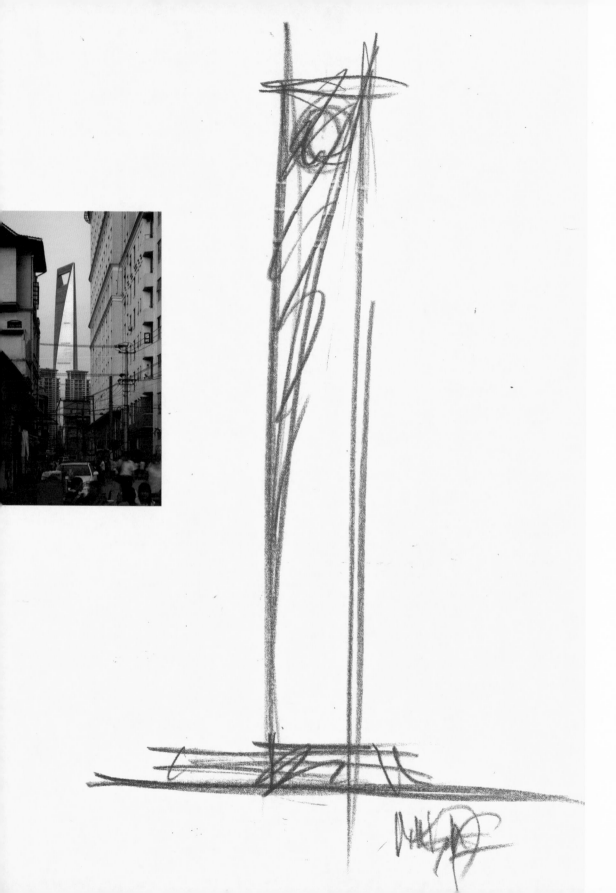

WILLIAM PEDERSEN

William Pedersen is the founding design partner of Kohn Pedersen Fox Associates (KPF), which he started with A. Eugene Kohn and Sheldon Fox in 1976. Fourteen years later, they became the youngest firm to receive the National AIA Firm Award for design excellence. Of particular concern Pedersen is the development of what he calls the "fundamental building block of the modern city": the high-rise commercial office building. Throughout his career, he has systematically sought ways for buildings of this seemingly mundane type to gesture and connect to other participants, joining in an active architectural conversation with them. In addition to numerous state and local AIA awards, he received recognition from the Council for Tall Buildings and Urban Habitat (CTBUH) for the Shanghai World Financial Center as the "Best Tall Building in the World" in 2009.

Shanghai World Financial Center (SWFC)
Shanghai, China
China pencil on tracing paper
21.6 x 27.9 cm
Sketch: 1997
Building: 2008
William Pedersen/Kohn Pedersen Fox Associates

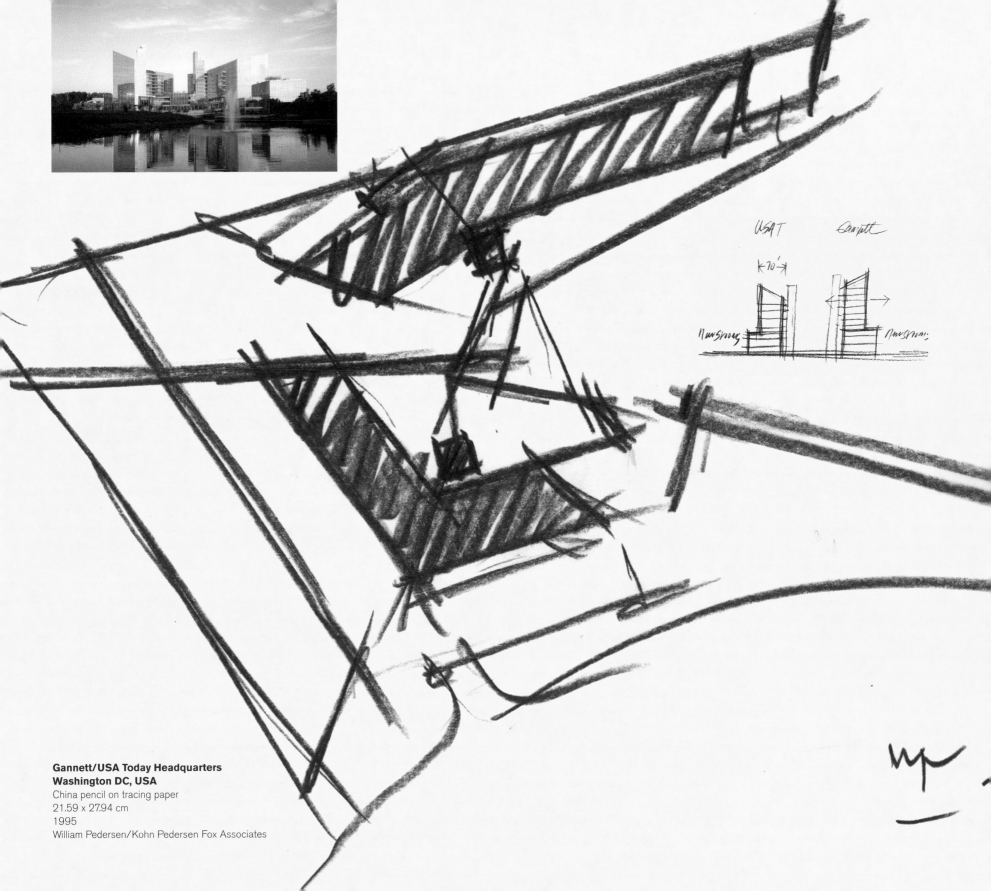

Gannett/USA Today Headquarters
Washington DC, USA
China pencil on tracing paper
21.59 x 27.94 cm
1995
William Pedersen/Kohn Pedersen Fox Associates

GUSTAV PEICHL

Gustav Peichl (born in Vienna, Austria, 1928) studied architecture at the Academy of Fine Arts in Vienna from 1949 to 1953. He then worked in Roland Rainer's atelier from 1952–1954, before founding his own company in 1956. Peichl has also worked as a cartoonist under then Pseudonym "Ironimus". In 1991 he founded Peichl & Partner, which was re-established as Peichl & Partner ZT GmbH. Peichl's buildings are characterized by their technical aesthetic, classical proportions and symbolic form. The simple elegance of his buildings share similarities with the Second Modernity, although his work also plays with details that are influenced by the Postmodern. Peichl's best-known works include the Austrian Pavilion and the Millennium Tower in Vienna. In 1986, he received the Mies van der Rohe Award for European Architecture.

Bundeskunsthalle
Bonn, Germany
Pencil and colored pencil on tracing paper
Building: 1992
Gustav Peichl

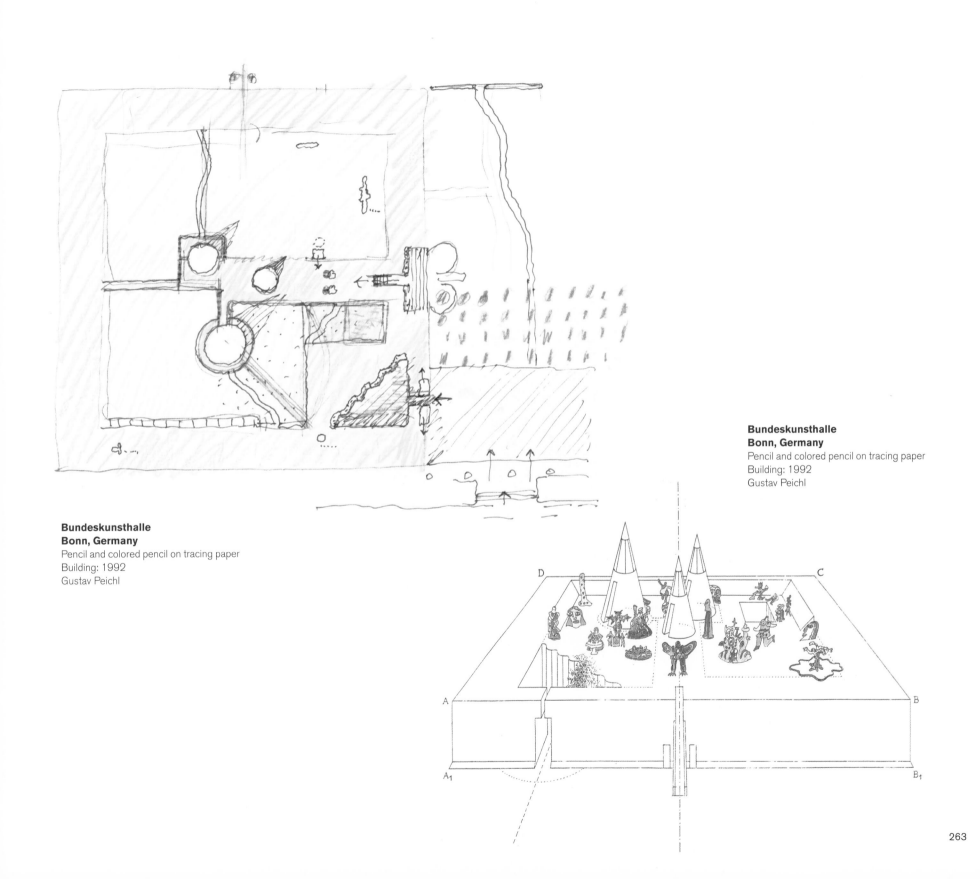

Bundeskunsthalle
Bonn, Germany
Pencil and colored pencil on tracing paper
Building: 1992
Gustav Peichl

Bundeskunsthalle
Bonn, Germany
Pencil and colored pencil on tracing paper
Building: 1992
Gustav Peichl

263

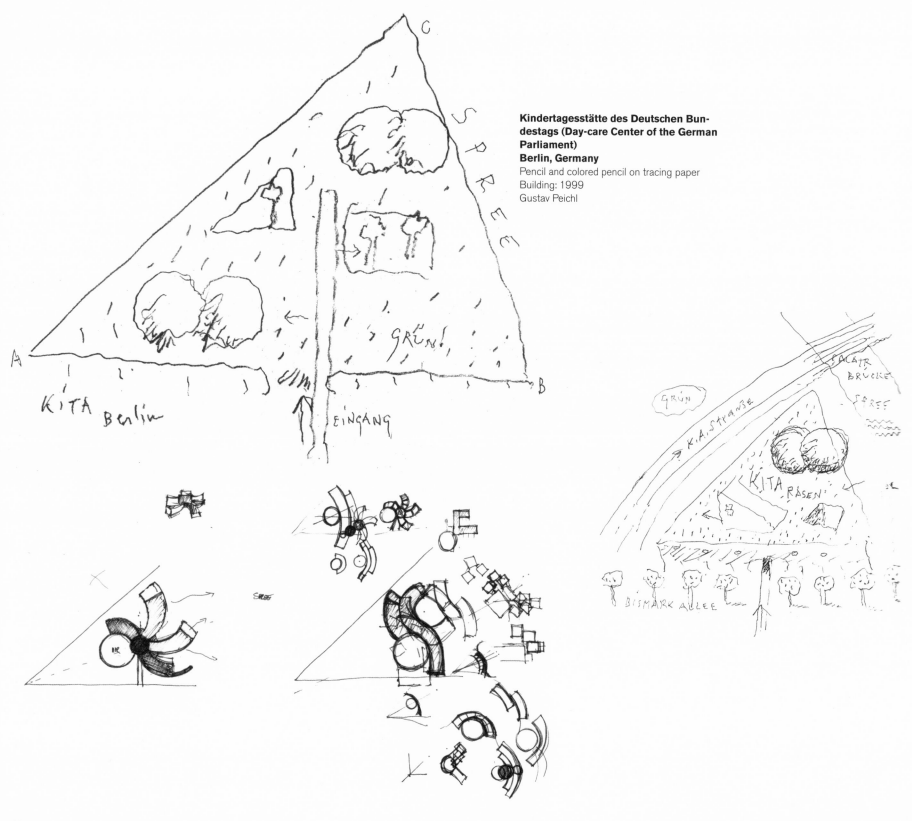

Kindertagesstätte des Deutschen Bundestags (Day-care Center of the German Parliament)
Berlin, Germany
Pencil and colored pencil on tracing paper
Building: 1999
Gustav Peichl

264

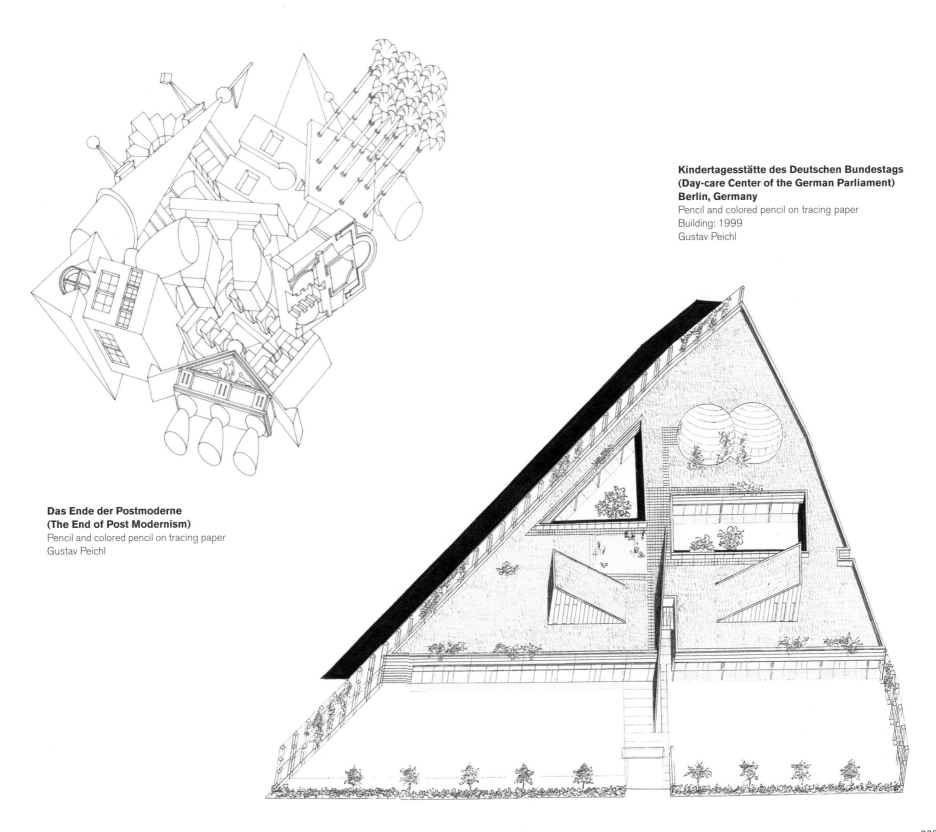

**Kindertagesstätte des Deutschen Bundestags
(Day-care Center of the German Parliament)
Berlin, Germany**
Pencil and colored pencil on tracing paper
Building: 1999
Gustav Peichl

**Das Ende der Postmoderne
(The End of Post Modernism)**
Pencil and colored pencil on tracing paper
Gustav Peichl

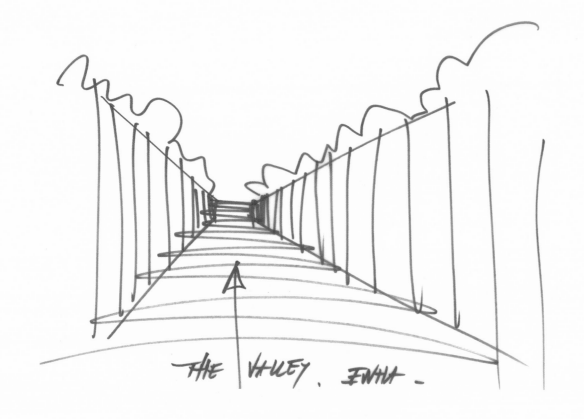

THE VALLEY. EWHA -

2006 - PARIS - EWHA

DOMINIQUE PERRAULT

Internationally renowned French architect Dominique Perrault (born in Paris, France, 1953) gained international recognition after winning the competition for the National French library in 1989 at the age of 36. This project marked the starting point for many other public and private commissions abroad, such as the Velodrome and Olympic swimming pool in Berlin, the extension of the European Court of Justice in Luxembourg, the Olympic tennis center in Madrid, the campus of Ewha's University in Seoul and the Fukoku Tower in Osaka, Japan. Ongoing projects include the rehabilitation/extension of the former mechanical engineering halls and the central library, as well as the construction of the Teaching Bridge of the Ecole Polytechnique Fédérale in Lausanne, Switzerland. Perrault has received many prestigious prizes and awards, including the AFEX Award for the Ewha Womans University in Korea, the Mies van der Rohe prize (1997), and the Equerre d'argent prize for the Hotel Industriel Berlier (1989).

**Ewha Woman's University
Seoul, South Korea
International Competition
by Invitation**
Winning project: 2004
Sketch: 2006
Building: 2008
Felt-tip pen on tracing paper
42 x 30 cm
Dominique Perrault/Adagp

**Ewha Woman's University
Seoul, South Korea**
Felt-tip on tracing paper
42 x 30 cm
Sketch: 2006
Building: 2008
Dominique Perrault/Adagp

THE VALLEY EWHA

**Ewha Woman's University
Seoul, South Korea**
Felt-tip pen on tracing paper
42 x 30 cm
Sketch: 2006
Building: 2008
Dominique Perrault/Adagp

THE VALLEY EWHA

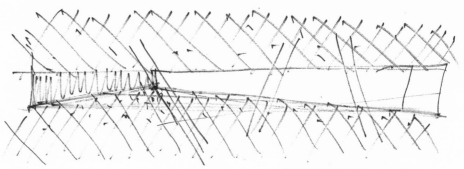

**Ewha Woman's University
Seoul, South Korea**
Felt-tip on tracing paper
42 x 30 cm
Sketch: 2006
Building: 2008
Dominique Perrault/Adagp

**Ewha Woman's University
Seoul, South Korea**
Felt-tip and highlighter on tracing paper
42 x 30 cm
Sketch: 2006
Building: 2008
Dominique Perrault/Adagp

IN THE LANDSCAPE = THE "VALLEY"

HISTORICAL BUILDING.

THE VALLEY.

Ewha Woman's University
Seoul, South Korea
Felt-tip pen and highlighter on tracing paper
42 x 30 cm
Sketch: 2006
Building: 2008
Dominique Perrault/Adagp

269

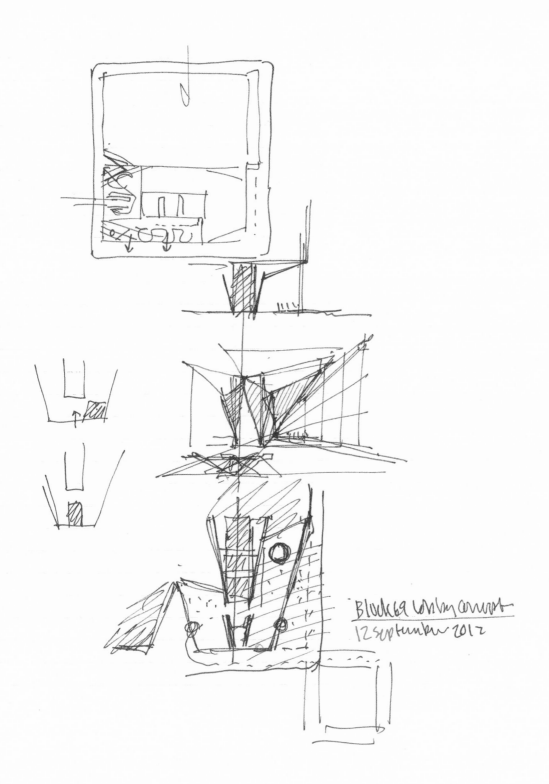

Block 69 lobby concept
12 September 2012

JON PICKARD

Pickard Chilton Principal Jon Pickard (born in Des Moines, IA, USA, 1954) has been recognized internationally for his achievements in architecture. He has designed or collaborated in the design of some of the world's most recognized buildings, including such prominent projects as the Exxon-Mobil Office Complex in Houston, Texas; the Devon Energy Center in Oklahoma City, Oklahoma; and The Atrium, a luxury residential building in Dubai. Prior to founding Pickard Chilton, he collaborated with Cesar Pelli in the design of numerous landmark and award-winning projects, including the World Financial Center and Kuala Lumpar City Center. Jon Pickard received his Bachelor of Architecture degree from Iowa State University and his Master of Architecture from the Yale School of Architecture.

609 Main
Houston, TX, USA
Felt-tip pen on paper
27.9 x 21.6 cm
2012
Jon Pickard/Pickard Chilton

609 Main
Houston, TX, USA
Pencil on tracing paper
30.5 x 43.2 cm
2012
Jon Pickard/Pickard Chilton

271

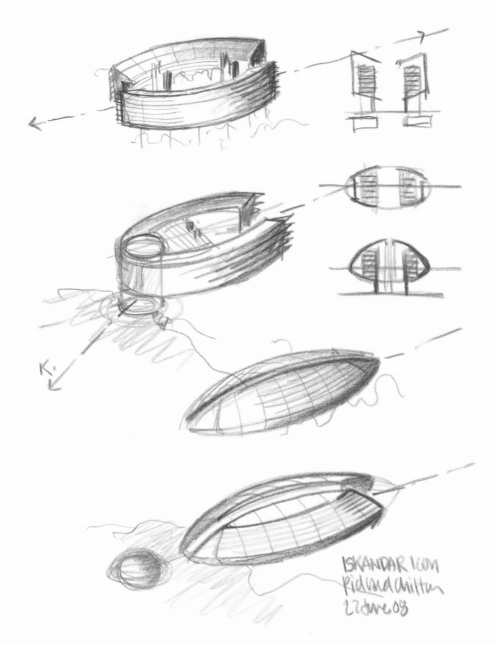

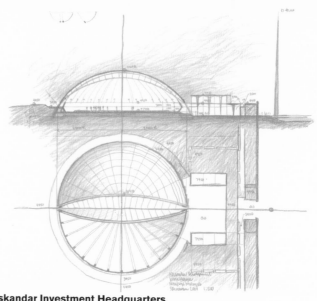

Iskandar Investment Headquarters
Pencil on tracing paper
19.8 x 21.8 cm
2009
Jon Pickard/Pickard Chilton

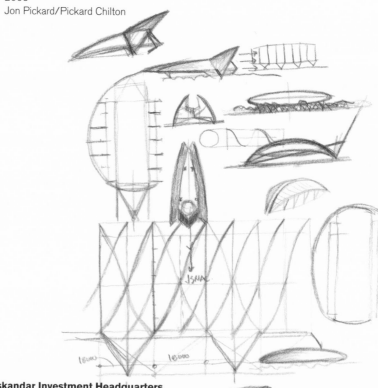

Iskandar Investment Headquarters
Pencil on tracing paper
30.5 x 22.9 cm
2009
Jon Pickard/Pickard Chilton

Iskandar Investment Headquarters
Pencil on tracing paper
30.5 x 20.3 cm
2009
Jon Pickard/Pickard Chilton

Wells Fargo
Des Moines, IA, USA
Felt-tip pen on tracing paper
26.7 x 45.7 cm
Sketch: 2004
Building: 2006
Jon Pickard/Pickard Chilton

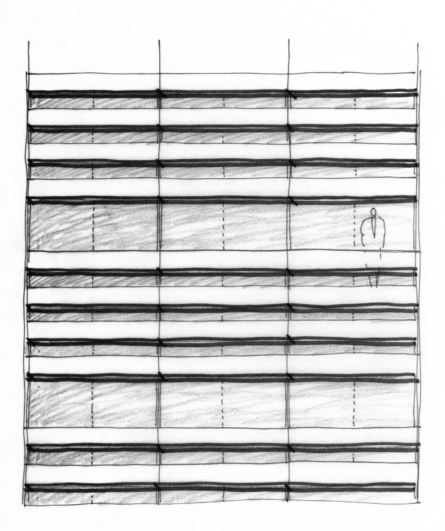

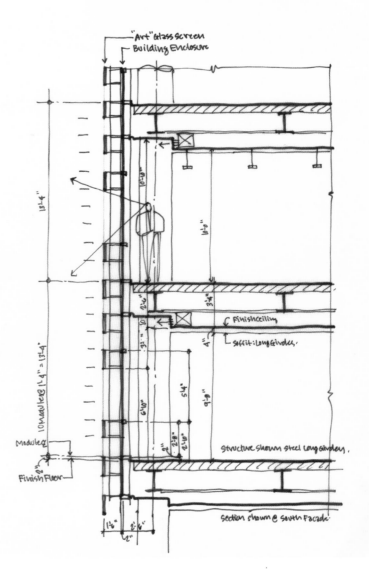

Eighth Avenue Place
Calgary, Canada
Pencil on tracing paper
45.7 x 38.1 cm
Sketch: 2007
Building: 2011
Jon Pickard/Pickard Chilton

Eaton Center
Beachwood, OH, USA
Pencil on tracing paper
29.2 x 47 cm
Sketch: 2008
Building: 2013
Anthony Markese/Pickard Chilton

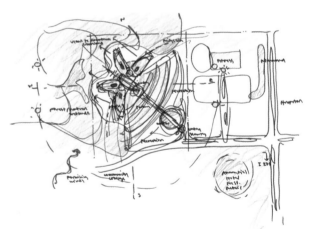

Eaton Center
Beachwood, OH, USA
Pencil on tracing paper
38.1 x 50.8 cm
Sketch: 2008
Building: 2013
Anthony Markese/Pickard Chilton

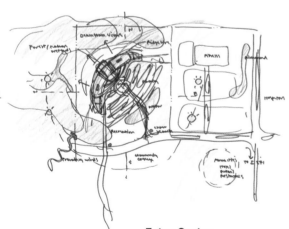

Eaton Center
Beachwood, OH, USA
Felt-tip pen on tracing paper
31.8 x 43.2 cm
Sketch: 2008
Building: 2013
Anthony Markese/Pickard Chilton

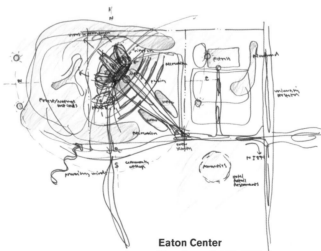

Eaton Center
Beachwood, OH, USA
Felt-tip pen on tracing paper
34.5 x 46.5 cm
Sketch: 2008
Building: 2013
Anthony Markese/Pickard Chilton

Eaton Center
Beachwood, OH, USA
Felt-tip pen on tracing paper
42.7 x 34.04 Inches
Sketch: 2008
Building: 2013
Anthony Markese/Pickard Chilton

River Point
Chicago, IL, USA
Felt-tip pen on tracing paper
35.6 x 22.9 cm
2006
Anthony Markese/Pickard Chilton

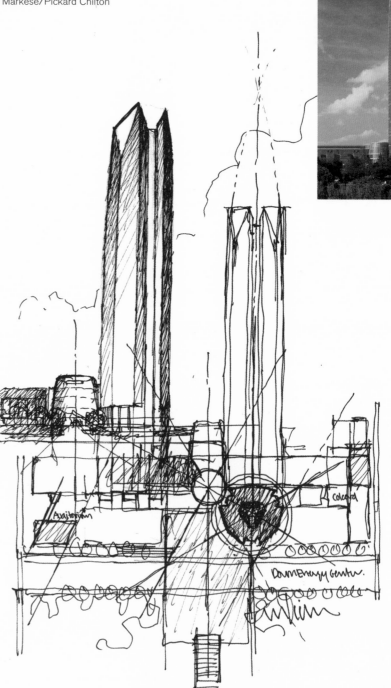

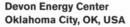
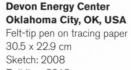

Devon Energy Center
Oklahoma City, OK, USA
Felt-tip pen on tracing paper
30.5 x 22.9 cm
Sketch: 2008
Building: 2012
Jon Pickard/Pickard Chilton

276

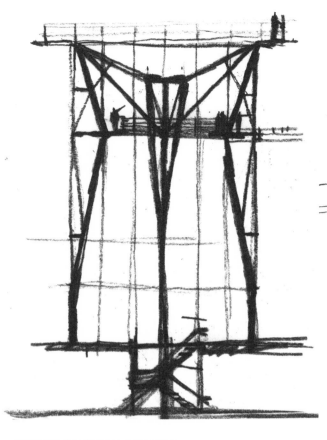

**CalPERS Headquarters Complex
Sacramento, CA, USA**
Pencil on tracing paper
11.43 x 8.9 cm
Sketch: 1999
Building: 2005
Anthony Markese/Pickard Chilton

**CalPERS Headquarters Complex
Sacramento, CA, USA**
Pencil on tracing paper
20.3 x 27.2 Inches
Sketch: 1999
Building: 2005
Anthony Markese/Pickard Chilton

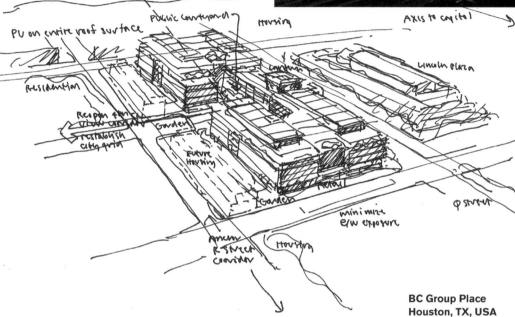

**BC Group Place
Houston, TX, USA**
Felt-tip pen on tracing paper
58.2 x 77.5 cm
2007
Jon Pickard/Pickard Chilton

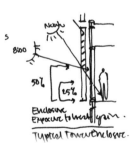

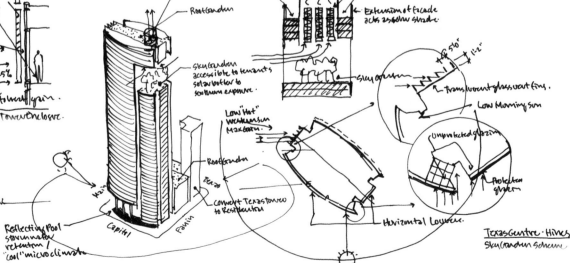

277

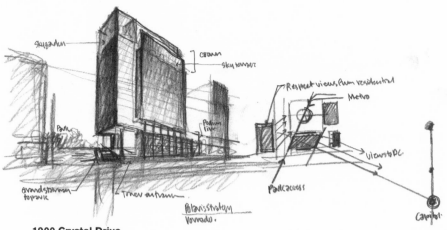

1900 Crystal Drive
Arlington, VA, USA
Pencil on tracing paper
22.9 x 33 cm
2012
Jon Pickard/Pickard Chilton

1900 Crystal Drive
Arlington, VA, USA
Felt-tip pen and pencil on tracing paper
27.9 x 43.2 cm
2012
Robert McClure/Pickard Chilton

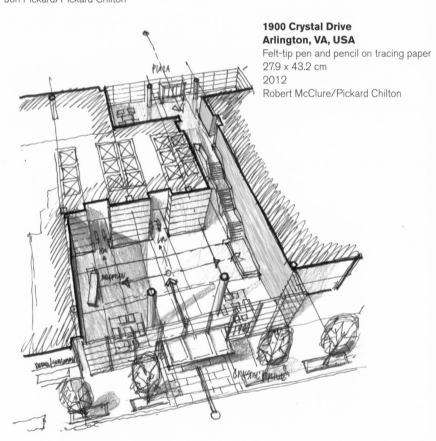

1900 Crystal Drive
Arlington, VA, USA
Pencil on tracing paper
21.6 x 31.5 cm
2012
Robert McClure/Pickard Chilton

900 New York Avenue
Washington DC, USA
Felt-tip pen on tracing paper
33 x 33 cm
2008
Anthony Markese/Pickard Chilton

900 New York Avenue
Washington DC, USA
Pencil on tracing paper
76.2 x 61 cm
2008
Anthony Markese/Pickard Chilton

CHRISTIAN DE PORTZAMPARC

Christian de Portzamparc (born in Casablanca, Morocco, 1944) studied at the École des Beaux-Arts in Paris from 1962 to 1969. Soon after completing his studies, he set his mark on the landscape of the new town of Marne-la-Vallée with his Water Tower, a "poetic monument". In 1975, he designed a neighborhood in Paris with 210 dwellings: Rue des Hautes-Formes was completed in 1980 and marked a turning-point in the history of urban design. Christian de Portzamparc works all over the world, theorizing on the present and future of the city, fragmentation, a case-by-case approach and the "open block" concept. From an individual building to an entire neighborhood, the city is fundamental to his work, which is dominated by three overlapping themes: flagship public buildings, which bring people together; sculptural towers; and neighborhoods and blocks of residential and office buildings.

Les Hautes-Formes
Paris, France
On layer, India ink & watercolor
Competition: Pan VII 1975
Drawing: 1975
Building: 1979
Christian de Portzamparc

Les Hautes-Formes
Paris, France
Pen
Competition: Pan VII 1975
Drawing : 1975
Building: 1979
Christian de Portzamparc

Les Hautes-Formes
Paris, France
On layer, India ink and watercolor
Competition: Pan VII 1975
Drawing: 1975
Building: 1979
Christian de Portzamparc

281

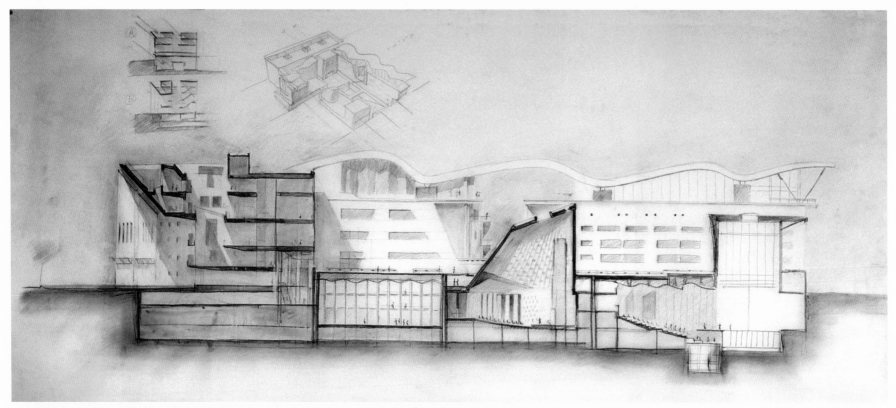

Cité de la Musique
Paris, France
Pastel on paper
Competition: 1984, first prize
Drawing: 1985
Building: 1990
Christian de Portzamparc

Cité de la Musique
Paris, France
Watercolor on paper
Competition: 1984, first prize
Drawing: 1985
Building: 1990
Christian de Portzamparc

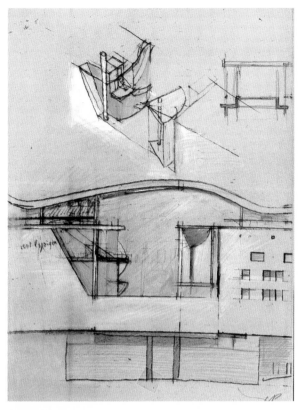

Cité de la Musique
Paris, France
Pastel on paper
Competition: 1984
Drawing: 1985
Building: 1990
Christian de Portzamparc

Cité de la Musique
Paris, France
Pastel on paper
Competition: 1984, first prize
Drawing: 1985
Building: 1990
Christian de Portzamparc

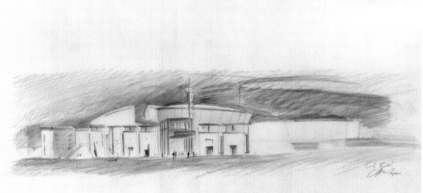

Cité de la Musique
Paris, France
Pastel on paper
Competition: 1984, first prize
Drawing: 1985
Building: 1990
Christian de Portzamparc

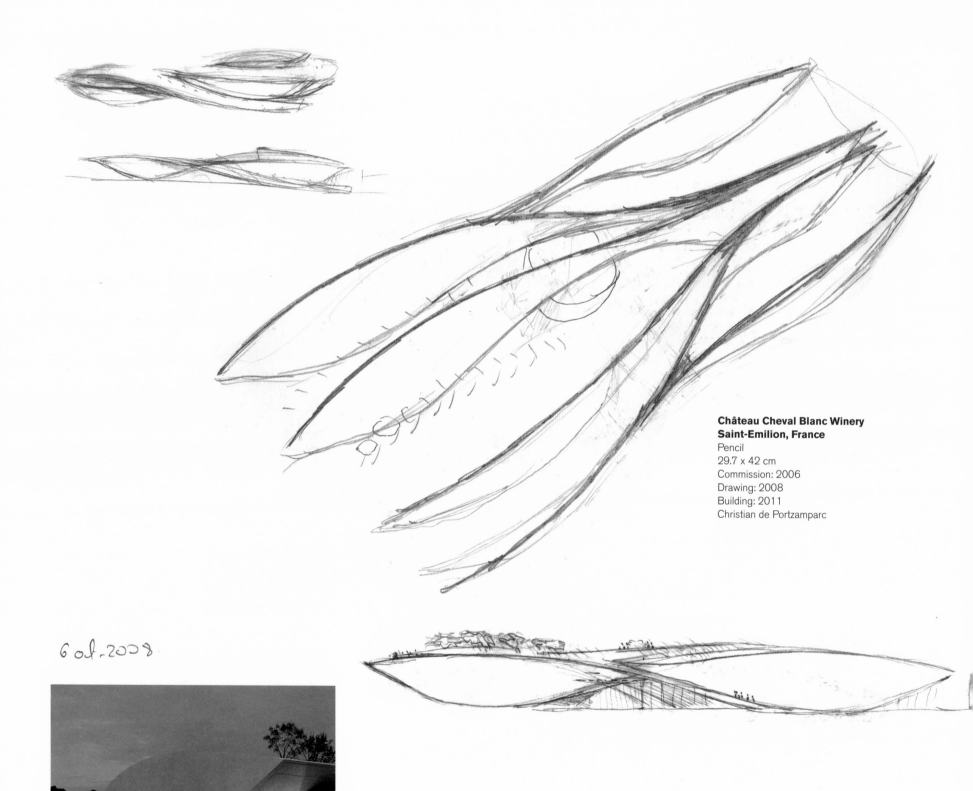

Château Cheval Blanc Winery
Saint-Emilion, France
Pencil
29.7 x 42 cm
Commission: 2006
Drawing: 2008
Building: 2011
Christian de Portzamparc

6 oct. 2008

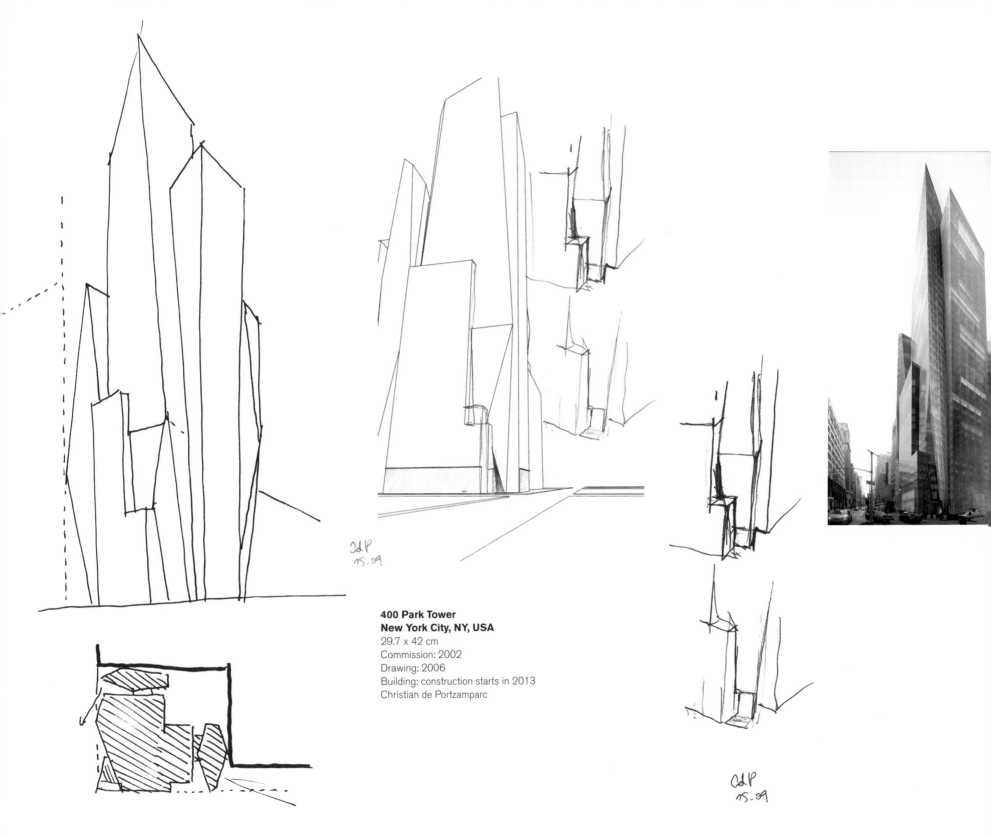

400 Park Tower
New York City, NY, USA
29.7 x 42 cm
Commission: 2002
Drawing: 2006
Building: construction starts in 2013
Christian de Portzamparc

285

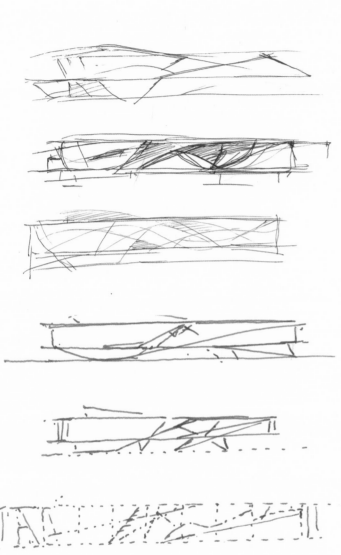

Cidade das Artes
Rio de Janeiro, Brazil
Pencil drawing
29.7 x 42 cm
Drawing: 2008
Commission: 2002
Building: to be completed in 2013
Christian de Portzamparc

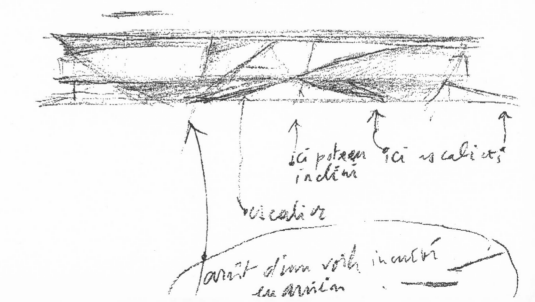

Herge Museum
Louvain-la-Neuve, Belgium
Pencil on paper
29.7 x 42 cm
Commission: 2001
Drawing: 2001
Building: 2009
Christian de Portzamparc

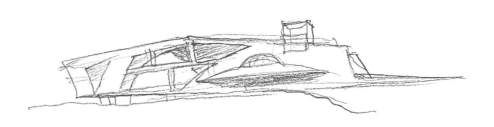

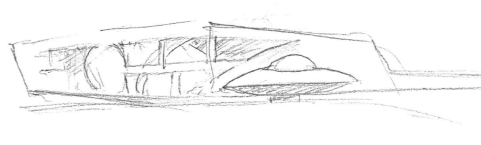

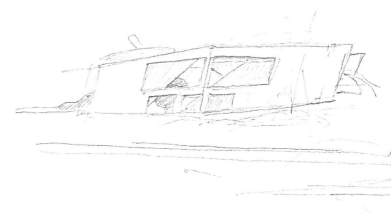

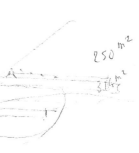

Herge Museum
Louvain-la-Neuve, Belgium
On layer pencil drawing
42 x 29.7 cm
Commission: 2001
Drawing: 2001
Building: 2009
Christian de Portzamparc

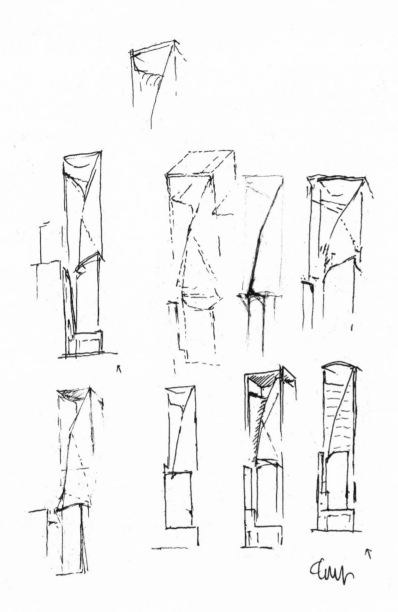

LVMH Tower
New York City, NY, USA
Pencil drawing on paper
29.7 x 42 cm
Commission: 1995
Drawing: 1995
Building: 1999
Christian de Portzamparc

18.06.95

LARGEUR TOUR
OPTIMISÉE

PANS INCURVÉS

LVMH Tower
New York City, NY, USA
Pastel on paper
29.7 x 42 cm
Commission: 1995
Drawing: 1995
Building: 1999
Christian de Portzamparc

LVMH Tower
New York City, NY, USA
Pastel on paper
42 x 29.7 cm
Commission: 1995
Drawing: 1995
Building: 1999
Christian de Portzamparc

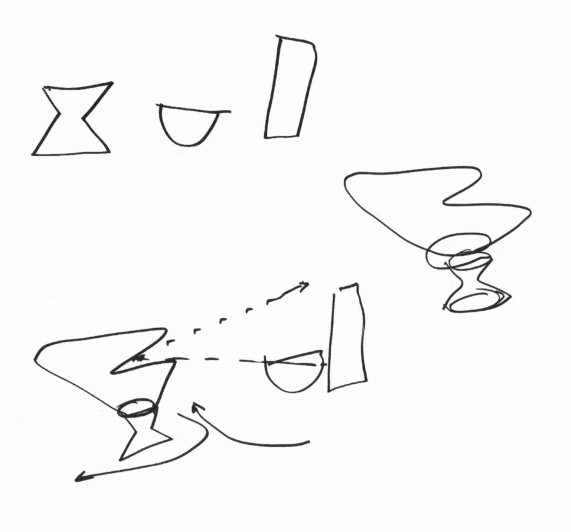

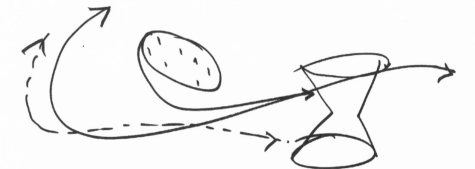

WOLF D. PRIX

Wolf D. Prix (born in Vienna, Austria, 1942) is co-founder, Design Principal and CEO of Coop Himmelb(l)au. He studied architecture at the Vienna University of Technology, the Architectural Association of London, and the Southern California Institute of Architecture in Los Angeles. Most formative among his many international teaching positions was his tenure at the University of Applied Arts Vienna. He taught as a visiting professor at the Architectural Association in London in 1984 and at Harvard University in Cambridge, Massachusetts in 1990. In 2004 he received the Annie Spink Award for Excellence in Architectural Education for his commitment to teaching and training and was awarded with the Jencks Award: Visions Built prize in 2008. The work of Wolf D. Prix has been published in numerous books and his architectural designs have been featured in many museums worldwide.

BMW Welt
Munich, Germany
Marker on tracing paper
42 x 29.7 cm
Sketch: 2007
Building: 2007
Wolf D. Prix

BMW Welt
Munich, Germany
Marker on tracing paper
42 x 29.7 cm
Sketch: 2007
Building: 2007
Wolf D. Prix

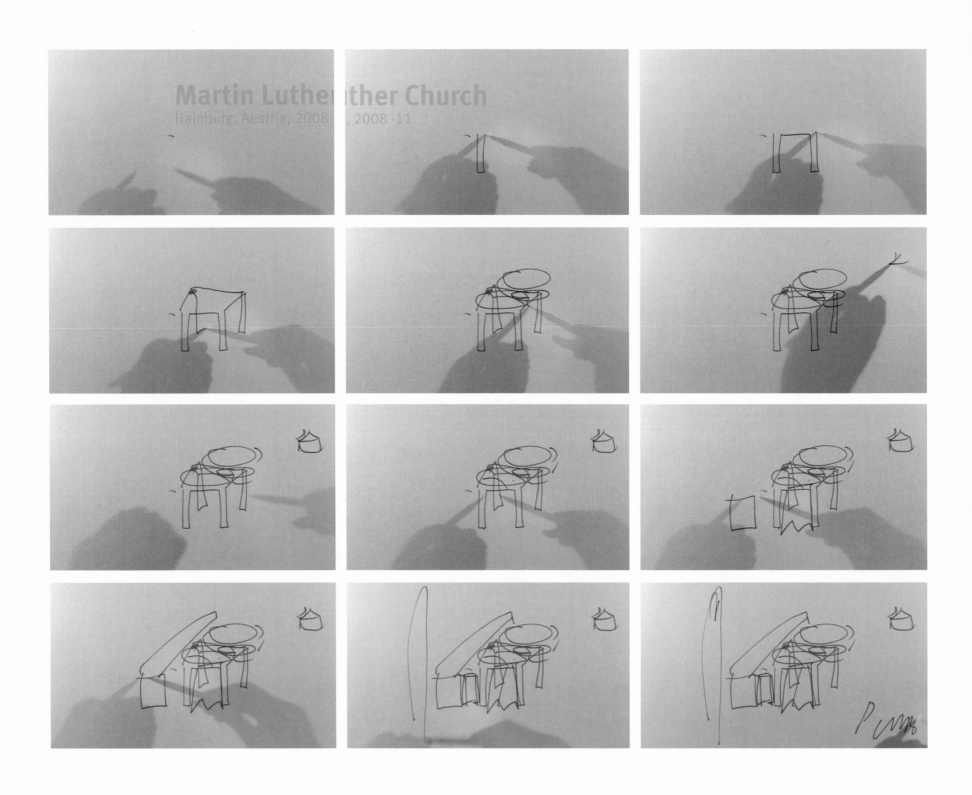

Martin Luther Church
Hainburg, Austria, 2008 ..., 2008 -11

**Martin Luther Church
Hainburg, Austria**
Marker on bond paper
29.7 x 21 cm
Sketch: 2008
Building: 2011
Wolf D. Prix

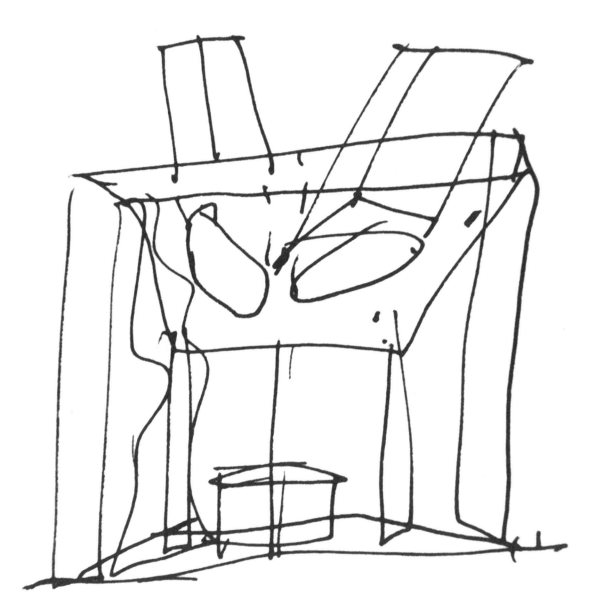

**Martin Luther Church
Hainburg, Austria**
Marker on bond paper
60 x 30 cm
Sketch: 2012
Building: 2011
Wolf D. Prix

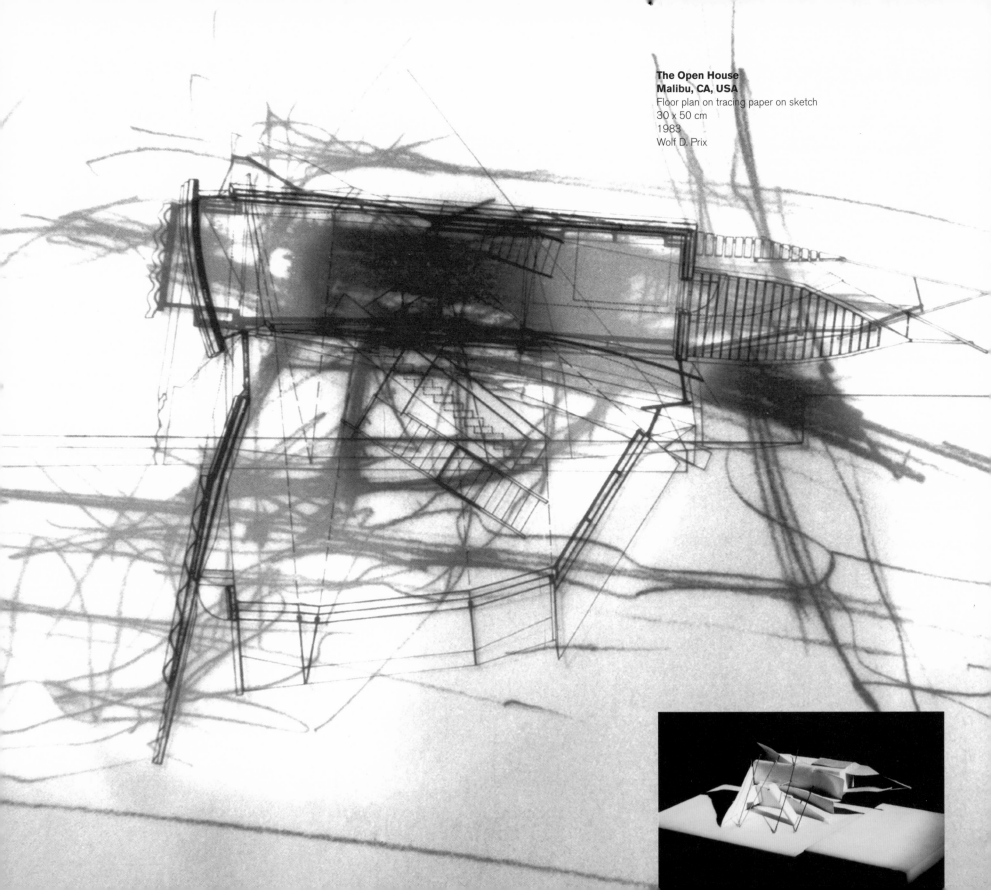

The Open House
Malibu, CA, USA
Floor plan on tracing paper on sketch
30 x 50 cm
1983
Wolf D. Prix

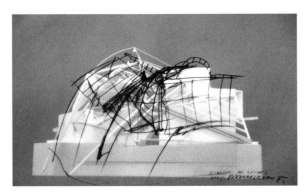

**Rooftop Remodeling Falkestraße
Vienna, Austria**
Concept sketch on model photo
1984
Wolf D. Prix

**Rooftop Remodeling Falkestraße
Vienna, Austria**
Pencil on tracing paper
50 x 60 cm
1984
Wolf D. Prix

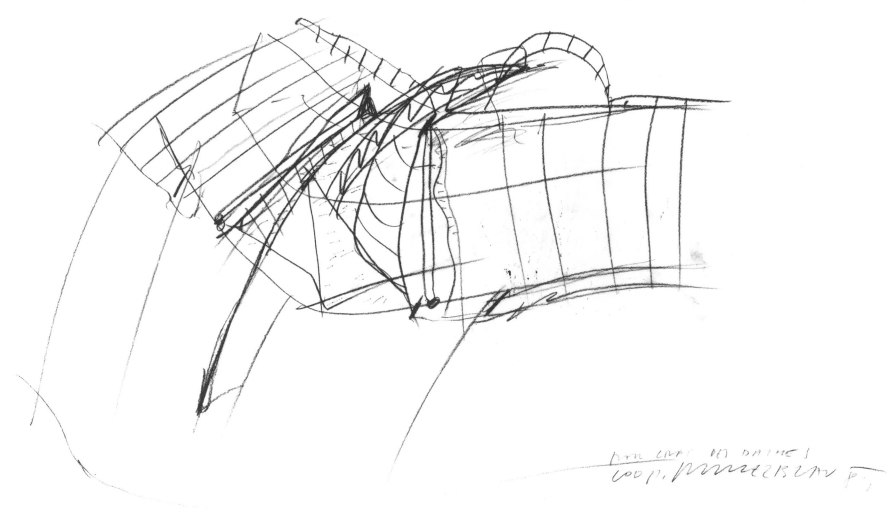

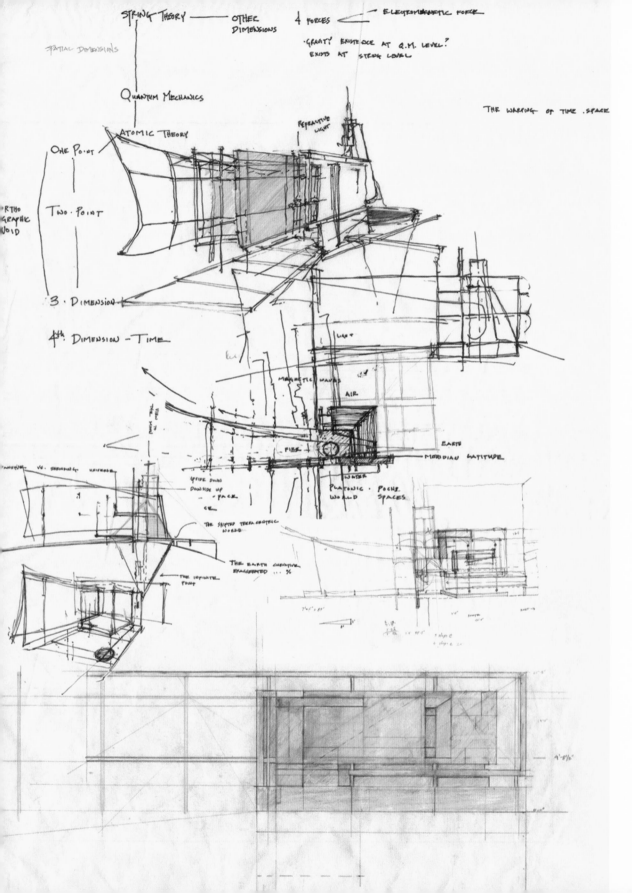

STEVE QUEVEDO

Steve Quevedo (born in Dallas, TX, USA, 1962) received his Bachelor of Science in Architecture, 1985, and his Master of Architecture, 1989, from the School of Architecture at the University of Texas in Arlington. His professional experience includes working with the following offices: Andrea Clark Brown, HOK International, Ltd., and the Office of Graham Greene, Texas. In 1992, he was one of the founding members of Firm X, Richard B. Ferrier Architecture, Hampton Quevedo King, a small collaborative focusing on institutional, residential, public service and design competitions. Quevedo's drawings have received several awards in the Ken Roberts Delineation Competition. Steve Quevedo is an Associate Professor of Architecture at UTA, where he teaches basic design and urban design. His research involves the construction of conceptual drawings using hand drawings and digital hybrid methods.

XYZ House of Multiple Dimensions
Shinkenchiku Residential Design Competition
Ink and graphite on yellow tracing paper
20 x 31 cm
2004
Steve Quevedo

Convergence Space:
XYZ House of Multiple Dimensions
Shinkenchiku Residential Design Competition
Ink, chalk pastel and acrylic on mylar
43 x 61 cm
2004
Steve Quevedo

Level Two +12"-0"
Convergence of the Solitude World

Level One + 0'- 0"
Convergence of the Real World

Lower Level - 12'- 0"
Convergence of the Virtual World

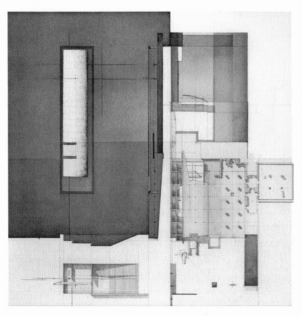 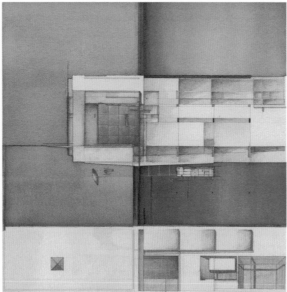 

Enigmatic Constructions
Graphite and watercolor
on 300lbs Arches
56 x 84 cm
2005
Steve Quevedo

Paradise Bridge
Phoenix, AZ, USA
Graphite and watercolor on 300 lbs Arches
20 x 20 cm
1997
Steve Quevedo

Monument to the Moon
Graphite on strathmore paper
43 x 61 cm
2012
Steve Quevedo

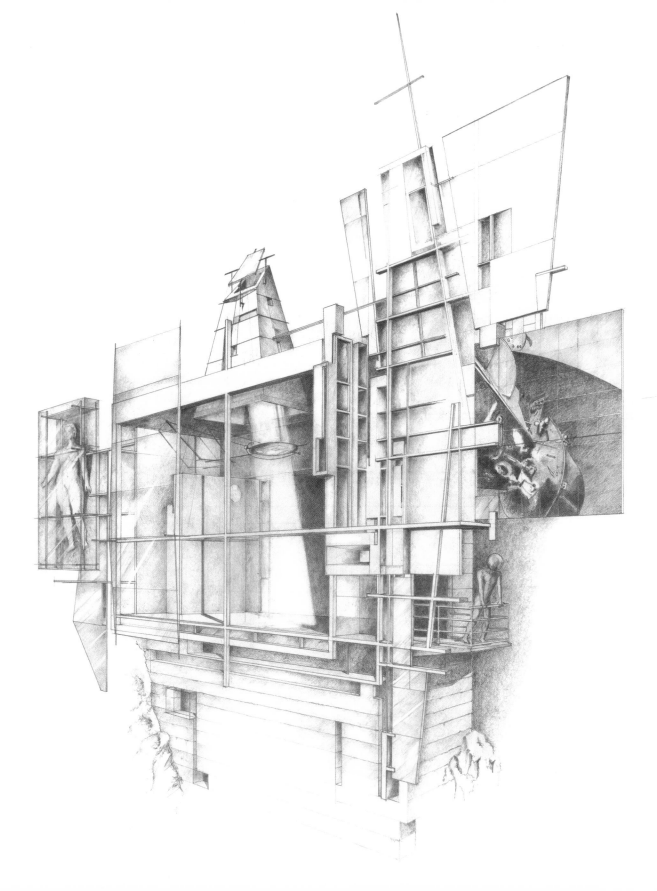

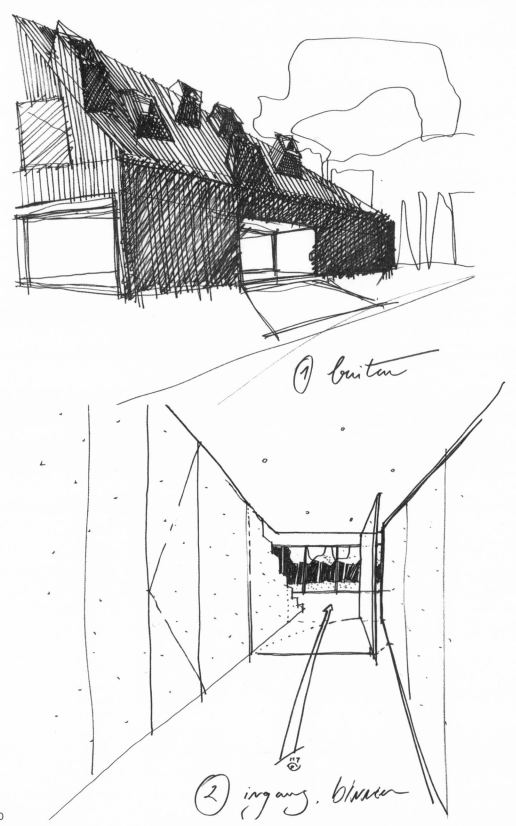

① buiten

② ingang, binnen

ANA ROCHA

Ana Rocha (born in Portugal, 1972) graduated from the Faculty of Architecture at Porto University in 1996. She worked for Mecanoo architecten from 1996–2004 and later at Döll Atelier voor Bouwkunst, Rotterdam. She founded Rocha Tombal architecten, together with Michel Tombal in 2006. Their projects focus on the role of light in architecture; how light can be guided into narrow dark spaces. House Ijburg, for example, is a house of contrasts; a light-route has been created behind the closed façade and the contrast between the light-filled ground floor and darker stairwells becomes a design element in itself.

House Bierings
Utrecht, The Netherlands
Ink on paper
30 x 20 cm
2007
Ana Rocha

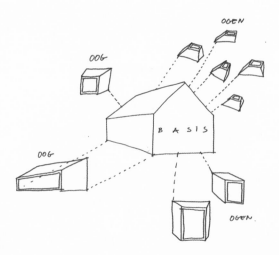

300

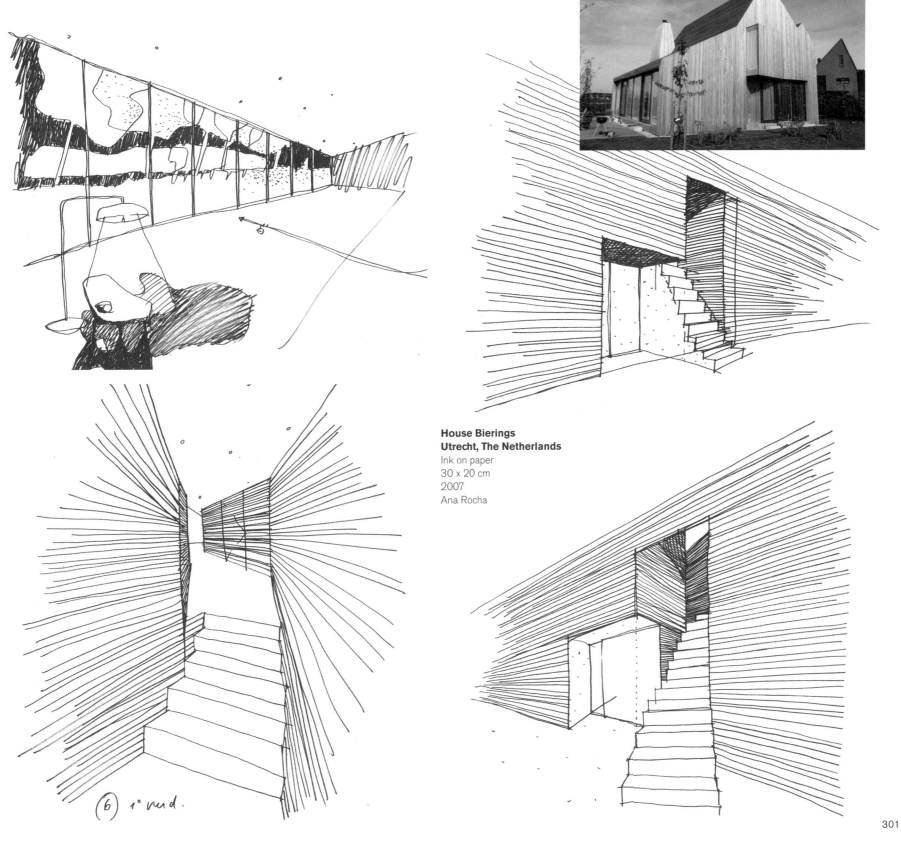

House Bierings
Utrecht, The Netherlands
Ink on paper
30 x 20 cm
2007
Ana Rocha

301

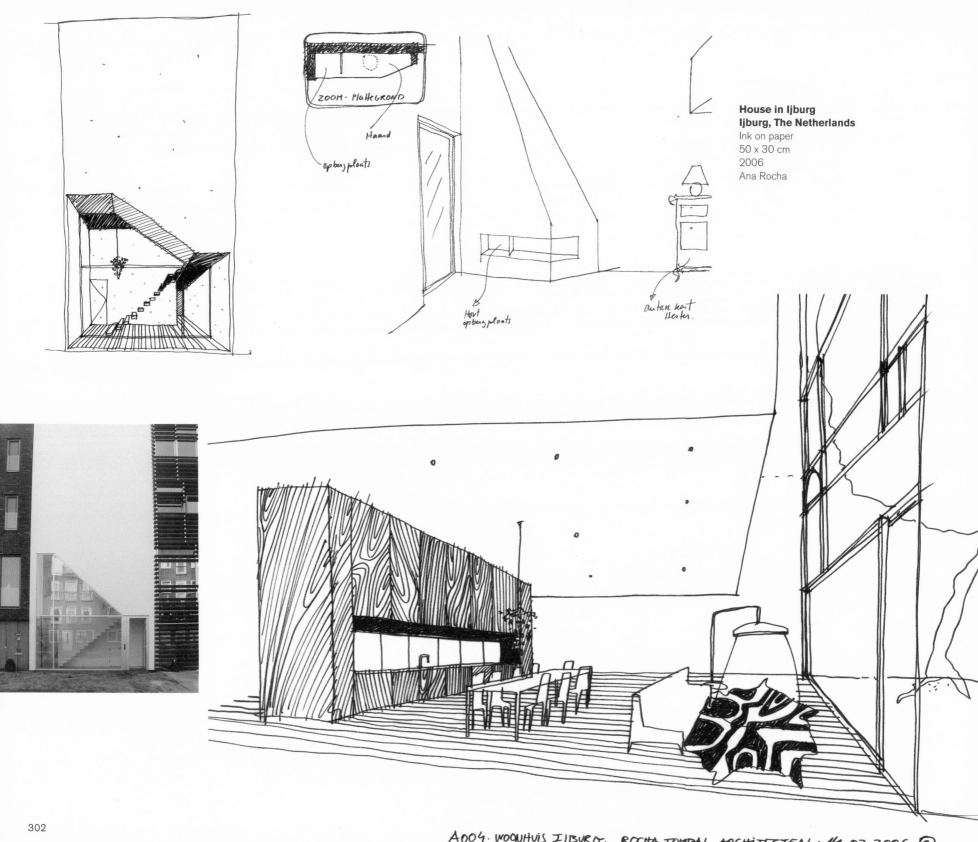

House in Ijburg
Ijburg, The Netherlands
Ink on paper
50 x 30 cm
2006
Ana Rocha

ZOOM - PlatteGROND

Haard

opbergplaats

Hout opbergplaats

antien hait Hester.

AOO4. WOONHUIS IJBURO. ROCHA TOMBAL ARCHITECTEN · 14·03·2006 ©

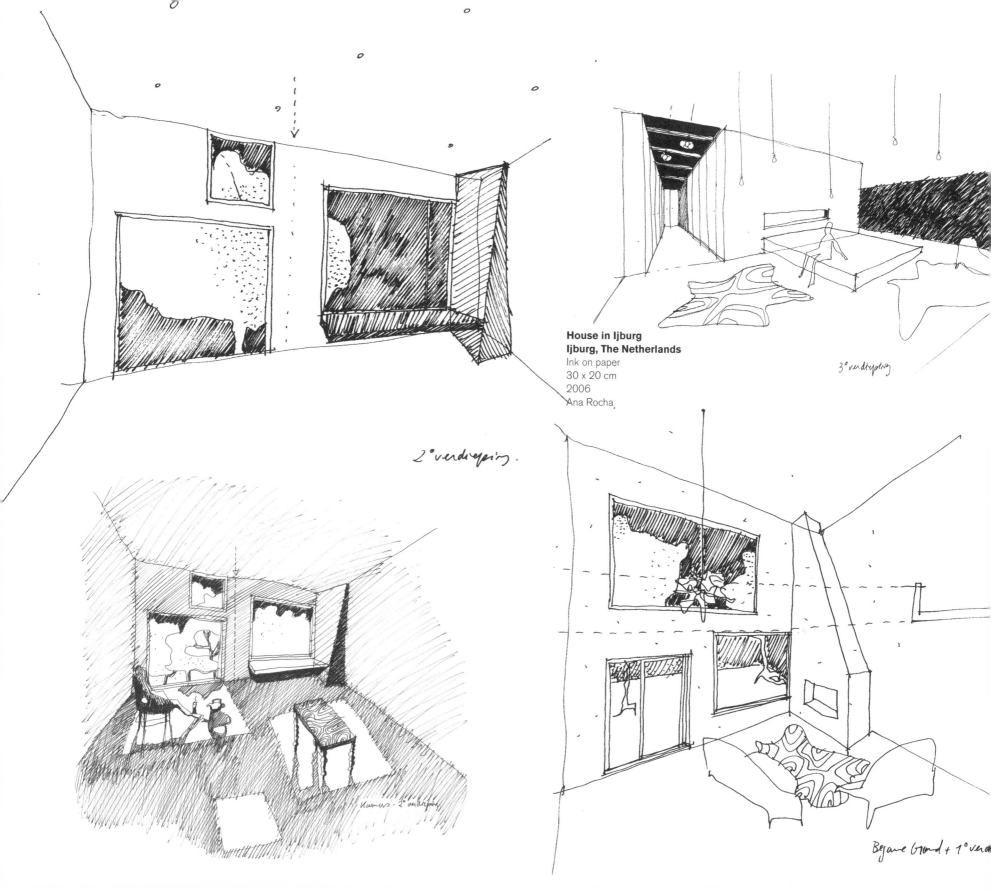

House in Ijburg
Ijburg, The Netherlands
Ink on paper
30 x 20 cm
2006
Ana Rocha

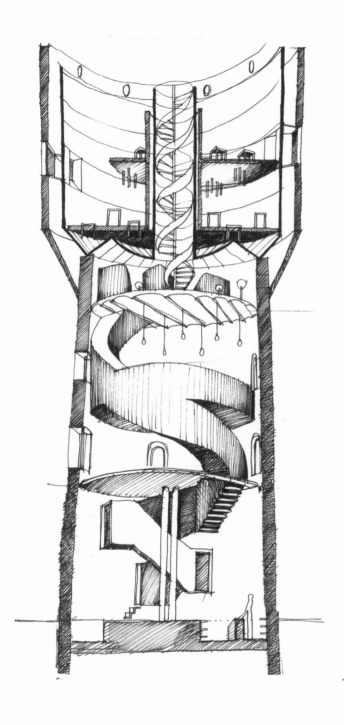

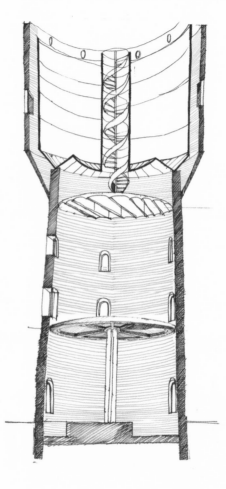

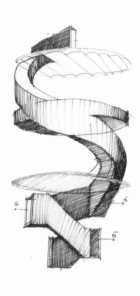

Water Tower
Delft, The Netherlands
Ink on paper
50 x 20 cm
2007
Ana Rocha

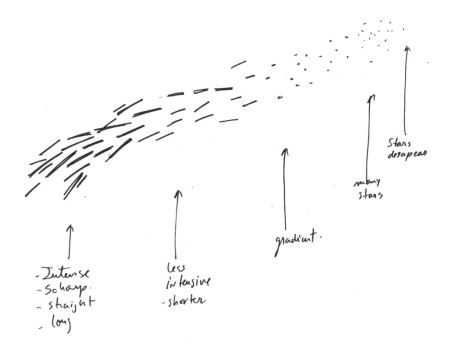

↑
- Intense
- scharp.
- straight
- long

↑
less
intensive
- shorter

↑
gradient.

↑
many
stars

↑
Stars
desapear

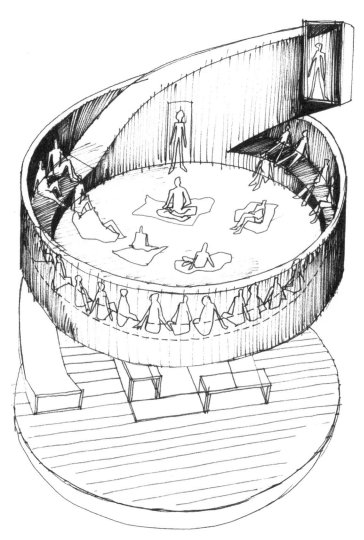

Water Tower
Delft, The Netherlands
Ink on paper
35 x 50 cm
2007
Ana Rocha

Water toru · cursuszalu

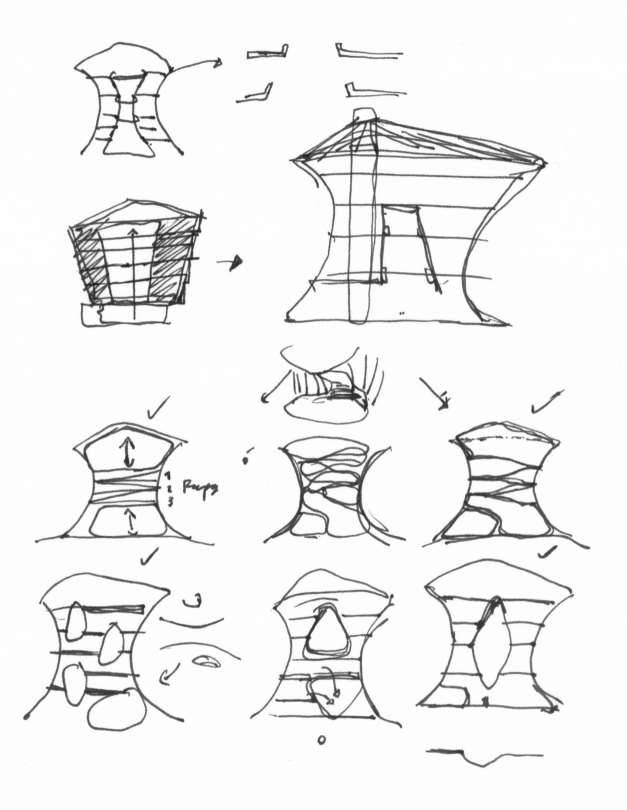

FERNANDO ROMERO

Fernando Romero (born in Mexico, 1971) is a Mexican architect and founder of FREE. The company's ambition is to use design to translate conditions into sustainable solutions based on economic viability as well as social and environmental integrity. Romero worked with Rem Koolhaas in Rotterdam where he was main designer of the Casa da Música project. His approach to architecture has been influenced by a strong focus on research and innovation, giving him insight into related topics such as urbanization, climate change, social housing and visual arts. As an acknowledgment of his contribution to contemporary architecture, Fernando Romero has received various awards, including the Global Leader of Tomorrow Award at the World Economic Forum (2002). In 2010 he opened his New York City office for international operations.

The Soumaya Museum
Mexico City, Mexico
Pencil on paper
Sketch: 2013
Building: 2011
Fernando Romero

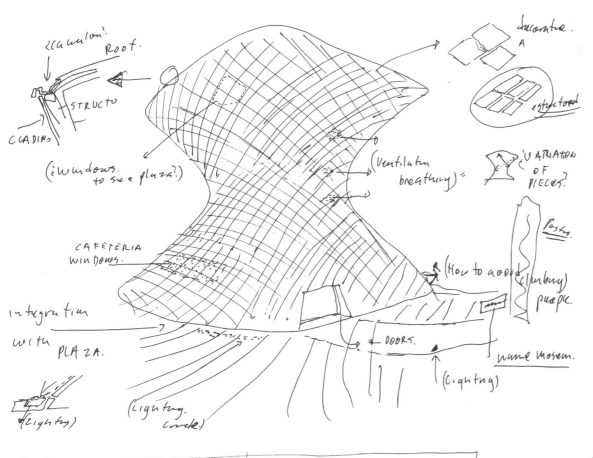

The Soumaya Museum
Mexico City, Mexico
Pencil on paper
Sketch: 2013
Building: 2011
Fernando Romero

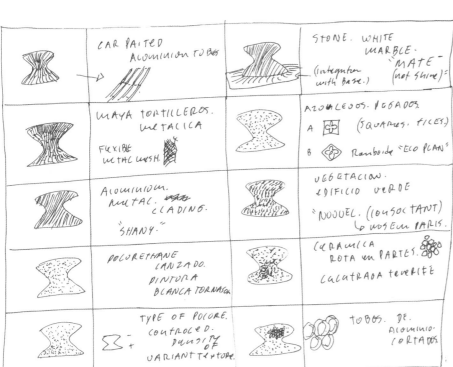

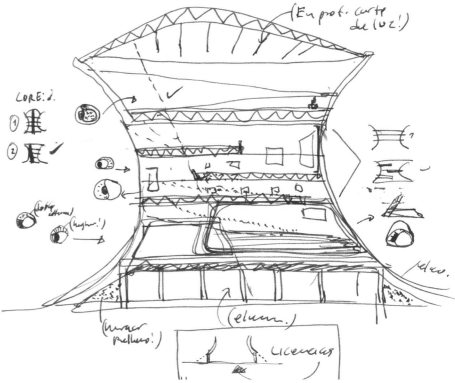

Mortuary Houses
Beja, Portugal
Ballpoint pen
21 x 29.7 cm
2007
João Santa-Rita

JOÃO SANTA-RITA

João Santa-Rita (born in Lisbon, Portugal, 1960) graduated from Lisbon's Superior School of Fine Arts in 1983.
He founded his own office, Santa-Rita Arquitectos,
together with José D. Santa-Rita in 1990. He was elected
vice president of the Portuguese Architects' Chamber from
2011–2013 and has taught at a number of universities,
including; Autónoma University; the Superior School of
Theater and Cinema; and the School of Art and Design in
Lisbon. His work has been presented in a number of solo
exhibitions and in 2010 he participated in an exhibition
of architectural drawings at La Galerie D'Architecture in
Paris. He was nominated for the Mies van der Rohe prize
in 2012.

Mortuary Houses
Beja, Portugal
Ballpoint pen
21 x 29.7 cm
2007
João Santa-Rita

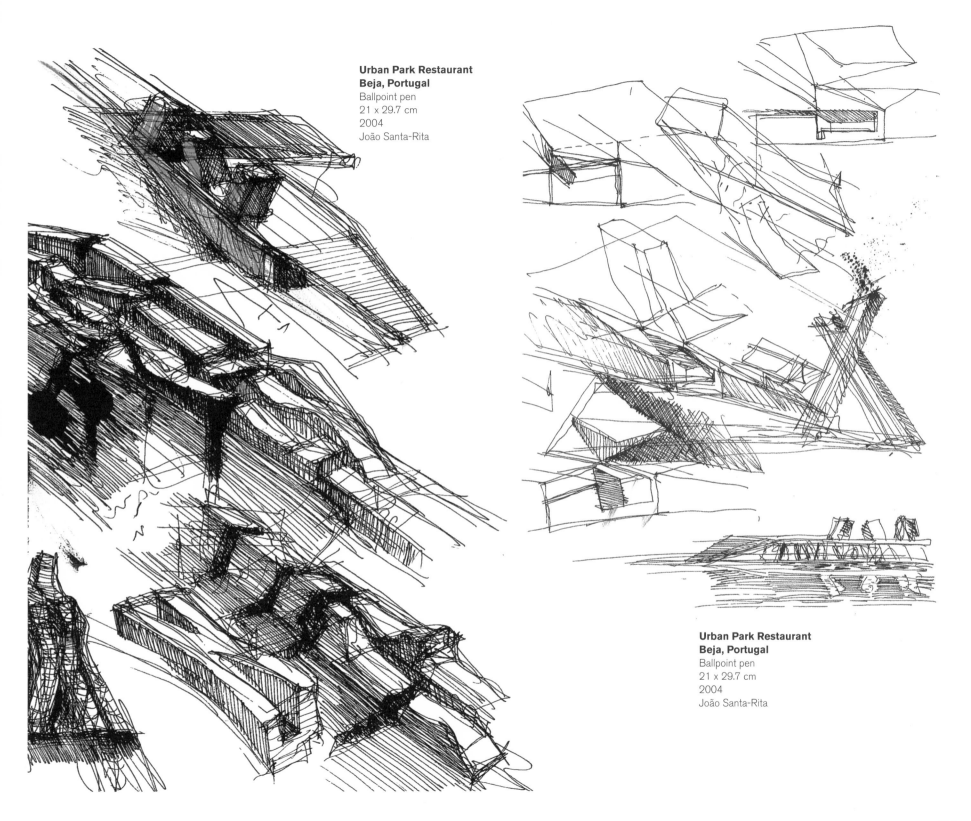

Urban Park Restaurant
Beja, Portugal
Ballpoint pen
21 x 29.7 cm
2004
João Santa-Rita

Urban Park Restaurant
Beja, Portugal
Ballpoint pen
21 x 29.7 cm
2004
João Santa-Rita

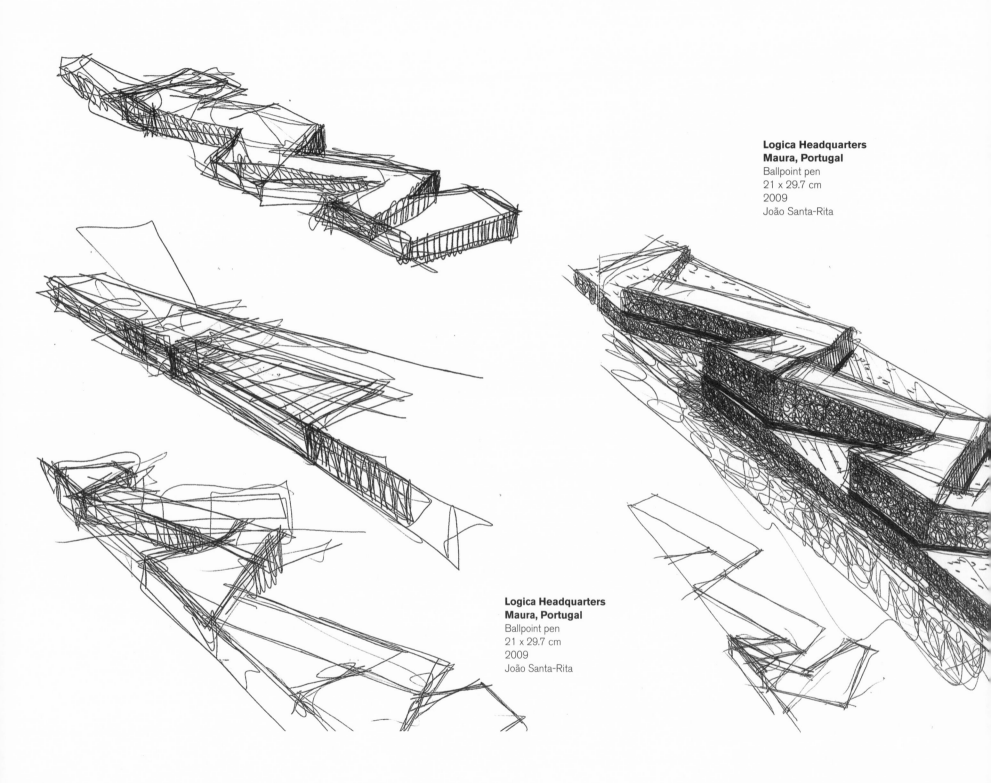

**Logica Headquarters
Maura, Portugal**
Ballpoint pen
21 x 29.7 cm
2009
João Santa-Rita

**Logica Headquarters
Maura, Portugal**
Ballpoint pen
21 x 29.7 cm
2009
João Santa-Rita

Rotunda Subway Station
Lisbon, Portugal
Ballpoint pen
21 x 29.7 cm
1995
João Santa-Rita

Rotunda Subway Station
Lisbon, Portugal
Ballpoint pen
21 x 29.7 cm
1995
João Santa-Rita

311

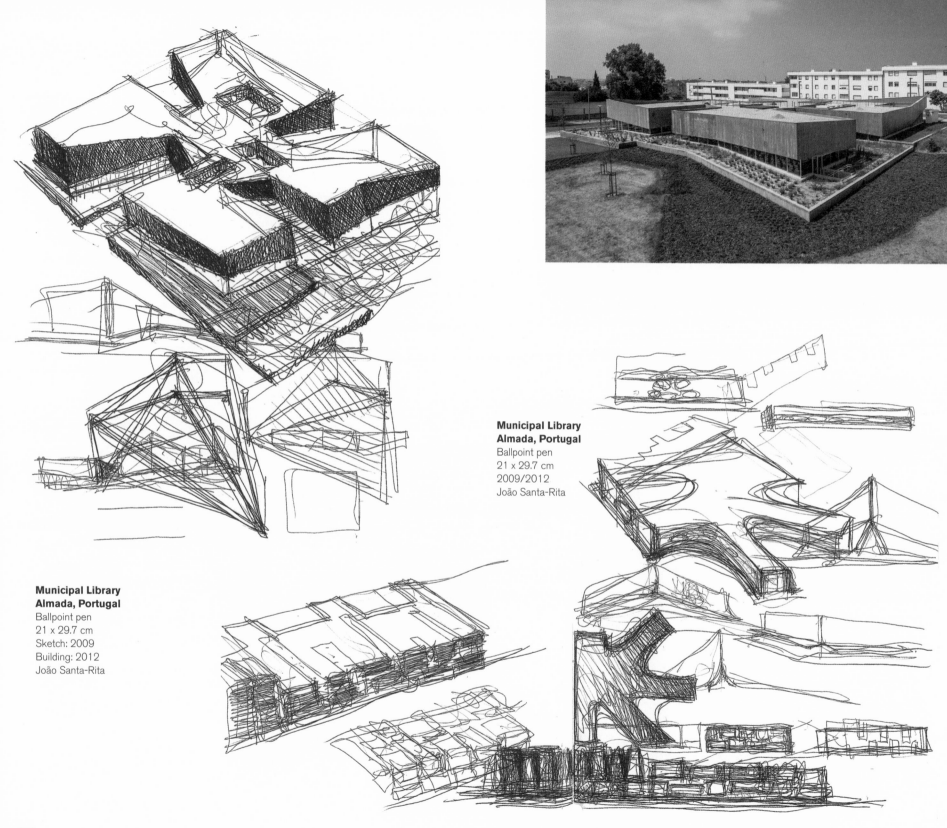

**Municipal Library
Almada, Portugal**
Ballpoint pen
21 x 29.7 cm
2009/2012
João Santa-Rita

**Municipal Library
Almada, Portugal**
Ballpoint pen
21 x 29.7 cm
Sketch: 2009
Building: 2012
João Santa-Rita

312

Exhibition Post It
Lisbon, Portugal
Ballpoint pen
21 x 29.7 cm
2012
João Santa-Rita

Exhibition Post It
Lisbon, Portugal
Ballpoint pen
21 x 29.7 cm
2012
João Santa-Rita

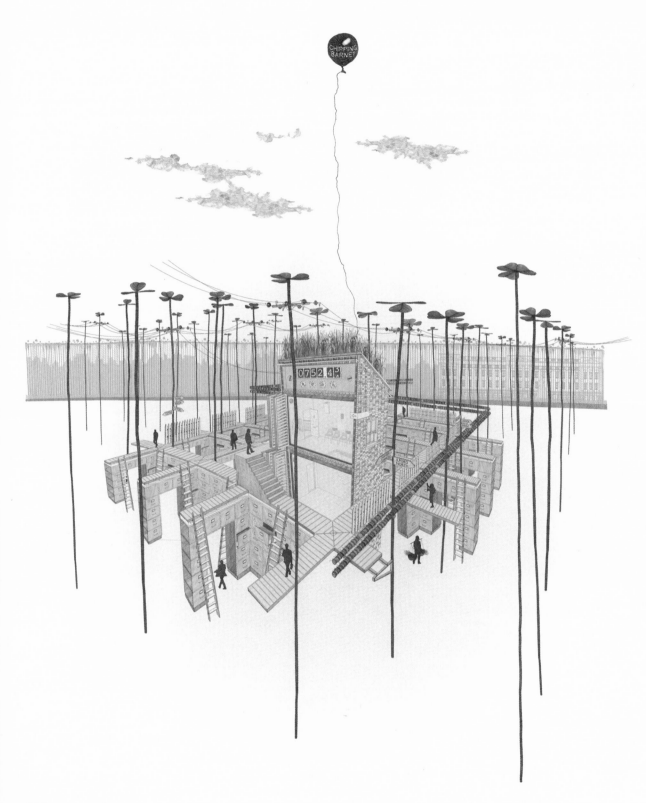

NED SCOTT

Ned Scott (born in London, United Kingdom, 1985) graduated from The Bartlett, UCL in 2012, receiving his MArch in Architecture with distinction. He works for London-based architecture studio We Made That. He is also the co-founder of the Warsaw Summer School, a tutor at The Bartlett Summer School and a member of the London-based architecture collective ADA. Ned Scott's work has been internationally published and exhibited and is primarily concerned with the interpretation of cultural, social and environmental program and narratives to challenge and re-imagine the function and utility of certain aspects of cities.

**The MP's House for
Chipping Barnet**
Pencil on paper
70 x 100 cm
2012
Ned Scott

Aerial Perspective
Pencil on paper
70 x 100 cm
2012
Ned Scott

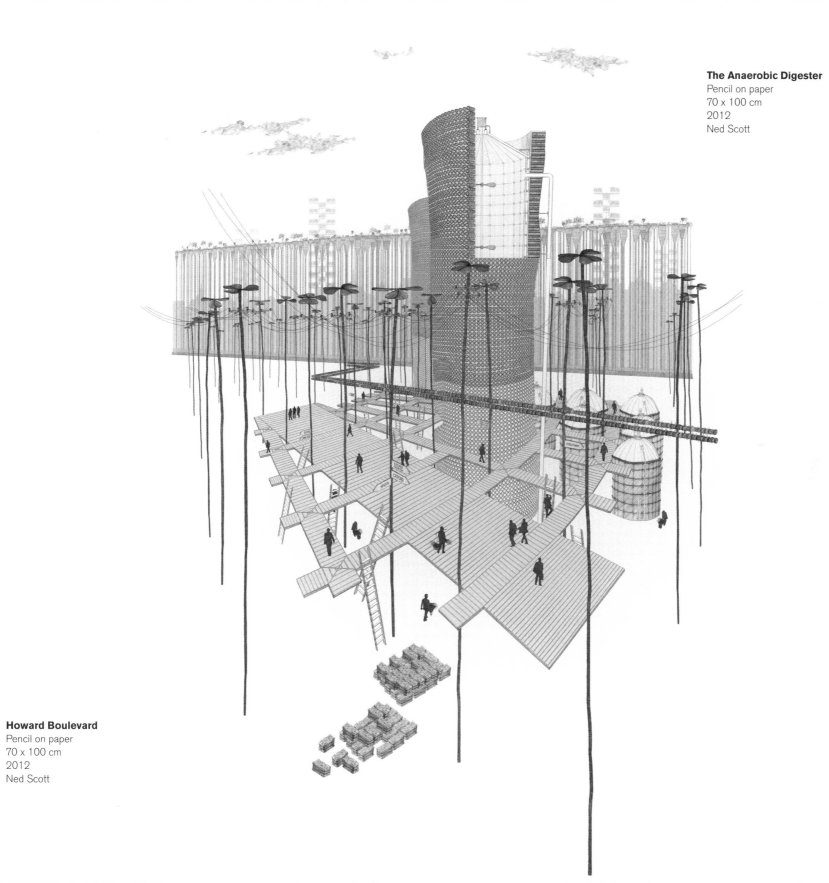

The Anaerobic Digester
Pencil on paper
70 x 100 cm
2012
Ned Scott

Howard Boulevard
Pencil on paper
70 x 100 cm
2012
Ned Scott

The Energy Crop Tower
Pencil on paper
70 x 100 cm
2012
Ned Scott

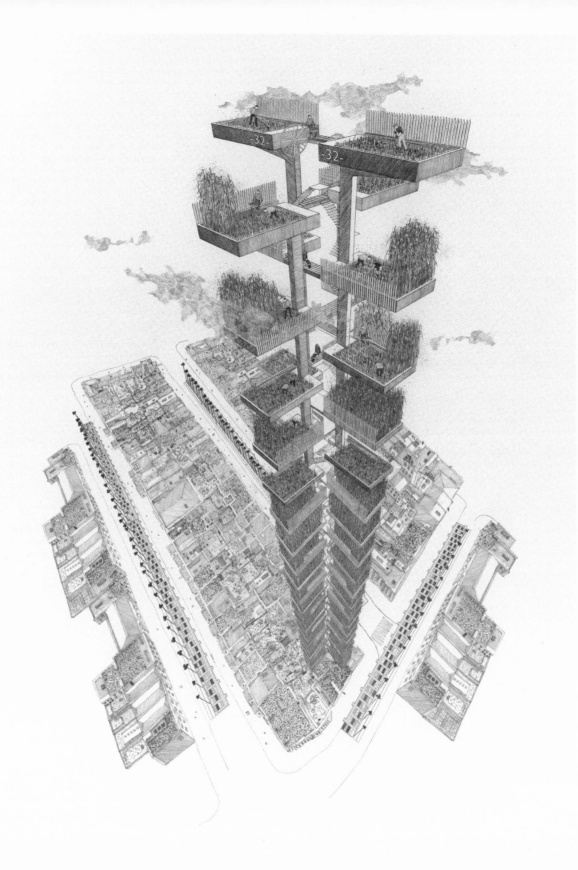

The Instrument
Pencil on paper
70 x 100 cm
2012
Ned Scott

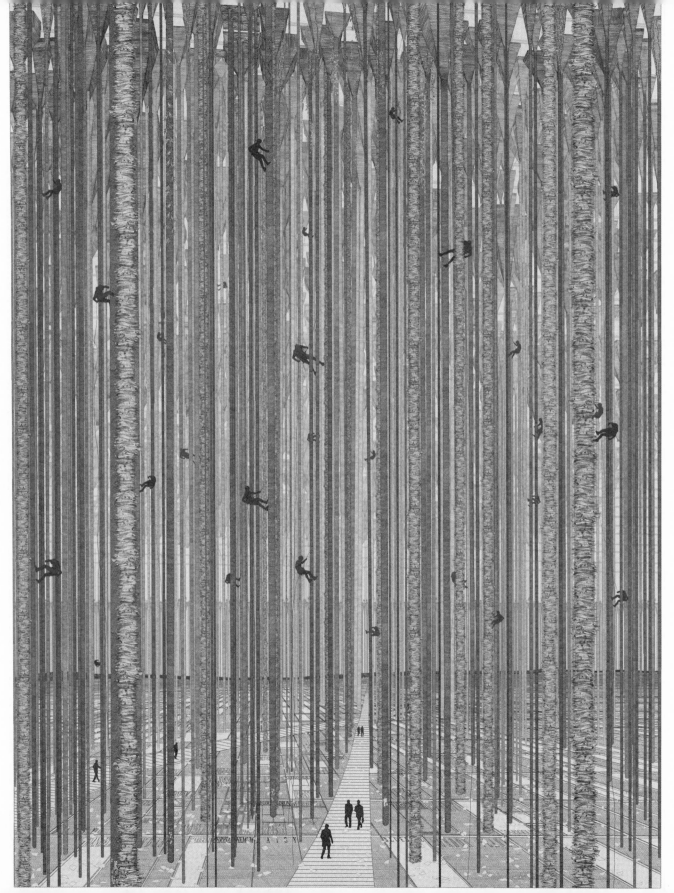

The New St. James's Park
Pencil on paper
70 x 100 cm
2012
Ned Scott

The Smart Grid
Pencil on paper
70 x 100 cm
2012
Ned Scott

321

THOMAS GORDON SMITH

Thomas Gordon Smith (born in Oakland, CA, USA, 1948) is a professor of architecture at the University of Notre Dame in Indiana and a practicing architect. He received his Bachelor of Arts and Master of Architecture from the University of California, Berkeley. He won the Rome Prize at the American Academy in Rome for 1979–80. His façade and architectural designs contributed to the Strada Novissima Venice Biennale exhibition, The Presence of the Past, in 1980. His books include Classical Architecture: Rule and Invention and Vitruvius on Architecture. His professional projects include Annunciation Abbey, Guadalupe Seminary, university buildings in California, Indiana, and Wyoming; museums in New York and Indiana, and private residences in five states.

**Watercolor of Vitruvian Man and
Eustylos Portico
South Bend, IN, USA**
Watercolor
61 x 86 cm
2000
Thomas Gordon Smith

House in Wisconsin
WI, USA
Watercolor and pencil
43 cm x 59
2001
Thomas Gordon Smith

Our Lady of Guadalupe Seminary
Denton, NE, USA
Watercolor and pencil
54 x 70 cm
1999
Thomas Gordon Smith

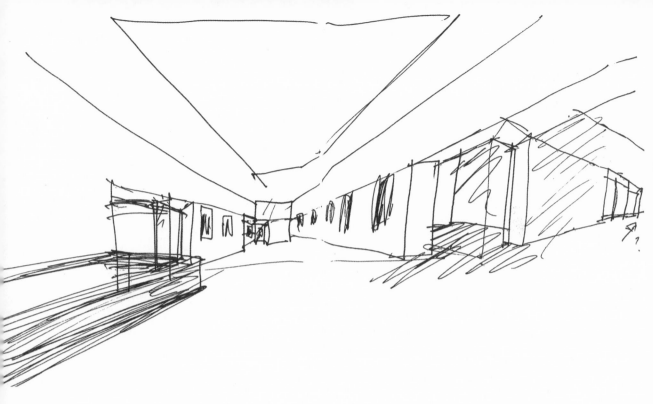

EDUARDO SOUTO DE MOURA

Eduardo Souto de Moura (born in Porto, Portugal, 1952) graduated from the School of Architecture of Oporto (ESBAP) in 1980. He then worked as assistant professor at the Faculty of Architecture of Oporto (FAUP) from 1981 to 1991. He also worked with Noé Dinis in 1974, Álvaro Siza between 1975 and 1979, and with Fernandes de Sá. He founded his own company, Souto Moura Arquitectos, in 1980. He was employed as a guest professor at various prestigious universities, including Paris-Belleville, Harvard, Dublin, Zurich and Lausanne and has received many awards for his work, including; the FAD Award "Ciutat i Paisatge" for the Project "Metro do Porto", the Secil Award 2010 for the "Paula Rego Museum" in Lisbon and the Wolf Prize. Recent projects include the winery in Valpaços, Portugal, 2010; and the La Berge du Lac residential buildings in Bordeaux, France.

**Museu Paula Rego
Cascais, Portugal**
Black pen on paper
29.7 x 21 cm
Sketch: 2006
Building: 2008
Eduardo Souto de Moura

Museu Paula Rego
Cascais, Portugal
29.7 x 21 cm
Sketch: 2006
Building: 2008
Eduardo Souto de Moura

327

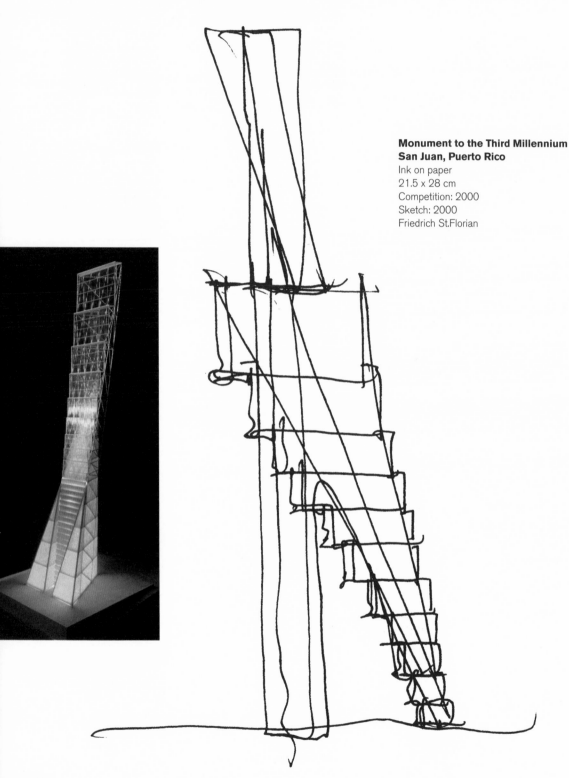

FRIEDRICH ST.FLORIAN

**Monument to the Third Millennium
San Juan, Puerto Rico**
Ink on paper
21.5 x 28 cm
Competition: 2000
Sketch: 2000
Friedrich St.Florian

Friedrich St.Florian (born in Graz, Austria, 1932) belonged to a group of young architects during the 1960s and 1970s whose search for a new architecture was fueled by their fascination with new technologies and new materials. St.Florian never insists on applying the same approach twice. There are, however continuing themes in his work, such as the careful use of light, a developed sense of spatial composition, a responsible understanding of materials, scale and proportions. For the past 42 years, St.Florian has worked as Professor of Architecture at the Rhode Island School of Design. He served as Dean of Architectural Studies for eight years and Chief Critic of the European Honors Program in Rome for four years. St.Florian has won numerous awards for his achievements in the field of architecture and his visionary drawings are in the permanent collection of the Museum of Modern Art in New York City and the Centre Georges Pompidou in Paris. He is a fellow of the American Academy in Rome and a fellow of the American Institute of Architects.

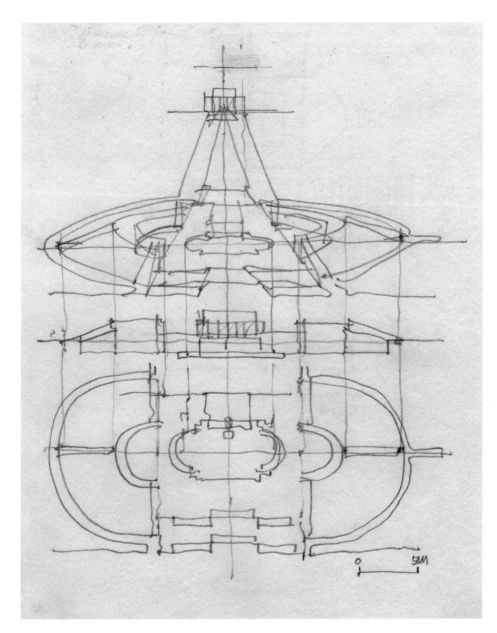

World War II Memorial
Washington, DC, USA
Competition Winning Design
Pencil on paper
20.5 x 25.5 cm
1996
Friedrich St.Florian

St.Florian House
Providence, RI, USA
Pencil on Paper
21.5 x 28 cm
1998
Friedrich St.Florian

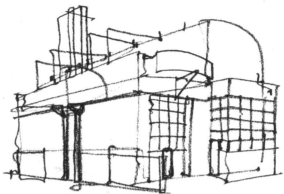

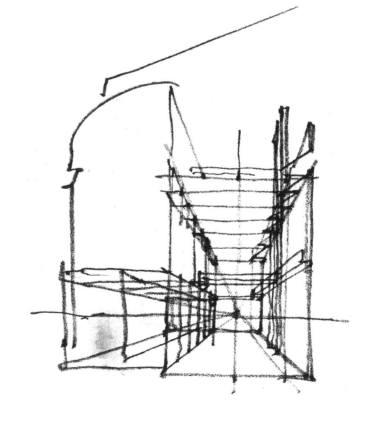

Bunde Fire Station
Bunde, Germany
Sketch ink on smooth white paper
21.6 x 27.9 cm
Building: 2001
Randall Stout/Randall Stout Architects, Inc.

RANDALL STOUT

Randall Stout, FAIA, (born in Knoxville, TN, USA) received his Masters of Architecture at Rice University in 1988. He is the president and principal-in-charge of LA-based Randall Stout Architects, Inc. Directing projects worldwide, Stout's design experience includes cultural, civic, educational, commercial, institutional, industrial, recreational, and residential facilities. In addition to his position as president of Randall Stout Architects, Inc. he is professor of Architecture at the University of Nevada, Las Vegas and a Fellow of the American Institute of Architects.

Bunde Fire Station
Bunde, Germany
Sketch ink on smooth white paper
21.6 x 27.9 cm
Building: 2001
Randall Stout/Randall Stout Architects, Inc.

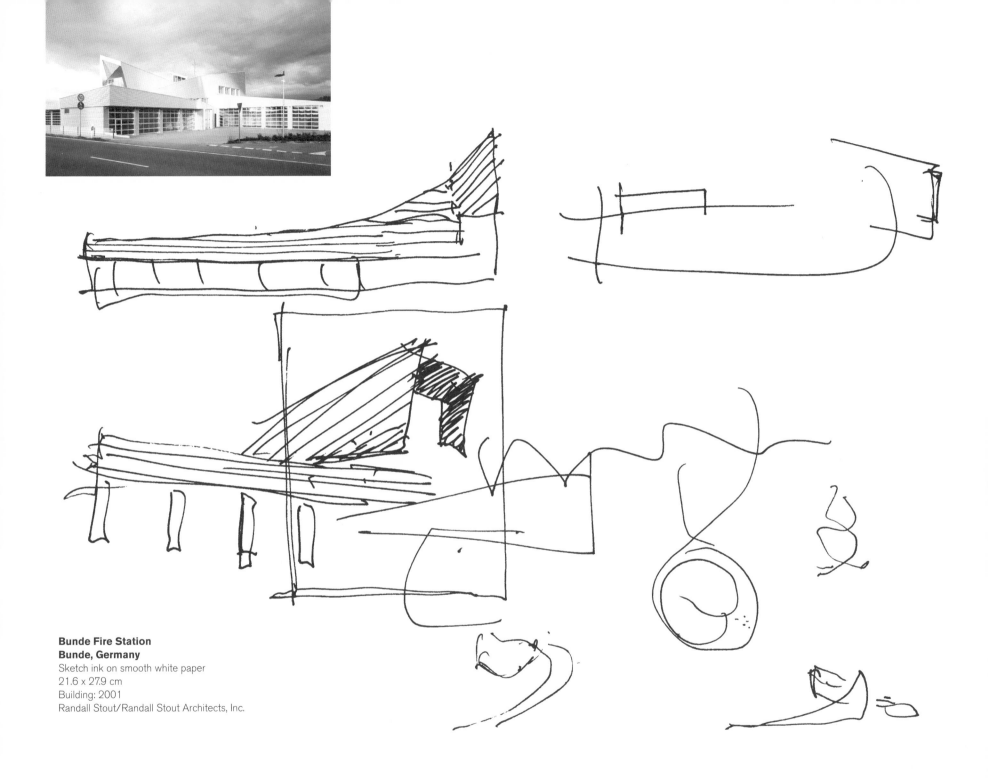

Bunde Fire Station
Bunde, Germany
Sketch ink on smooth white paper
21.6 x 27.9 cm
Building: 2001
Randall Stout/Randall Stout Architects, Inc.

**Art Gallery of Alberta Edmonton
Alberta, Canada**
Ink on smooth white paper
21.6 x 27.9 cm
Building: 2010
Randall Stout/Randall Stout Architects, Inc.

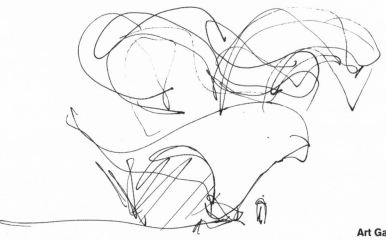

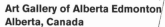

**Art Gallery of Alberta Edmonton
Alberta, Canada**
Ink on acid free 140lb coldpress watercolor paper
22.9 x 30.5 cm
Sketch: 2006
Building: 2010
Randall Stout/Randall Stout Architects, Inc.

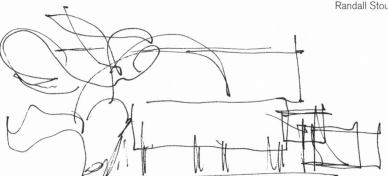

**Art Gallery of Alberta Edmonton
Alberta, Canada**
Ink on smooth white paper
21.6 x 27.9 cm
Building: 2010
Randall Stout/ Randall Stout Architects, Inc.

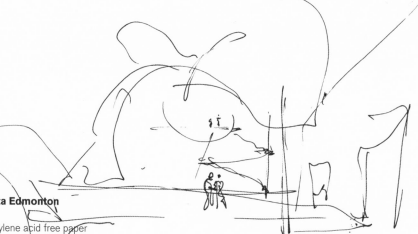

**Art Gallery of Alberta Edmonton
Alberta, Canada**
Ink on 100% polypropylene acid free paper
27.9 x 36.6 cm
Sketch: 2006
Building: 2010
Randall Stout/Randall Stout Architects, Inc.

Steinhude Sea Recreational Facility
Steinhude, Germany
Sketch ink on fine grain white
writing paper
17.8 x 10.5 cm
Building: 2000
Randall Stout/Randall Stout Architects, Inc.

Steinhude Sea Recreational Facility
Steinhude, Germany
Sketch ink on fine grain white
writing paper
35.6 x 21.6 cm
Building: 2000
Randall Stout/Randall Stout Architects, Inc.

Steinhude Sea Recreational Facility
Steinhude, Germany
Sketch ink on tracing paper
66.04 x 60.96 cm
Building: 2000
Randall Stout/Randall Stout Architects, Inc.

Taubman Museum of Art
Roanoke, VA, USA
Sketch ink on 20lb white paper
27.9 x 21.6 cm
Building: 2008
Randall Stout/Randall Stout Architects, Inc.

Taubman Museum of Art
Roanoke, VA, USA
Ink on smooth white paper
36.97 x 28.7 cm
Building: 2008
Randall Stout/Randall Stout Architects, Inc.

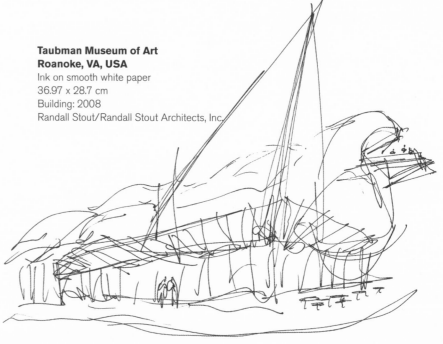

Taubman Museum of Art
Roanoke, VA, USA
Ink on smooth white paper
71.12 x 21.6 cm
Building: 2008
Randall Stout/Randall Stout Architects, Inc.

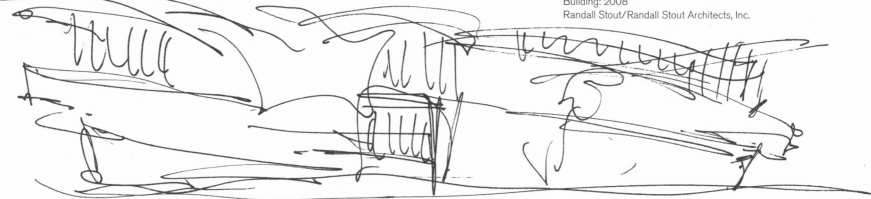

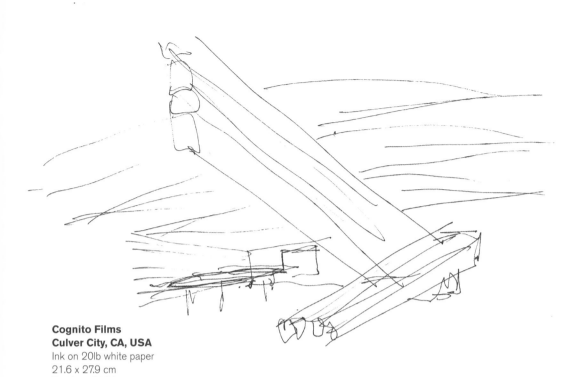

Cognito Films
Culver City, CA, USA
Ink on 20lb white paper
21.6 x 27.9 cm
Building: 2001
Randall Stout/Randall Stout Architects, Inc.

Cognito Films
Culver City, CA, USA
Ink on 20lb white paper
21.6 x 27.9 cm
Building: 2001
Randall Stout/Randall Stout Architects, Inc.

Cognito Films
Culver City, CA, USA
Ink on 20lb white paper
21.6 x 27.9 cm
Building: 2001
Randall Stout/Randall Stout Architects, Inc.

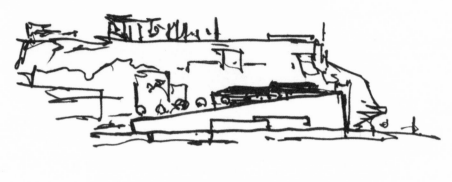

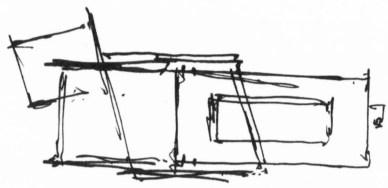

19.5.01

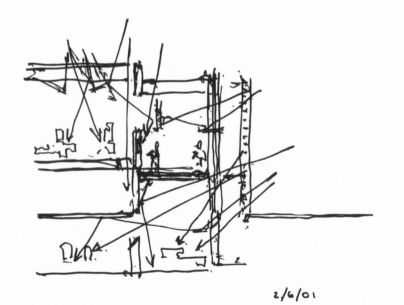

2/6/01

ALEXANDROS TOMBAZIS

Alexandros Tombazis (born in India, 1939) spent his childhood in India, England and Greece. As a child, he first showed a talent for art before turning to architecture. The first oil crisis encouraged him to consider new ways of designing in a sustainable way. He began investigating the possibilities of solar energy and later became a pioneer in bioclimatic design in Greece. Tombazis has always divided his time between his architectural practice, drawing, photography and traveling. He has been awarded prizes in more than 115 architectural competitions. Apart from numerous projects in Greece, he has also worked in Cyprus, Portugal, the Netherlands, the Ukraine, the United Arab Emirates, Oman and China. In 1991 he was elected as an honorary fellow of the American Institute of Architects. In 2006 he received an honorary Doctor of Philosophy (PhD) from the University of Thessaloniki.

**New Acropolis Museum
Athens, Greece**
Felt-tip pen on tracing paper
2001
Alexandros Tombazis

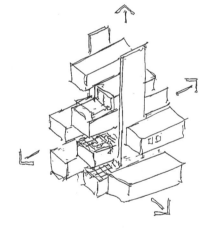

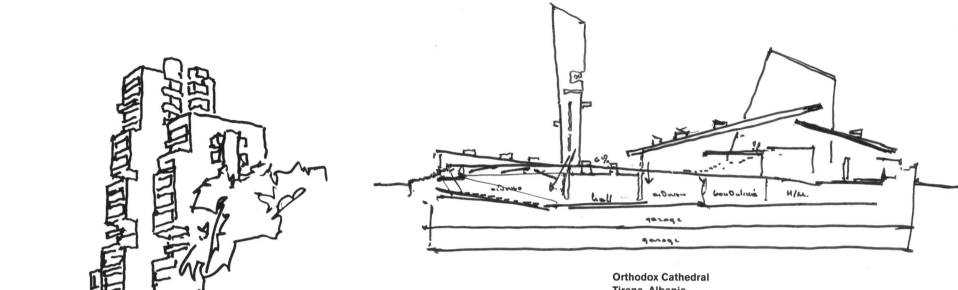

**Orthodox Cathedral
Tirana, Albania**
2001
Alexandros Tombazis

**DIFROS Highrise Residential
Complex
Athens, Greece**
Felt-tip pen on t racing paper
Alexandros Tombazis

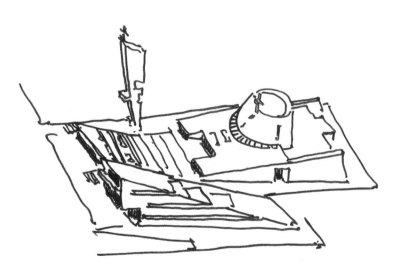

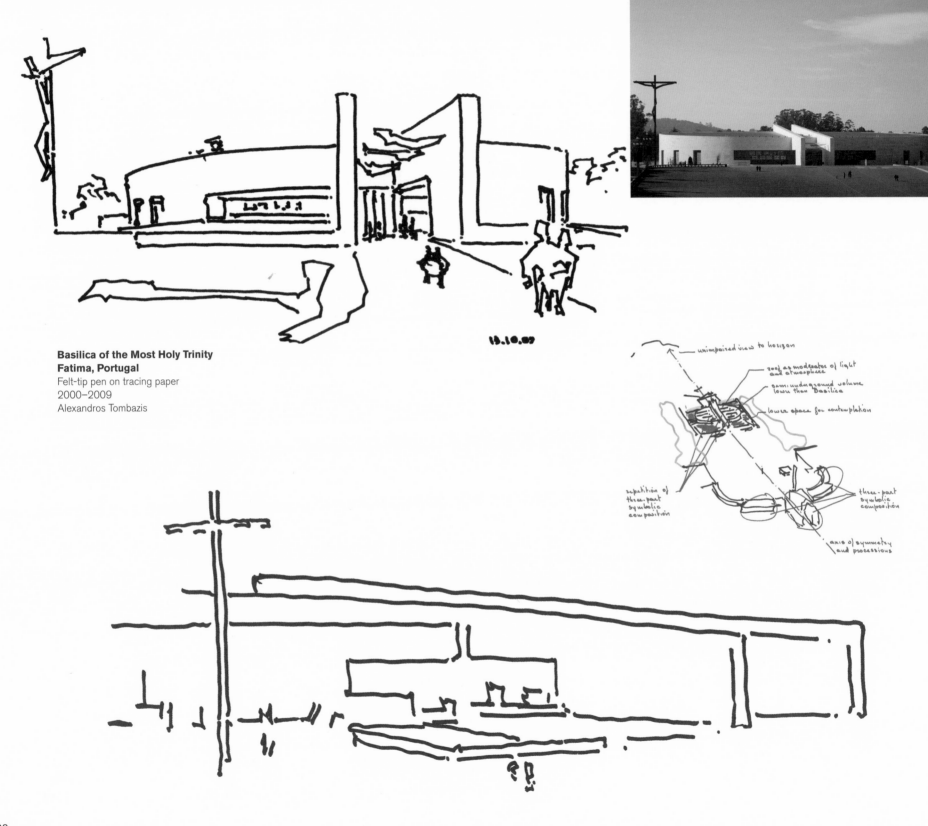

Basilica of the Most Holy Trinity
Fatima, Portugal
Felt-tip pen on tracing paper
2000–2009
Alexandros Tombazis

unimpaired view to horizon

roof as moderator of light
and atmosphere

semi-underground volume
lower than Basilica

lower space for contemplation

repetition of
three-part
symbolic
composition

three-part
symbolic
composition

axis of symmetry
and processions

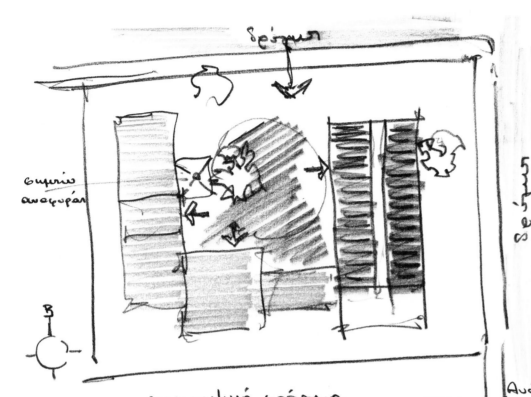

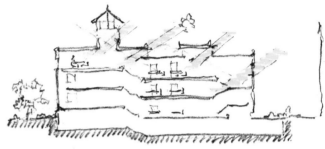

Office Building Complex
Athens, Greece
Felt-tip pen and water marker on paper
1994–1996
Alexandros Tombazis

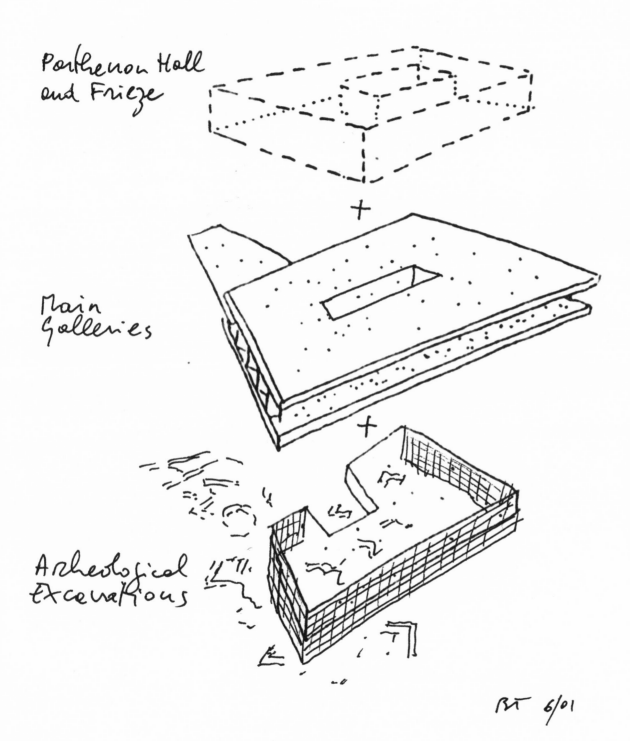

Parthenon Hall
and Frieze

Main
Galleries

Archeological
Excavations

BT 6/01

BERNARD TSCHUMI

Bernard Tschumi (born in Lausanne, Switzerland, 1944) is an architect based in New York City and Paris. First known as a theorist, he exhibited and published The Manhattan Transcripts in 1981 and wrote Architecture and Disjunction, a series of theoretical essays (MIT Press, 1994). In 1983, he won a prestigious competition to design and build the Parc de la Villette in Paris. Since then, he has gained a reputation for producing groundbreaking designs that include the New Acropolis Museum, Le Fresnoy Center for the Contemporary Arts, and the Vacheron-Constantin Corporate Headquarters, amongst others. He served as Dean of the Graduate School of Architecture, Planning and Preservation at Columbia University in New York City from 1988 to 2003.

New Acropolis Museum
Athens, Greece
Ink on paper
14 x 20 cm
Sketch: 2001
Building: 2009
Bernard Tschumi/Bernard Tschumi Architects

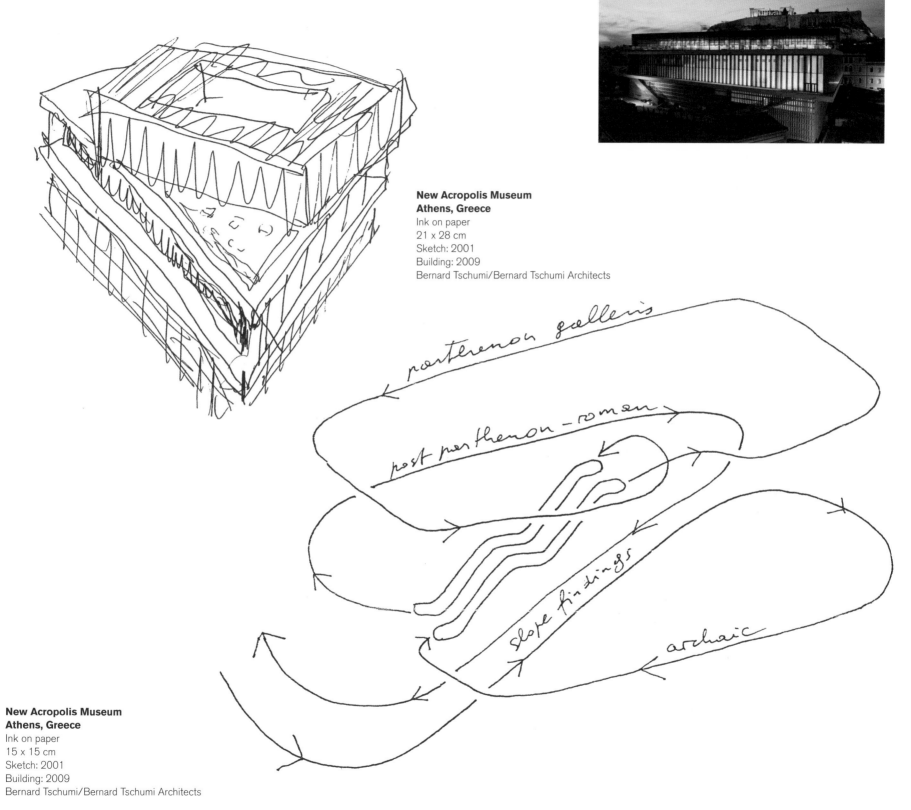

New Acropolis Museum
Athens, Greece
Ink on paper
21 x 28 cm
Sketch: 2001
Building: 2009
Bernard Tschumi/Bernard Tschumi Architects

parthenon galleries

post parthenon – roman

slope findings

archaic

New Acropolis Museum
Athens, Greece
Ink on paper
15 x 15 cm
Sketch: 2001
Building: 2009
Bernard Tschumi/Bernard Tschumi Architects

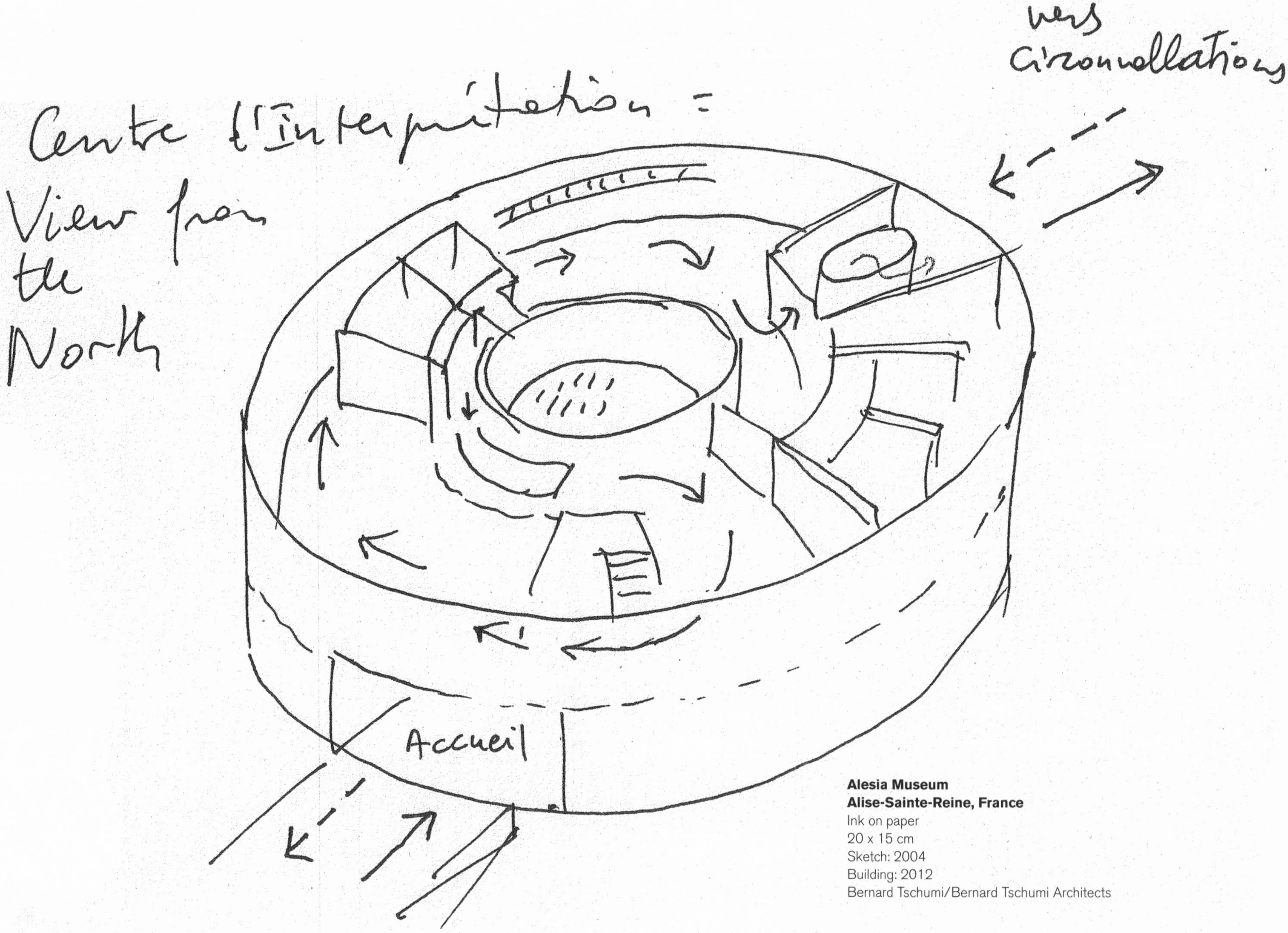

Centre d'Interpretation =
View from the North

vers Circonvallations

Accueil

Alesia Museum
Alise-Sainte-Reine, France
Ink on paper
20 x 15 cm
Sketch: 2004
Building: 2012
Bernard Tschumi/Bernard Tschumi Architects

Alesia Museum
Alise-Sainte-Reine, France
Ink on paper
21 x 28 cm
Sketch: 2004
Building: 2012
Bernard Tschumi/Bernard Tschumi Architects

Alesia Museum
Alise-Sainte-Reine, France
Ink on paper
22 x 19 cm
Sketch: 2004
Building: 2012
Bernard Tschumi/Bernard Tschumi Architects

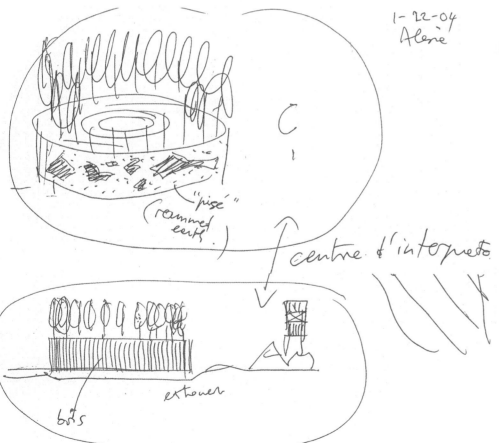

343

the view
from below

22 Nov. 03

The In-between
Beijing 798

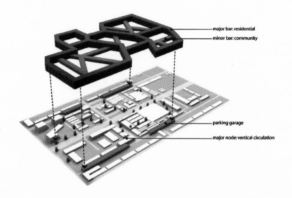

major bar: residential
minor bar: community

parking garage
major node: vertical circulation

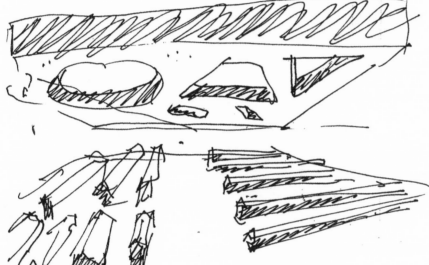

Factory 798
Beijing, China
Ink on paper
21 x 28 cm
Sketch: 2003
Building: 2004
Bernard Tschumi/Bernard Tschumi Architects

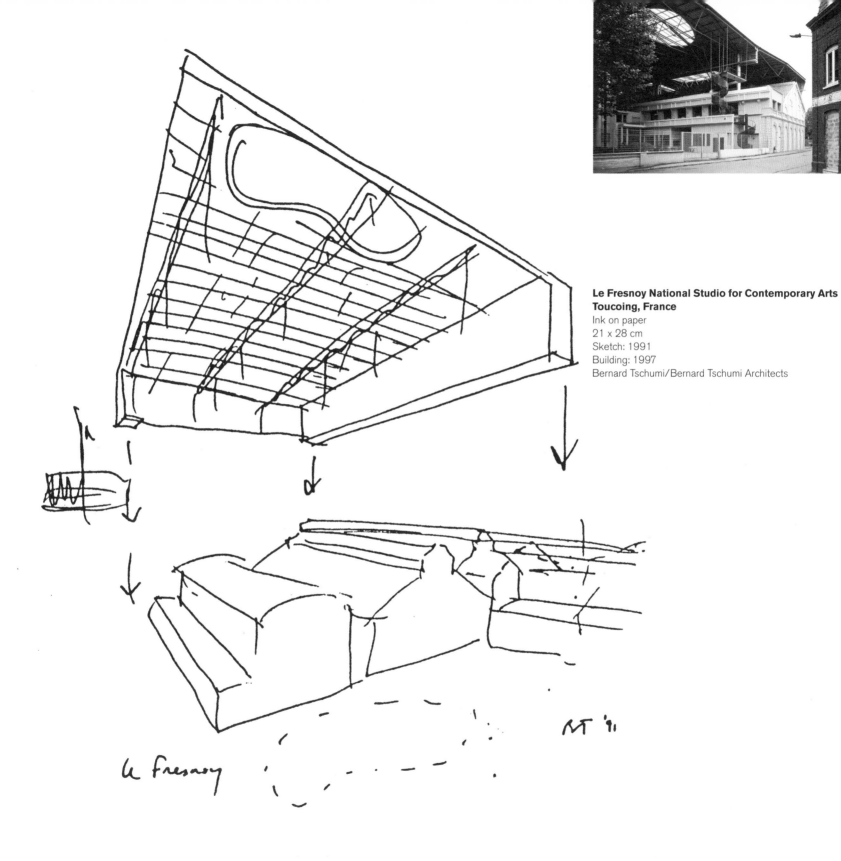

**Le Fresnoy National Studio for Contemporary Arts
Toucoing, France**
Ink on paper
21 x 28 cm
Sketch: 1991
Building: 1997
Bernard Tschumi/Bernard Tschumi Architects

Le Fresnoy

345

Parc de la Villette
Paris, France
Ink on paper
25 x 15 cm
Sketch: 1983
Building: 1998
Bernard Tschumi/Bernard Tschumi Architects

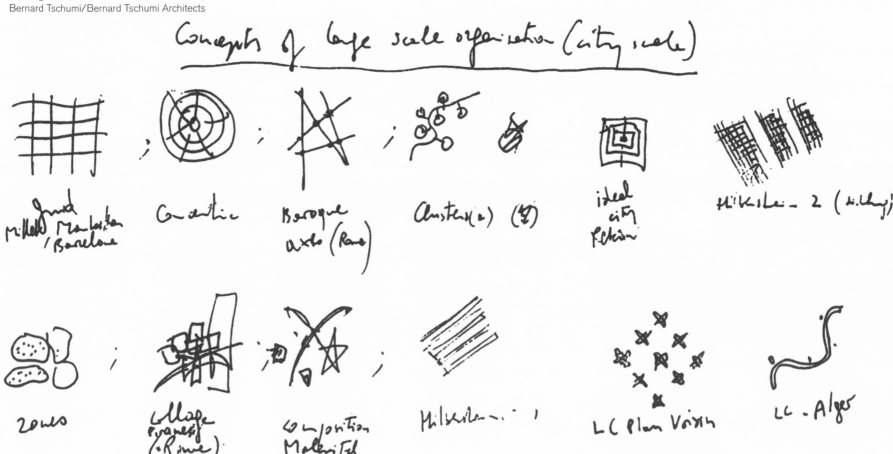

Concepts of large scale organisation (city scale)

Grid / Manhattan / Barcelona ; Concentric ; Baroque axis (Rome) ; Amsterdam (a) (b) ; ideal city Pekin ; Hilberseimer 2 (sillage)

zones ; village piranese (+Rome) ; composition Malevitch ; Hilberseimer 1 ; LC Plan Voisin ; LC - Alger

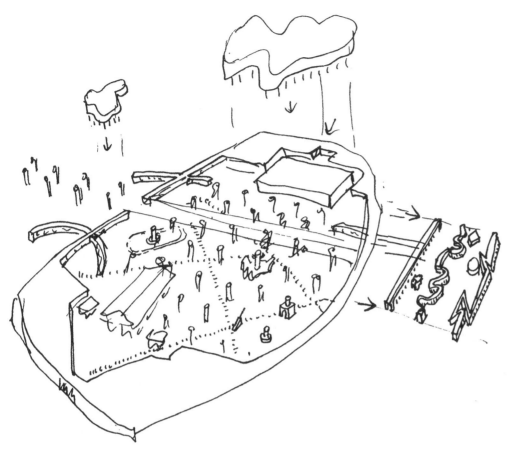

Parc de la Villette
Paris, France
Ink on paper
21 x 28 cm
Sketch: 1983
Building: 1998
Bernard Tschumi/Bernard Tschumi Architects

Parc de la Villette
Paris, France
Ink on paper
35 x 35 cm
Sketch: 1983
Building: 1998
Bernard Tschumi/Bernard Tschumi Architects

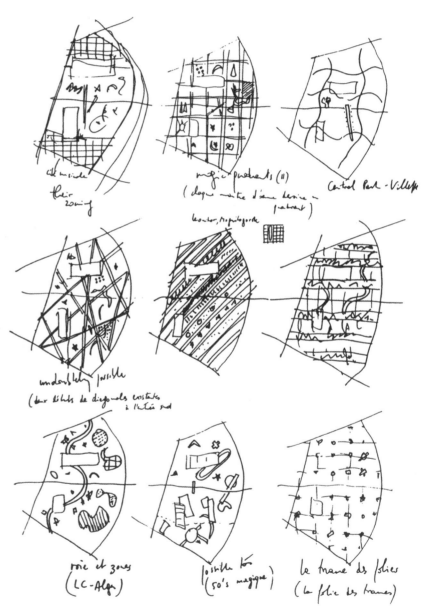

RAFAEL VIÑOLY

Rafael Viñoly (born in Montevideo, Uruguay, 1944) has been practicing architecture for 45 years and his designs have been consistently driven by the belief that the essential responsibility of architecture is to generate the most elegant solution within the economy of each project, and maximizing the opportunity for civic investment. Viñoly holds a Masters in architecture from the University of Buenos Aires, and has lived in New York City since 1978 from where he oversees an international practice that has developed more than 400 designs for projects around the world. He is a member of the American Institute of Architects, the Royal Institute of British Architects, the Japan Institute of Architects, and the Sociedad Central de Arquitectos in Argentina.

The Covered Courtyard
"Access from the Parking"

↑ Museum Shop.

Cleveland Museum of Art
Cleveland, OH, USA
Felt-tip pen and China colored marker
Sketch: 2001
Building: 2012
Rafael Viñoly

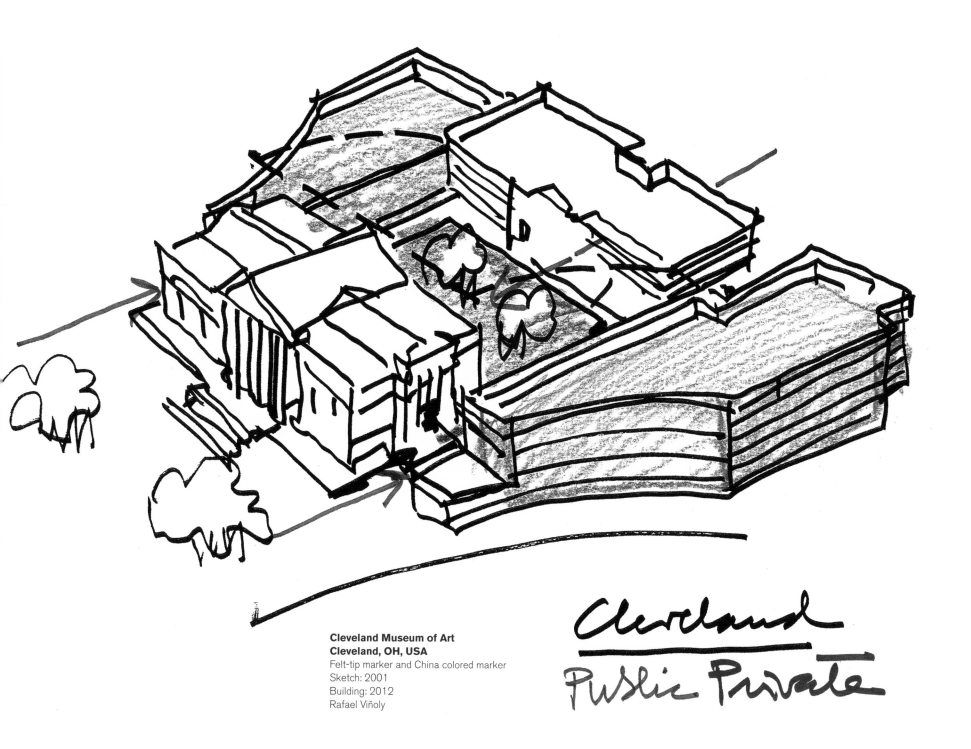

Cleveland Museum of Art
Cleveland, OH, USA
Felt-tip marker and China colored marker
Sketch: 2001
Building: 2012
Rafael Viñoly

Cleveland
Public Private

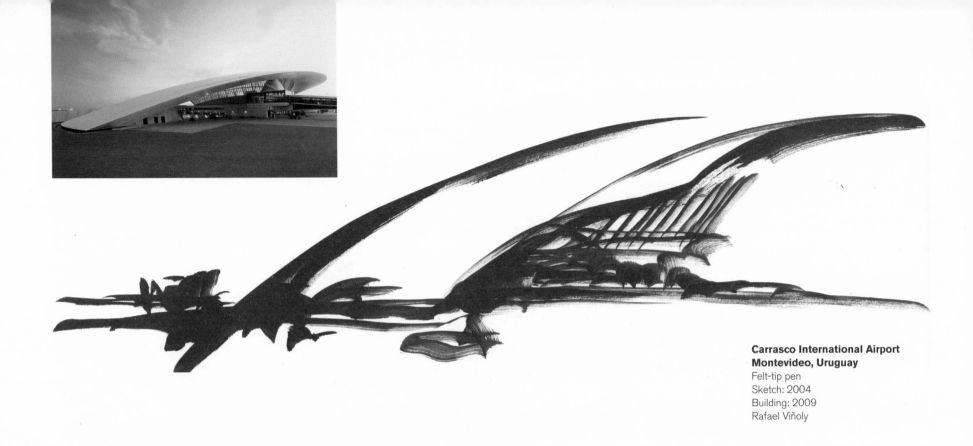

**Carrasco International Airport
Montevideo, Uruguay**
Felt-tip pen
Sketch: 2004
Building: 2009
Rafael Viñoly

**Howard Hughes Medical Institute
Janelia Farms Campus
Ashburn, VA, USA**
Felt-tip pen
Sketch: 2002
Building: 2006
Rafael Viñoly

Tokyo International Forum
Tokyo, Japan
Felt-tip pen
Sketch: 1989
Building: 1996
Rafael Viñoly

University of Chicago
Graduate School of Business
Chicago, IL, USA
Felt-tip pen and watercolors
Sketch: 2000
Building: 2004
Rafael Viñoly

University of Chicago
Graduate School of Business
Chicago, IL, USA
Felt-tip pen and watercolors
Sketch: 2000
Building: 2004
Rafael Viñoly

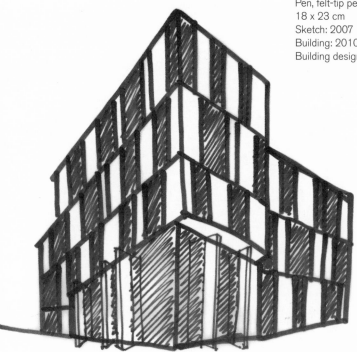

De Kroon
Hoofddorp, The Netherlands
Pen, felt-tip pen and marker
18 x 23 cm
Sketch: 2007
Building: 2010
Building design: Bart van der Vossen/Rijnboutt

BART VAN DER VOSSEN, MATTIJS RIJNBOUTT, FREDERIK VERMEESCH

Rijnboutt bv originated from the Architectengroep in 2005 and designs and advises in the full width of architecture, urbanism and landscape architecture. The current board of management consists of Richard Koek, Renée Liefting, Kees Rijnboutt, Bart van der Vossen, Mattijs Rijnboutt and Frederik Vermeesch. Bart van der Vossen studied architecture at the Eindhoven University of Technology. From 1996 on Bart van der Vossen worked at the Architectengroep and since 2005 he is joint director of Rijnboutt. In addition to executing building commissions, he is also urban designer and supervisor. Mattijs Rijnboutt studied architecture and urban design at the Delft University of Technology. As a member of the Architectengroep, he has been joint director of Rijnboutt since 2005. He is currently working on various urban design projects and buildings. Frederik Vermeesch graduated from the Faculty of Engineering, Department of Architecture, at the Free University of Brussels. He has been architect at Rijnboutt since 2006 and was made joint director in 2009. Frederik Vermeesch is working on a wide variety of buildings, urban design projects and interior design.

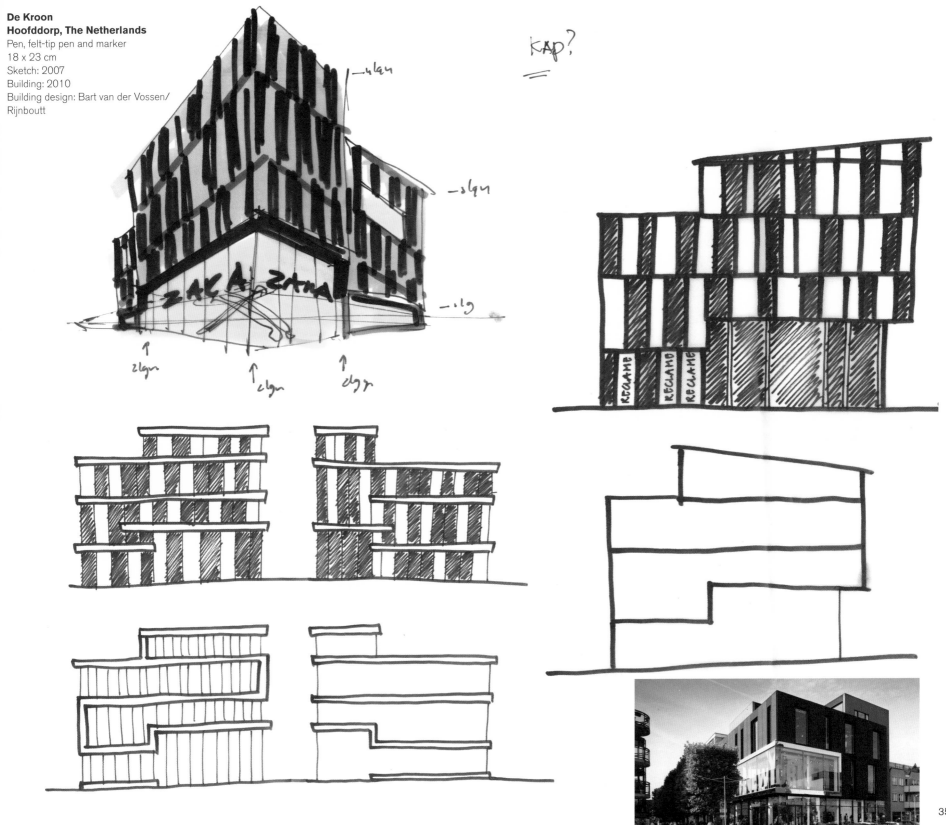

De Kroon
Hoofddorp, The Netherlands
Pen, felt-tip pen and marker
18 x 23 cm
Sketch: 2007
Building: 2010
Building design: Bart van der Vossen/
Rijnboutt

355

LET OP:
voor leuk 'oude' doorsnede

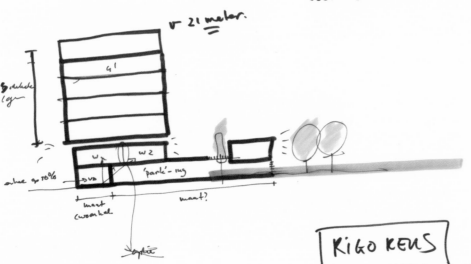

v 21 meter.

RIGO KENS

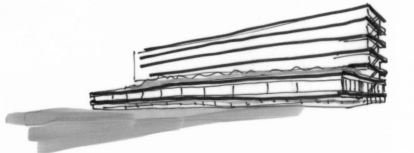

Zalmweide
Hoogvliet, The Netherlands
28 x 39 cm
Pen, felt-tip pen and marker
Sketch: 2007
Building: 2010
Building design: Bart van der Vossen/
Rijnboutt

1005
d. 2010.

Cinema Eemplein
Amersfoort, The Netherlands
Pen and marker
12 x 22 cm
Sketch: 2010
Building: 2012
Building design: Designer: Frederik Vermeesch/
Rijnboutt

**ermitage Shopping, De Tsaar
ustenburg
andam, The Netherlands**
n, felt-tip pen and marker
x 10 cm
etch: 2004
lding: 2010
lding design: Mattijs Rijnboutt/
boutt

**Hermitage Shopping, De Tsaar
Rustenburg
Zaandam, The Netherlands**
Pen, felt-tip pen and marker
11 x 15 cm
Sketch: 2004
Building: 2010
Building design: Mattijs Rijnboutt/
Rijnboutt

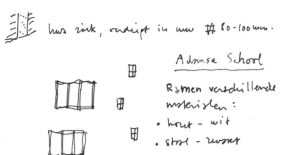

**ermitage Shopping, De Tsaar
ustenburg
aandam, The Netherlands**
en, felt-tip pen and marker
2 x 15 cm
ketch: 2004
uilding: 2010
uilding design: Mattijs Rijnboutt/
jnboutt

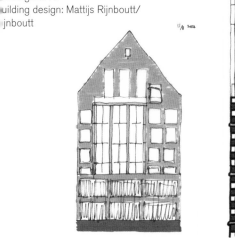

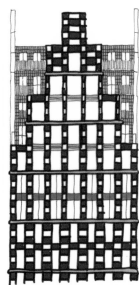

**Hermitage Shopping, De Tsaar
Rustenburg
Zaandam, The Netherlands**
Pen, felt-tip pen and marker
15 x 9 cm
Sketch: 2004
Building: 2010
Building design: Mattijs Rijnboutt/
Rijnboutt

The Bank
Amsterdam, The Netherlands
Pen
25 x 40 cm
Sketch: 2007
Building: 2010
Building design: Frederik Vermeesch/
Rijnboutt

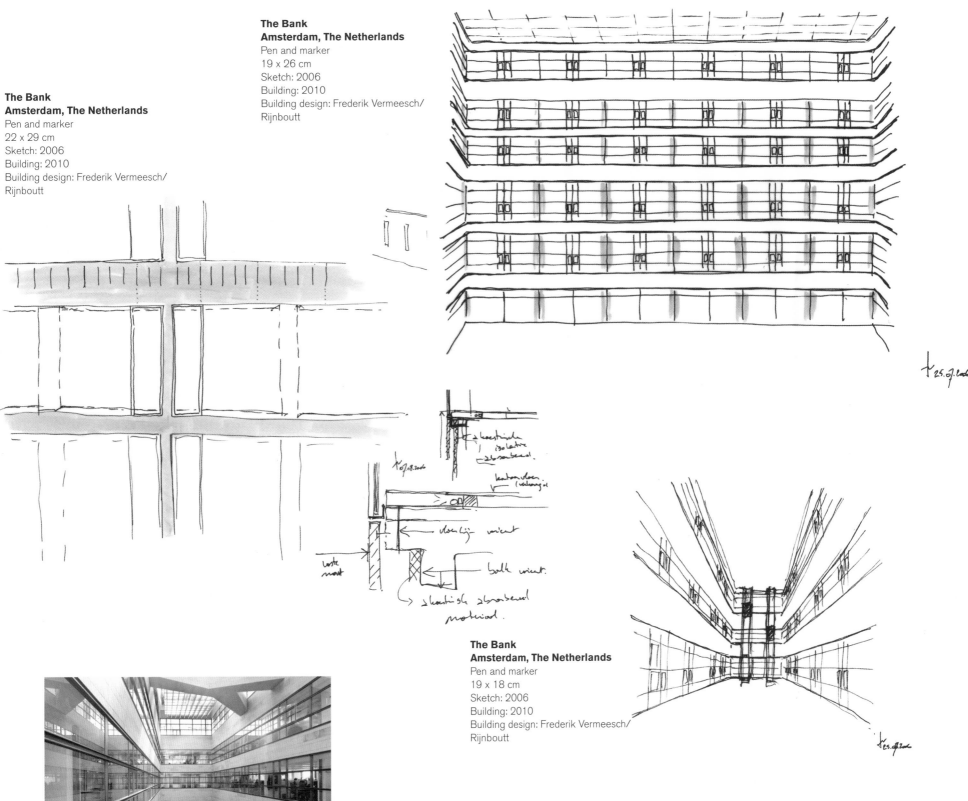

The Bank
Amsterdam, The Netherlands
Pen and marker
22 x 29 cm
Sketch: 2006
Building: 2010
Building design: Frederik Vermeesch/
Rijnboutt

The Bank
Amsterdam, The Netherlands
Pen and marker
19 x 26 cm
Sketch: 2006
Building: 2010
Building design: Frederik Vermeesch/
Rijnboutt

The Bank
Amsterdam, The Netherlands
Pen and marker
19 x 18 cm
Sketch: 2006
Building: 2010
Building design: Frederik Vermeesch/
Rijnboutt

359

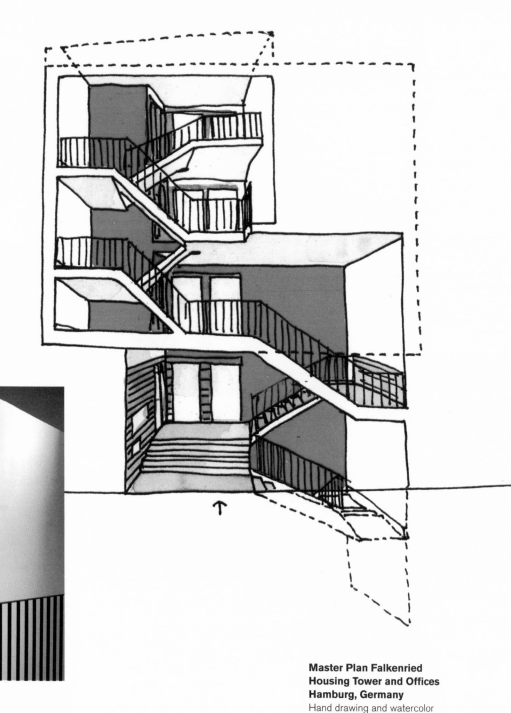

PETER WILSON

Peter Wilson (born in Melbourne, Australia, 1950) studied at, and subsequently became one of the figurehead teachers of London's legendary Architectural Association School of Architecture in the 1970s and 1980s. His evocative, nuanced drawings were at that time widely published. Since winning the competition for the Münster City Library the office of Bolles+Wilson has operated from Germany, and has worked on a wide range of projects including the Luxor Theater Rotterdam, the Monteluce Quartier Perugia and currently the New National Library of Luxembourg. Bolles+Wilson have been the subject of three El Croquis monographs – their books include 'Western Objects-Eastern Fields' 1989 and 'A Handful of Productive Paradigms' 2009. Wilson was guest professor at the Accademia di Architettura, Mendrisio, 2006–2008.

Master Plan Falkenried
Housing Tower and Offices
Hamburg, Germany
Hand drawing and watercolor
8 x 8.6 cm
Sketch: 2002
Building: 2004
Peter Wilson/Bolles+Wilson

Master Plan Falkenried
Housing Tower and Offices
Hamburg, Germany
Hand drawing and watercolor
12.6 x 12.5 cm
Sketch: 2002
Building: 2004
Peter Wilson/Bolles+Wilson

City Library
Helmond, The Netherlands
Hand drawing and watercolor
6.6 x 9.3 cm
Sketch: 2006
Building: 2010
Peter Wilson/Bolles+Wilson

City Library
Helmond, The Netherlands
Hand drawing and watercolor
14.9 x 9.4 cm
Sketch: 2006
Building: 2010
Peter Wilson/Bolles+Wilson

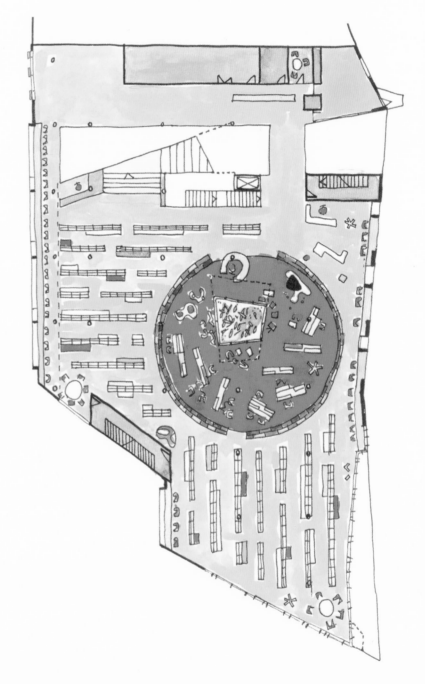

**St. Sebastian – Church Remodeled
as Kindergarten**
Hand drawing and watercolor
9.6 x 15.5 cm
Sketch: 2011
Building: 2013
Peter Wilson/Bolles+Wilson

Raakspoort – City Hall and Bioscoop
Haarlem, The Netherlands
Hand drawing
6.4 x 10.0 cm
Sketch: 2009
Building: 2011
Peter Wilson/Bolles+Wilson

364

Raakspoort – City Hall and Bioscoop
Haarlem, The Netherlands
Hand drawing and watercolor
10.3 x 21.0 cm
Sketch: 2009
Building: 2011
Peter Wilson/Bolles+Wilson

366

Spuimarkt Block
The Hague, The Netherlands
Shopping Center of the Year NL 2009
Hand drawing and watercolor
6.6 x 8.3 cm
Sketch: 2004
Building: 2008
Peter Wilson/Bolles+Wilson

Spuimarkt Block
The Hague, The Netherlands
Shopping Center of the Year NL 2009
Hand drawing and watercolor
9.2 x 12.1 cm
Sketch: 2004
Building: 2008
Peter Wilson/Bolles+Wilson

Spuimarkt Block
The Hague, The Netherlands
Shopping Center of the Year NL 2009
Hand drawing and watercolor
8.2 x 10.2 cm
Sketch: 2004
Building: 2008
Peter Wilson/Bolles+Wilson

Picture Credits

Peter Aaron/Esto	82, 83, 195
Peter Aaron/Otto	273, 277 a.
Courtesy Rafael Viñoly Architects/© Daniela Mac Adden	350 a.
AECDP	285
B+W	360, 362
Iwan Baan	343
Peter Bennetts	238, 240, 241
Helene Binet	143
Maria Birulés	244 (portrait)
Sandor Bodo, Providence	329
Tom Bonner	294
Nicolas Borel	283, 287, 289
Tamás Bujnovszky	290
Gregori Civera	64
Crystal	216, 217
Marc Detiffe	26
Carolyn Djanogly	120 (portrait)
Herman van Doorn	164
Dream Hub	214
Cemal Emden	107
Mischa Erben	152 a.
H.G. Esch/courtesy of KPF	260
Torben Eskerod	249
Courtesy Rafael Viñoly Architects/© Brad Feinknopf	348, 352, 353
Luis Ferreira Alves	327
Courtesy Rafael Viñoly Architects/© Paul Fetters	350 b.
James Foster	22
Art Gray	18, 20
Fernando Guerra	FG+SG	237, 312, 338
Martine Hamilton-Knight	243
Markus Hauschild	363
Peter Hubbe	331, 333
Hufton+Crow	221
Kevin Hui	239
Kees Hummel	355–357, 359
Tim Hursley/courtesy of KPF	261
Timothy Hursley	334
Yasushi Ichikawa	197
Aker Imaging	277 b.
Vimal Jain	32–35

Miran Kambi	92
Alan Karchmer	276 a.
Courtesy Rafael Viñoly Architects/© Kawasumi Architectural Photography	351
Toshiharu Kitajima	232
Eric Laignel	59
Daniel Lee	91
Nic Lehoux	84, 86, 89
Ducio Malagamba	163, 291, 293, 295
Michael Marsland	270 (portrait)
E. Maru & S. Koshimizu	68
Peter Mauss/Esto	341, 345, 346
Alan McIntrye Smith	322–324
André Morin/DPA/Adagp	267
Nacása & Partners	67
NFP	158 (portrait)
Claude O'sughrue	70
Hiroyuki Oki	259
paul ott photografiert	152 b., 153
Matevž Paternoster	93
Rui Pires	38
Andrew Pogue	21
Rheinzink	145
Christian Richters	57, 361, 365, 367
Ed Riddell	87
Nigel Rigden	110
Erick Saillet	284
Günter Schneider	219
Silverstein Properties	213
Rui Morais de Souza	266 (portrait)
Studio 8 Architects	226, 229
Studio AMD	271, 274, 275
Andre Viera	286
Rainer Viertlboeck	180–182
Joshua White	335
Rainer Wührer	155
Nigel Young/Foster + Partners	122
Xia Zhi	168, 169
Wade Zimmerman	281

All other photographs were provided directly by the architectural firms.

Imprint

The Deutsche Nationalbibliothek lists this publication in the Deutsche Nationalbibliografie; detailed bibliographic data are available in the Internet at http://dnb.dnb.de

ISBN 978-3-03768-150-3
© 2014 by Braun Publishing AG

www.braun-publishing.ch

1st edition 2014

Project coordination: Editorial Office van Uffelen
Editorial staff: Lisa Rogers
Graphic concept and layout: Michaela Prinz, Berlin